Dawn Of The Metal Gods

My Life In Judas Priest And Heavy Metal

by Al Atkins & Neil Daniels

Including An Introduction By Judas Priest Bassist Ian Hill

I.P. Verlag Jeske/Mader GbR
Haydnstr. 2
12203 Berlin
Germany

All rights reserved. No part of this publication may be reproduced, stored in a retrieval system, or transmitted in any form or by any means, electronic, mechanical, photocopying, recording or otherwise, without the prior permission of the publisher.

ISBN 978-3-931624-56-9
April 2009

Copyright © 2009 by Al Atkins & Neil Daniels

Photo Credits: John Santee/Showcase Promotions (cover, page 209); Norman Hood (backcover, page 68 on top, 99, 101, 109); Caroline Johnson (page 76, 77, 78 below, 203); Emma Kilgannon (page 8); Beverley Stone (page 67); Jessica Patel (page 74, 75); John England (page 141, 152, 154, 157); Richard Ward/Classic Rock Photography (page 7, 80, 196); Joe D'Agostino (page 47, 85); James Cumpsty (page 135); Jörg Schulz (page 207) all other pictures: Al Atkins archive

Content

Foreword By Judas Priest Bassist Ian Hill   5

Introduction By Al Atkins   6

Introduction By Neil Daniels   8

Chapter 1
Born & Bred In The Midlands (1947-1962)   10

Chapter 2
Birmingham Beat Boom & The Rockin' Sixties (1963-1968)   20

Chapter 3
The Ballad Of Al Atkins & Judas Priest (1969-1973)   49

Chapter 4
Life After Priest & The Story Of Lion (1974-1978)   111

Chapter 5
Off The Road (1979-1983)   141

Chapter 6
Travels In Europe (1984-1988)   148

Chapter 7
Heavy Thoughts: My Solo Career Begins (1989-2001)   152

Chapter 8
Living In The Shadow Of The Past: Embracing The Priest (2002-2004)   180

Chapter 9
**Demon Deceivers: Al Atkins & The Holy Rage
(2005-2009)** 189

Epilogue – What More Can I Say? 205

Appendix
I: A Personal Tribute To Judas Priest 206
II: Judas Priest Line-Up History (1969-1973) 210
III: Judas Priest Tour Dates (1969-1973) 211
IV: Miscellaneous Tour Dates (1974-2008) 216
V: Full Career Discography 218
VI: A Q&A With Al Atkins & The Holy Rage 220

Acknowledgements & Sources 224
About The Authors 224

Al Atkins' Dedication:
To my loving family and all the musicians I have had the pleasure of playing with over the past 40 years …

Neil Daniels' Dedication:
To my parents, Ann and Andrew Daniels …

"He's a lovely geezer with a great voice ..."
Dennis Stratton (ex-Iron Maiden/Praying Mantis)

"Al's songs influenced heavy metal from the sixties to today."
Jess Cox (ex-Tygers Of Pan Tang/Metal Nation Records)

"Al is the co-writer of an absolute metal classic ..."
Brian Tatler (Diamond Head)

"Priest are simply one of the all time greats of metal."
Paul Dianno (ex-Iron Maiden)

"Al's in your face ... his voice is in command"
Graham Bonnet (ex-Rainbow)

"Al is one of metal's all time greats"
Simon Lees (ex-Budgie)

"Al is a great metal singer ..."
Taz Taylor (Taz Taylor Band)

"Al Atkins must be one of the most dedicated musicians I have ever worked with ..."
Pete Boot (ex-Budgie/Fill Your Head With Rock)

"I've got a lot of time for Allan – nice bloke ..."
Bruno Stapenhill (Bassist in Judas Priest Mark I)

"He's an amazing vocalist, songwriter and a very good friend ..."
Chris Johnson (The Holy Rage)

"Allan did most of the writing. He was a Jack of all trades."
John Ellis (Drummer in Judas Priest Mark II)

"Al Atkins formed the band ..."
David Howells (Co-founder of Gull Records)

"Al is a great singer and a nice guy."
Johnny Lokke (Kansas USA)

"... he could play guitar, harmonica, and drums and also write his own songs."
Dave Corke (Judas Priest's manager from 1970-76)

"Al Atkins has written great songs, past, present, and future – truly a genius ..."
Juan Garcia (Agent Steel)

"You can have great sex with the right partner: 20 years on and five albums later, making music with Al still feels like great sex!"
Paul May (A.N.D/Temple Dogs/V-Rats/Al Atkins)

"His 'Victim Of Changes' and other greats set the precedence for all to follow."
Rob Grohl (RG Concert Promotionz)

Foreword By Judas Priest Bassist Ian Hill

I had the great fortune to have spent my spotty adolescence, and nascent musical career during the 1960's. It was a time when most forms of contemporary music was in its experimental infancy. Pop, soul, modern blues, progressive rock, jazz rock, heavy metal, of course, and most of what followed can trace its roots back to this special time …

Looking back, what strikes me now more than ever, was the sheer diversity of styles, even in a single genre – Clapton, Hendrix, Beck, and Page, for instance, all had vastly different techniques and although all went on to great fame in other genres, were all at one time regarded as blues guitarists. This was mirrored throughout the other genres.

In the large part, these and all other unique styles were due to the pioneering nature of the time. Everyone was striving for something new, to be different, and above all played and sang what they felt, rather than what they thought others wanted them to do. There were no rules, no yardsticks, and no boundaries, no one to copy! This was a philosophy that Allan, as well as K.K., John Ellis and myself emphatically believed in, when we first got together, and is carried forward by Allan and Judas Priest to the present day.

One of the big differences between then and now was the great number of venues to play. Live music was the norm rather than the novelty back then. Even West Bromwich, a comparatively small industrial town a few miles north of Birmingham, where I (like Allan and K.K.) was brought up, boasted at least half a dozen venues in the town centre alone. These consisted of everything from pubs and clubs through dance halls to the gala baths and the town hall. The magical part, of course, was the bands that played in them back then. I can remember Cream, Pink Floyd, Fleetwood Mac, Taste, Free, amongst a myriad others, coming through these venues during the sixties and early seventies, (the largest of which couldn't have had a capacity of more than a couple of thousand or so). Amongst these early trail blazers were the many upcoming bands that would eventually go on to success, including Allan and an embryonic Judas Priest!

In the course of these coming pages, Allan will cover these topics, and much, much more in great detail; so although I could go on, as these times hold very fond memories for me, I'll quit now and let Allan write his own book!

March, 2009

Introduction By Al Atkins

ver the years I have been asked by lots of Judas Priest fans from all over the world if I am ever going to write my autobiography. Well, here it is, finally, my version of events from the past seven decades that my crazy life has spanned.

On many occasions I have been asked all sorts of questions regarding the early years of Judas Priest: when was I introduced to rock music? Who or what inspired me? Where did the name Judas Priest come from? When exactly did Priest form? Where did we play our very first gig? Why did you leave the band? Do you still keep in touch with the band? And so on and so forth. I hope that this book provides adequate answers for all of those questions (and more).

Indeed, it is a privilege to say that I played an integral part in the genesis of British heavy metal giants Judas Priest. Having formed the band way back in the late sixties and sang with them for their first four years of their illustrious career, I still feel that a part of me is with them as they spread the metal cause around the globe from country to country, city to city. From the early sixties onwards, as British blues music was dominating major cities such as Birmingham and London, I joined or formed several rock and roll bands, but Judas Priest was the only one that survived from that competitive decade and made it to the big league to the point where they have become universally recognised as the archetypal British heavy metal band. They still define the term HEAVY METAL, carrying the torch for the genre and especially for British metal in general.

With the help of rock writer Neil Daniels who wrote his own book on the band called »The Story Of Judas Priest: Defenders Of The Faith« this book is about us placing the foundations of the band into context; realistically it was not all fame and glory, there was a lot of hard work in those earlier years and a lot of hardship before and after Mr. Rob Halford joined the band in 1973, having replaced me after I decided to call it a day once and for all. But having said that, there was also a lot of fun and memories to treasure which is why I want to share them with you right here.

I have also included lots of rare band photos and pictures of memorabilia, which have never been seen before. It is also fitting that I have included a selection of interesting interviews with people who played an important part in the earlier phase of my career and that of Judas Priest's. Without them, the great beast would not have been born!

There is also an extensive appendix in the book which I hope many of you will find useful. Over the years I have compiled lots of tour dates, random facts and trivia so it's good to share them with those of you who are interested.

»Dawn Of The Metal Gods« is also my chance to talk about my career after Judas Priest, which has been a struggle to say the least, but I have made some music I am proud of and toured with and supported some legendary bands such as the Heavy Metal Kids, Skid Row, Sex Pistols, The Stranglers, Warrior Soul and Graham Bonnet. I have recorded and released five albums so far: »Judgement Day«, »Dreams Of Avalon«, »Victim Of Changes«, »Heavy Thoughts« and »Demon Deceiver«. The latter album gave me the best reviews of my career! I have also set up a website www.alatkins.com which archives my entire career and makes a nice companion to this book. I have witnessed the rise of rock and roll music in all its guises and I feel that now is the right time to share my stories and thoughts with you.

I have spent most of my life scribbling down lyrics and many of them have made it on to my solo albums (many of them have not) so I have included several of those lyrics in this book. Scattered amongst the details of my life, my lyrics tell a story about how I was feeling at a particular point in my life. I've had some rough times and have learned to express myself through a verse and a chorus. There really isn't a better way for a songwriter to express himself; the power of a lyric is unchallenged. But there are lots of things I'm not able to express in a song, hence this book.

»Dawn Of The Metal Gods: My Life In Judas Priest And Heavy Metal« is dedicated to all the musicians I have had the honour and pleasure to have played with over the years, sadly some of them have left us. All of them should have been stars – and to me they all are – but just a few can make it to the top of the tree in this very competitive and sometimes ruthless business known as heavy metal. Judas Priest made it to the top but I'm not bitter, quite the opposite in fact, and I will tell you why if you keep on reading.

There's no easy way to the top but some people are born stars and some get lucky, being in the right place at the right time has a lot to do with it. With Judas Priest, it was a long hard road from the pubs and clubs of the West Midlands when I was singing in the band to such popular and extensive sports venues as Madison Square Garden with Rob as the band's charismatic frontman; and we all know that during the eighties the Americans in particular took an obvious liking to Rob and the rest of the band. As AC/DC put it: "It's a long way to the top if you want to rock and roll."

I never reached the top and at this point in my life, I never will, but I gave it a bloody good go and this is my story, my life in heavy metal. I hope you enjoy the ride!

March, 2009

Introduction By Neil Daniels

Al Atkins has a story, it's definitely a story worth telling and I'm glad I am involved in the process. I first met Al during the research period of my own book on the band and I have to say I was knocked back at just how helpful he was, answering my many e-mails and offering advice on how to lay out the details of the early years of Judas Priest. Believe me, it was not an easy task especially as I had never written a book before. Speaking to several ex-members of Judas Priest between 1969 and 1973 I can honestly say that the likes of Ernie Chataway, Bruno Stapenhill and John Ellis had nothing but generous words for Al. They praised him for all his hard work and dedication to music proclaiming him to be a talented and overlooked songwriter and I'm inclined to agree with their comments. Suffice to say Al has had a tumultuous career, having tried to make it to the big time but missing out. Nevertheless, you have to admire somebody so willing to put his life on hold to pursue his career in rock and roll. Finally, after leaving a series of bands in the sixties right through to the end of the eighties, Al finally started to record some albums that display his obvious talents.

Evidently he is, and forever will be, linked to the heavy metal legends Judas Priest. Like his friend, the controversial former Iron Maiden singer Paul Di'Anno, Al has often been criticised for capitalising on his brief but important and mostly overlooked career in Judas Priest. One question has to be asked to those critics: if you formed one of the most impor-

tant bands in popular music – a band that literally created heavy metal – wouldn't you be proud of it? Wouldn't you gloat too? This book is a chance for Al to set his side of the story straight whilst fondly reminiscing about the sixties blues boom in Birmingham that spawned such singers as Robert Plant, Noddy Holder and Steve Winwood et al. Al has seen rock and roll go through many changes and played an integral part in the creation of heavy metal and in this book he will narrate much of rock music's history.

While his career may not have reached such dizzying heights of success as the aforementioned singers, he has created a reputation that is, in some respects, enviable: to metal fans in the West Midlands he is something of a local legend and to Judas Priest fans he is a cult star who co-wrote the classic heavy metal screamer "Victim Of Changes" as well as a small selection of songs that appeared on the band's debut album, 1974's »Rocka Rolla« (released through Gull Records) and their sophomore album »Sad Wings Of Destiny«, which was also released via Gull.

Despite years of inactivity in the music business, Al has managed to record five excellent solo albums since leaving Priest in 1973 and garnered some robust reviews in the rock and metal press along the way to his current position as lead singer of his band The Holy Rage. His most recent album »Demon Deceiver« was awarded with some noticeably good reviews in the likes of Classic Rock and other important rock magazines. And the power and talent The Holy Rage display on stage shows that they have a very promising future ahead of them.

It's been an honour and a pleasure to have been involved with the writing of this book and to have shared Al's memories with him.

Like the man himself, his songs have stood the test of time and some of those songs he wrote all those years ago have been covered by artists like Gamma Ray (Germany), Armoured Saint (L.A.), Skyclad (UK) and the American power metal band Steel Prophet. Rob Halford has also included a version of Al's song "Never Satisfied" on the bonus DVD in the 2007 collection »Metal God Essentials Volume 1«.

In a sense, Al's career has come full circle and although he shows no signs of slowing down at the age of 60, there is no better time than now to pen the story of his life …

March, 2009

Chapter 1
Born & Bred In The Midlands (1947-1962)

It's the first week of January in 1970 and Judas Priest are about to go on stage at some club in Scotland. I'm in the changing room with Ernie, the guitarist, and Bruno who plays bass. Our drummer John decided to stay back home in West Bromwich because he had the flu, so I had to play drums and sing. I wasn't feeling too good because we'd had an awful time travelling in the bad weather and had already been in Scotland for about two weeks. I just wanted to go home.

"Bloody hell, what a great way to start the New Year", I said, sarcastically, to the lads. It was Judas Priest's first ever tour …

Let's begin by telling you a little bit about my life before I started playing in rock and roll bands. I was born Allan John Atkins on October 14th, 1947 at 2 Marsh Lane in a town called West Bromwich (West Brom to the locals), which lies a few miles outside of the industrial city of Birmingham, England. World War II had finished two years before my birth and the country was struggling financially; the war had almost bankrupted our economy and the glory years of the once powerful and seemingly indestructible British Empire had long since passed. My parents were proud Brits who believed in the Empire and her Majesty the Queen. But my generation were not quite so lucky because we grew up after the Second World War; lots of my peers moved to Australia or America in the sixties whilst others settled in other, more attractive and prosperous parts of the UK.

Most Brits who were born before me and my generation had been in the army and fought in wars. We got lucky. I don't know much about my paternal and maternal grandparents but I do know that, like many young, fit and patriotic British males, my paternal grandfather Joe Atkins had a career in the military; he was a Sergeant in the Red Cross and was shot between the eyes by a sniper while aiding other injured soldiers on the front line.

I also take great pride in the fact that my great uncle Joseph Davies was awarded a Victoria Cross – the highest accolade for a British soldier – in July, 1916 for his services during World War I. He was also awarded the Russian Order of St. George (First Class) by Tsar Nicholas II. I know quite a bit about my great uncle; he was born in Tipton, which is just outside of West Bromwich and he grew up to be a commendable British soldier. When the First World War commenced in 1914, he was actually in India but then he was transferred to France two years later and was promoted to the rank of Corporal after taking shrapnel wounds. His full title when he died was Corporal Joseph Davies V.C. 10th Battalion Royal Welch Fusiliers.

My Midlands peers include Ozzy Osbourne, Noddy Holder, Tony Iommi, Robert Plant, Roy Wood, Jeff Lyne, Steve Winwood and Bev Bevan. And like them, I was born at the arse end of the class system. Most families, certainly north of Birmingham, were poor but hard-working and modest. There weren't many decent jobs around in those days. There was definitely a distinction in England between the upper and lower classes: in the Midlands and the north of England, for example, the industries and coal mines provided jobs for working class men but at the same time the upper classes in the south of England were getting even richer. As I grew older, I began to hate the class system in this country.

There is also a big difference between our Midlands accent and the accents of those wealthier people of the South in places like London, Sussex and Surrey. But as a child I didn't really know much about this until I grew up and learned more about myself and my upbringing.

In those grim days, the men went to work and the women stayed at home. Even when women got the right to vote in 1928, in Britain we were still plagued by the class system and part of that meant that it was only proper that the wife stayed at home to look after the kids, clean the house and to have a hot meal ready for her husband when he returned home from work. It was not easy for my mother and other women like her. Raising a family is a bloody hard job. It's all bollocks now but in those days that was the way we lived. When I was a kid, I certainly saw a lot more of my mum than I did of my dad and that's because he worked a lot.

My family lived in a small house on a deprived council estate in an area of West Bromwich called Stone Cross; there was mum, dad, my older brother Brian, my older sister Valerie and me – the baby of the family. Another one of my sisters named Sheila died from pneumonia just before her fourth birthday. Sheila actually died before I was born but in many ways I felt close to her because my parents only planned to have three children. So in some morbid way I've always assumed that I'm alive because she died. I've seen photos of Sheila; she was a beautiful looking child. I was told that her death devastated my parents, especially my dad, because his mum, who lived with us, had died just a couple of weeks earlier. Having a double trauma like that was heartbreaking. I would often hear my mum crying at night while my dad managed to cope in his own way, like most men, he stayed quiet and kept his thoughts and emotions private.

We were brought up in a very religious environment, which felt suffocating at times, but in a way I'm grateful because we were secure and content. My dad, Joseph Atkins, always wanted to be a priest and my mum Alice was raised in a strict and regimented Catholic School taught by stern nuns. My mum's maiden name was Gibbs and her mum's maiden name was Davies; she originally came from Wales. My maternal grandfather originated from Cork in Ireland. My maternal grandparents had 13 children but two died at an early age; my mum was the eldest of the eleven children left.

My mum was a good, strong woman with a firm set of principles and beliefs. Bloody hell, some of the stories she told me about her school years made me thankful I wasn't raised by nuns. And I thought my parents were strict! Even to this day I don't ever recall hearing my mum curse and that's because of her upbringing.

"If I ever hear you swear or speak like that again, I'll wash your mouth out with soap and water", she said to me after I'd thrown a tantrum.

I think if I was raised by nuns, I would have made it my mission to provoke a nun so much that she'd burst out with a torrent of swear words. Ha! I can just hear one of them now.

"You fucking little bastard ... may God strike you down with a lightning bolt, you horrible little shit." We all have weak spots.

Because of my mum's rules, I had to learn quickly how to be obedient and when to say please and thank you; I did not want to get on the wrong side of my parents. My mum and dad never argued and never raised a hand to me or my brother and sister, although I was the worst behaved out of the three of us. Like any child raised by strict but caring parents, I knew the boundaries of acceptable behaviour; I knew which buttons to push and which

My brother Brian, me and my sister Valerie enjoying an English holiday.

to avoid. I kept on the straight and narrow … until I got into rock and roll and it all changed but that's a story for later.

Until I was about ten years old, my brother, sister and myself had to attend Sunday School every week, which was at a small Pentecostal Church just opposite where we lived in our modest council house; the only thing I liked was when we used to go out on day trips in an old Charabanc bus and on the way home my father always took out his harmonica and would play us a tune, and everyone would join in singing without a care in the world. We also had to attend our mum's Roman Catholic Church every now and then on Wednesday evenings at Stone Cross where we lived; again, I stayed there until I was about ten or eleven years old. I wasn't a big fan of church hymns but thinking back to those times, it was nice that we were so close and I guess it was through the hymns, and to an extent through religion, that made us a close knit family. You don't really see that kind of family anymore which is a shame. I couldn't really sing then either; it wasn't until my balls dropped that I started to sing.

My brother loved the friendliness and harmony of those days; consequently he became a pastor of his own congregation! Mum and dad used to make us kneel down by our beds at night and say our prayers before we went to sleep. It was even worse than brushing your teeth; I'd brush my teeth twice if I didn't have to say my prayers. But they made us do it because they said good things would happen if we obeyed God. I used to pray for silly things like a good mark at school so I wouldn't get into trouble, and I'd pray to God for some extra pocket money. So you can probably guess by now that religion never appealed to me at all; I really hated the daily regimes, meetings and sternness of religion and so when I became a teenager, I opted for a life in music which led to lots of sex, drugs and boozing. My parents never objected to this move in music (I never told them about the sex, drugs and boozing bit – I think they would have been mortified to learn that I liked to get pissed and stoned on a regular basis) until one of my future bands was called Judas Priest but I will talk about that in Chapter 3.

Charlemont Educational School was a very large and intimidating building; a lot of very old English schools are quite gothic buildings and Charlemont was no exception. I never appreciated the grandeur of the building until I got older and learned to love history and the beautiful historical sites in England.

I was at Charlemont right through from Infants to Juniors and even up into my Secondary School years. The British educational system is weird; why are public schools private? I never worked that one out. Anyway, Charlemont was public in the sense that anybody could go. It was at Charlemont that I got the unlikely nickname of Tatter. My form teacher, or class master as we used to say then, was named Mr. Ben Graham. He used to call me Tommy, which was taken from the common nickname of the British soldier Tommy Atkins during the First World War; basically if a German soldier wanted to speak to a Brit, they'd shout "Tommy" across no man's land so everyone started to call me Tommy. Later, the nickname got shortened to Tat and then it became Tatter, which has stuck with me all my life. Other school kids would say things like "Tatter, come over here" or "C'mon Tatter, let's skip class."

It was at Charlemont School when I was first introduced to music and although we had an upright piano at home, I didn't take much notice. As I've said, the hymns bored me; I wanted something more exciting than "Amazing Grace" or "Rock Of Ages". I wanted something with meaning, something I could relate to and something that would excite me.

I've mentioned that my dad had a harmonica; it was a button activated slide bar hohner chromatic harmonic, which he played very well and which I would steal from time to time. My very first recollection of attempting anything musical and being serious about it was doing an impersonation of Al Jolson. I blackened my face just like Al in the film »The Jazz Singer« and that was not because we didn't have any running water! I'd use black paint and I'd even wear my sisters white gloves to mimic Al's hand gestures. He was a white guy who made a career for himself as a black man. People who did that were called minstrels; you couldn't get away with that kind of thing nowadays without being called a racist. Al Jolson was a great entertainer, a legendary figure in the business who influenced an amazing array of artists; people like Frank Sinatra, Sammy Davis Jr. and even David Lee Roth. I think he appealed to so many different kinds of entertainers because he was such an eccentric character. I remember singing "Mammie" at Queen Elizabeth's coronation street party competition in 1953 when I was just six years old. Despite getting into rock and roll music, I have always been an Al Jolson fan.

Like most children raised in poor working class areas, West Bromwich was not the best looking or most glamorous of towns but it's my home and I love it, which is why I still live here; they say home is where the heart is and I believe that to be a hundred percent true. To outsiders it's probably one of the grimmest places in the country but to us locals it's where we belong. West Bromwich has given birth to quite a few famous people: Robert Plant, my Priest buddies Ian Hill and Kenny Downing, the comedian Frank Skinner and the Hollywood actor Matthew Marsden. Even the great Irish rocker Phil Lynott of Thin Lizzy was born in West Bromwich at Hallam Hospital (now Sandwell General) in 1949. We also have a famous football team called West Bromwich Albion. So you can't say we haven't given anything to the world!

West Bromwich didn't have a lot to offer. And because we were quite poor I was something of a naughty boy, skipping lessons and giving cheek to my parents but in all honesty I enjoyed growing up in those surroundings. I kept lots of animals and even before my teenage years I had pigeons, a dog and a cat. My parents, although they were strict, were quite forgiving too so I was lucky. Even now I keep a dog and rats!

Despite the size of our house, we had a large garden with an apple tree and a pear tree and I have some fond memories of spending my free time helping my mum make (and eat) apple pies. I love the smell of home cooked apple pies, there's nothing like it! I love my food. I prefer good English grub like steak and kidney pies and fish and chips.

Wednesbury cemetery looking a little bit spooky overlooking Ocker Hill in the early sixties.

I'm not an amateur historian but I do know quite a bit about my birthplace. West Bromwich – which means "little village on the heath of broom" – was for centuries a very rural farming town; there was a lot of greenery before the Industrial Revolution began at some point in the late 18th Century but the farming areas were replaced by coal mines and the choking fumes of industrialisation when vast deposits of coal were found. Industries were built all over West Bromwich and in similar Black Country/Northern towns, hence the saying "It's grim up North." I've always hated that saying, especially coming from people who have never seen the beauty of the Midlands; I can take you to grim and depressing areas of London, every place has its rough edges. And I doubt you'll find nicer people anywhere in Britain than in the Midlands. We're humble and friendly people.

Local novelist David Christie Murray has written passionately about the West Midlands. He once wrote about its Green Belt – a very large park with lakes – in Sandwell Valley, which shows that there is more to the Black Country than just factories, coal mines and industries that stain the sky from the smoke and soot and the hazardous smells. There is indeed some colour and a certain beauty to be found in the industrial Midlands and the North. The Green Belt is absolutely beautiful.

West Bromwich is in the borough of Sandwell which is part of the Black Country in the West Midlands. The Black Country is famous for many things; it's hard to define but I can tell you that it is a group of towns (essentially West Bromwich, Dudley, Walsall, Blackheath, Sandwell, Wolverhampton and Stourbridge) to the north and west of Birmingham. Birmingham is derived from the old name "Brummagem" but us locals just call the city "Brum" which is said with a great deal of affection. The Midlands is the birthplace of the famous British Industrial Revolution.

The Black Country used to be known as "Red by night and black by day" due to the amount of foundries, forges, collieries and chain making that went on there during the coal mining industry. In fact, I know of one story about the distinction between the North and the South of England: Queen Victoria once travelling on a train through the Black Country closed all the blinds in her carriage because the sight offended her so much. And the chains for the famous SS Titanic were made here at Noah Hingley & Sons at Netherton in 1911, so too was the 15-ton anchor. George Orwell wrote about the industrial North in his famous book »The Road To Wigan Pier«. For examples on what the Midlands and the North used to look like, you should take a look at the paintings by the Lancashire artist L.S. Lowry.

Whenever I read about Judas Priest and Black Sabbath and other heavy metal bands from the Black Country, certain band members always talk about their upbringing and the influence the steel companies, factories and coal mines have had on creating their particular style and sound of metal music. I do believe this to be true. It is difficult for us all not to be influenced by our surroundings; the same can be said of earlier gritty, garage rock of Iggy Pop and Alice Cooper who both come from Detroit which is akin to industrial Birmingham. If Iggy Pop had come from, say, Florida, I doubt he would have made punk rock with an obvious electric blues influence. Indeed, the Black Country itself not only turned out steel in the sixties and early seventies, it also turned out music with many top rock groups emerging, like Black Sabbath, Slade, Trapeze and Led Zeppelin. I'm sure Rob and the rest of Priest were inspired by the Black Country when they wrote songs like "Breaking The Law" and "Runnin' Wild" and when they made the video for "A Touch Of Evil", they probably thought of the Black Country factories. C'mon, they even named their most famous album »British Steel«, after the famous steel producing company. Check out "Made In Hell" on Rob's brilliant solo album »Resurrection« because that song sums up the era perfectly.

I'm going to talk a bit more about the Black Country and rock music in the next chapter but for now I've got a few more memories from my childhood that I'd like to share with you …

My own memories of the steel works and industries of the Midlands are from when I was a kid; I used to visit my uncle Bill Smith who lived just next door to us. He would come home covered head to foot in dirt and soot from his long laborious shifts at Johnson's Steel Works. He would stand by the kitchen sink and wash himself down with the hot water my aunt Harriet had boiled for him in one of those old stove kettles, and tell me all about his job rolling hot steel. Those stories horrified more than excited me; it was bloody hard work and deadly at times too. I always thought uncle Bill and his peers were heroes: "It's a tough job but somebody has to do it."

But those men like my uncle Bill had no choice; with families to support and bills to pay, they had to take whatever job was available. It's not like today where people have a lot of choice in employment; jobs in those days were very limited.

Sometimes I would walk up Church Lane at Black Lake Industrial Estate where he worked and I would watch him and his workmates through the rusty old barred windows; through those windows I would be able to see the fiery hot sparks from the steel producing machines shooting all around them. I'd see the hot mills bubbling with fire and producing enough smoke to fill the sky. They did that all day for little pay and there wasn't the kind of health and safety regulations there are now, so they were putting their lives at risk. They'd have a break long enough to eat their sandwiches and drink a cup of tea and that was it … back to work.

To a young child it looked really dangerous but I suppose to my uncle it was normal practice – it was a job. The pounding of the big hammers would cause the ground to shake and could be felt two miles away, and I used to think that this must be hell. In fact, one foundry in Netherton near Dudley was accurately called The Hell Hole. That's a good name for a song actually; I think I'll write a song about it one day.

The steel works and furnaces would let off an incredible heat that could have burned through the building like a fire; the heat would literally burn through Bill's work boots and I think in some way it contributed to his early death. He died before reaching his retirement when both his legs turned gangrene. It was not unusual for men to die young because of years spent working in steel furnaces or coal mines because the atmosphere was so toxic and even now in the 21st Century, you hear all the time about retired industry workers who have caught cancer or struggle to breathe because of the effects of their previous occupation.

After attempts to mimic Al Jolson, my next step in the world of music was joining the air scouts at 14 years old when I was in my Secondary School years at Charlemont. I joined just so I could learn to play a drum kit in the marching band with the help of my neighbour and friend Trevor Mumford. Marching bands were big businesses back then; it was a great British tradition. You still see them now and again at special occasions or at some grand function for the royal family but in those days you'd see them all the time. Not only did they sound great but they looked fantastic too, very smart and polished.

My brother and sister were not interested in music one little bit so I had to make friends with people who shared my interests. It was Trevor who showed me how to play every drum roll, so in actual fact, I was a drummer first and it was a few more years before I became a singer.

When I was a teenager, in the late fifties and early sixties, the British youth copied the Americans as seen on imported movies from the US and with this came authentic American music like traditional blues, rhythm and blues and rock and roll, which was copied and modified by our own (young) British artists during the sixties. The blues was alien to my parents but to my peers it was a glorious style of music that told stories of hardship, slavery and deprivation with such obvious emotion and the guitar work was simply magnetic.

During the Second World War between 1939 and 1945, American soldiers that were stationed in Britain would bring with them stuff like cigarettes (or pall malls as they say over there) and nudie magazines. But it was the dusty records they'd bring with them that had a major effect on us Brits. Of course, it was all American music, mostly the blues and jazz. However, hearing this supposedly new kind of music was very limited in the UK and the only way you could listen to non-British music was by tuning into Radio Luxemburg which was not exactly legal; these days it would be called pirate radio.

BBC Radio did have a Saturday morning show in the late fifties called »The Saturday Skiffle Club« and I remember that the presenters sounded like my school teachers. Commercial television arrived in Britain in the mid-fifties like a god send, us kids loved it. The BBC also broadcasted a Sunday afternoon review of the current music charts and later on it did get a little better in terms of exposing music with some late fifties television shows like Jack Good's »Oh Boy« and »Six Five Special«.

»Oh Boy«, in particular, played a huge apart in exposing pop groups but as a TV programme it appalled many Conservative voters and politicians. The most famous pop manager of the fifties was Larry Parnes; he used to promote his groups on »Oh Boy«. Parnes was like a Louis Walsh or Simon Cowell figure of his day, manufacturing the latest boy band although in those days we used to call them pop groups. Parnes managed some of the biggest British singers of the fifties: Billy Fury, Dickie Pride, Marty Wilde and Georgie Fame. He must have kicked himself in the arse when he watched The Beatles reach insane heights of success and popularity throughout the sixties; Parnes famously turned them down as a backing band for fellow Liverpudlian Billy Fury when they performed under the name The Silver Beetles.

Overall, the BBC had an important role in popularising American blues and other styles of American music in the immediate post-war years, certainly into the fifties and sixties. And because of this, many local radio stations started to notice the growing popularity of this kind of music. So the broadcasters began playing vintage blues songs and even pop music, which was then in its infancy with leading groups like The Shadows, on the radio as well as on the chart/review programmes on television. Of course, some individual broadcasters were sceptical and approached the blues and pop music with certain degrees of caution but it could have been much worse.

Radio was an important thing in the lives of many British people in those days. We had one of those old ones which stood up the corner of the room by my dad's favourite armchair and he would sit there listening to it every night whilst smoking his woodbine cigarettes. My dad would listen to anything: dramas, serials and especially comedies and the news. Roger Taylor of Queen was right when he wrote the song "Radio Ga Ga" which is about the downfall of radio and the uprising of the TV. Yeah Roger, I still love the radio, too.

Most portable radios in that era were bloody enormous things, like the size of a briefcase. I don't have an iPod or even a mobile phone (I'm like Ozzy – I hate the bloody things!) but I loved having a radio because until TV arrived it was the only way to listen to the latest music without spending money on records and money was not something that I had until I started working. I used to take a little transistor radio to bed with me every night at bedtime and lie under the sheets tuning it to various stations; I'd often hear a bit of blues, boogie-woogie and jazz. Television was less important to me back then; we were one of the last families in our street to get one and that would have been around 1957 when I was ten. I didn't know what to think of it at first, it was like an alien object.

My generation was the first post-war generation to fully appreciate the blues and even empathise with the lyrics because of what we had gone through during and immediately after the World War II; everybody was skint, angry and unwanted – the main traits of the blues. The central pre and post war blues players were people like Robert Johnson, Sonny Boy Williamson, John Lee Hooker, B.B. King, Muddy Waters, Willie Dixon, Howlin' Wolf and Elmore James. All these guys would influence the likes of Robert Plant, Jimmy Page, Eric Clapton, Jeff Beck, Steve Winwood, Peter Green, Paul Rodgers and Rod Stewart – all of them born in the forties. Some of the more popular songs that caught my attention were tunes like "Hoochie Coochie Man", "Sweet Home Chicago", "I Just Want To Make Love To You" and "How Many More Years". I, like many budding British musicians, was in awe of American blues. What's amazing about those classic blues songs is that they sound even better now in the new millennium.

Even though I was deeply fond of the blues, as I grew up in the late fifties and early sixties, like most of my mates, I was also into American pop artists like Buddy Holly and The Crickets, Jerry Lee Lewis, The Everley Brothers and, of course, the king himself, Mr. Elvis Presley. The late great Eddie Cochran – who was killed while touring England in a car accident on the old A4 road in Wiltshire in 1960 – was my childhood idol. He was just 21 when he died. What a sad story. Just day's earlier at one of Cochran's gigs at London's Hackney Empire, a 13 year old lad named Mark Feld had been allowed to carry his guitar to Cochran's limo. Several years later Mark changed his name to Marc Bolan and became a glam rock icon in the band T-Rex, but by a strange coincidence he too would die in a similar car accident. As fate would have it, their deaths have added to their legacies but at least Cochran and Bolan had enough time to make great music that will last forever.

I was – and still am – a fan of Cochran; his music has lived on decades after his untimely and unfortunate death and it will probably live on forever. Songs like "Summertime Blues", "C'mon Everybody", "Weekend" and "Something Else" still inspire me. I still get goose bumps every time I hear those songs on the radio or television; they remind me of my childhood. He only released one album during his lifetime and that was 1958's »Singin' To My Baby« – it's a cracker!

The likes of the revered electric guitarists Chuck Berry and Bo Diddley helped merge rockabilly (a sort of country-pop sound) with the blues to make an early incarnation of rock and roll. Lots of rockabilly singers such as Elvis were big fans of boogie-woogie piano-based blues while Chuck Berry, being an accomplished guitarist, was more interested in the electric blues from the gritty urban streets of Chicago. This unique sound was transported over the Atlantic, from America, and found its way to Birmingham and the West Midlands. Now that is one hell of a good story to tell!

The Americans dominated the pop scene in the late fifties and early sixties. The only British artist that I listened to at that time was Mr. Rock Island Line, himself, the late great Lonnie Donegan. "Rock Island Line" – a cover of the Leadbelly song – was rightly voted Number 38 in Mojo magazine's '100 Records That Changed The World' poll. He had a big influence on a lot of the early groups in Britain that were starting up at this time, including The Beatles. I have a little story to tell: in May, 1979, Lonnie turned up uninvited to a massive wedding party of Eric Clapton's. The guests included Ronnie Wood, Jeff Beck, Bill Wyman, Robert Palmer, Robert Plant, Jack Bruce and George, Paul and Ringo of The Beatles. When George Harrison saw Donegan, he said: "When I was a little boy I knocked on your door for your autograph." Lonnie replied: "Yes, that's why I'm here, I want it back."

Donegan first began playing to audiences in Chris Barber's jazz band and over the years Donegan built up a steady reputation because of his brilliant renditions of songs by Woody Guthrie and other famous folk/blues artists. He is popularly cited as the 'King Of Skiffle' and influenced the likes of Paul McCartney, Elton John, Bob Dylan and Brian May. There was nobody like him and there'll never be anybody like him again, he's one of a kind.

Skiffle was not to everybody's tastes; it was a sort of British homage to American folk, blues and jazz. People like Lonnie Donegan used all manner of items to make the skiffle sound, literally anything from a washboard to a kitchen sink. Skiffle players also used banjos like George Formby and acoustic guitars like Woody Guthrie. Skiffle paved the way for British rock and roll. Prior to meeting Paul McCartney, John Lennon formed a skiffle band in 1957 called The Quarrymen. McCartney met Lennon at a Quarrymen gig in Woolton, Liverpool and the rest as they say is history: McCartney joined The Quarrymen and brought a young George Harrison along with him.

1962 was the year I bought my first record – "Love Me Do" by The Beatles which I still have in my record collection and I'm sure it must be worth a few quid now. It was released in October of that year through Parlophone. I remember hearing Lennon's bluesy harmonica for the first time and being in complete awe of that sound. My parents weren't too keen on this new music I was listening to.

"This is the greatest thing I've ever heard", I said to my parents.

The Beatles were greatly influenced by American rhythm and blues and you can definitely hear that vibe on their first album »Please Please Me« although the blues is lost on some of their more famous pop singles. The Beatles and The Rolling Stones were two completely different bands, yet they shared similar musical influences; The Stones began as a blues covers band with Mick Jagger mimicking his idol Muddy Waters.

Music wasn't my only hobby; I loved horror movies and would go on my own to the Clifton Cinema in Stone Cross every Sunday night when they showed them. In cinemas, well, we used to say pictures back then, horror movies were popular with local kids.

My mum would say: "You're not going to watch those horrible monster films again, are you? I don't really approve of you spending so much time at the pictures."

I especially liked Boris Karloff and the home-grown »Hammer Horror« pictures with Christopher Lee and Peter Cushing. I wasn't surprised years later when a band called Earth changed their name to Black Sabbath having taken that from the Italian horror film which starred Mr. Karloff himself. So really, music and movies were my main interests and still are. I hated sport even though, as I've said, my hometown has a pretty good team called West Bromwich Albion. Sport tended to be for the really popular lads and I wasn't one of them.

My sister moved down to Kent when she was 17 years of age and I got to have my own bedroom after sharing with Brian for 14 years. Bliss.

I was a quiet lad in my early years because of my good family upbringing and schooling but there were so many bullies at Charlemont from the rough council estates in West Bromwich that I eventually got into their ways and was involved in a lot of fighting in my teenage years. By the time I left school aged 15 in 1962, I wore a leather jacket and a belt made up of metal hinges with a six-inch nail pushed down the front to hold it together. I'd also started smoking and met a girl called Janet Billingham; she was my age and we fell in love. It didn't last long; it was just a teenage romance. It's no wonder I got into heavy metal!

Chapter 2
Birmingham Beat Boom &
The Rockin' Sixties (1963-1968)

In the historic Beat Boom of the early sixties there were groups being formed in literally every street in every town across the country and personally I couldn't wait to play in one. The Beat Boom was especially popular in Liverpool and Birmingham so it was great for me because the whole scene was practically on my doorstep.

In 1963 I was just 16 years old and having already left school, I felt that the whole world was my oyster. My parents didn't want me to stay on at school, instead they wanted me to pursue a job and make some money; it was the normal thing to do in those days. I hung around with a right naughty bunch of lads who were always getting into trouble and we all ended up in court for stealing cars, which brought shame on my family.

I'd hear all kinds of things from my family: "You're an absolute disgrace, Allan."

As a consequence of my actions, my dad forbid me to see them anymore and told me to concentrate on what I liked best, which was music. The ironic thing about leaving school and having ambitions beyond academia was that I quickly found out there were hardly any jobs away from the industries and coal mines so I had lots of time on my hands and very little to do. I was as well staying on at school. Most working class kids in those days left school at 15 or 16, very few stayed in education. I finally found a small job to keep me busy. I worked at a garage as an apprentice motorbike mechanic, working mainly on BSA and Triumph motorcycles. Fixing them was more profitable than stealing them! The funny thing is, even though I worked as a mechanic, my family at that point didn't own a car. At least it was a steady job and not down the pits or in a factory.

One day in early 1963, I took my dad down to Wednesbury town centre in Sandwell and begged him to buy me a Stratford Besson drumset, which was on show in the front window of the music shop. As an eager kid I was full of promises to my parents and so I promised my dad I would keep out of trouble and stop stealing cars if I could have the drumset.

"Okay, but there better be an improvement in your behaviour or else I'll take it back."

My dad was a bit of a musician himself and he taught me a few drum beats to practice with and as a kid he had also taught me how to play harmonica but I wasn't a great drummer and at one time I was feeling really low and thought I'd never get a job in a group. I quickly became bored of the drums and I started practicing my vocal skills too and bought myself a new Vox P.A system and a mic (complete with a stand) from Yardley's in Birmingham which was one of the main music shops at the time, the other being George Clay's Music Centre.

Now that I was armed with all this brand new equipment I was confident that I would be able to get into my first group. Fortunately, I hooked up with two old school friends from Charlemont: Colin "Cosha" Bird who played guitar and Kenny Stein who played bass. We didn't have a name for our new group but we were full of excitement and enthusiasm at the prospect of playing music together. We practiced at every given opportunity and watched with keen eyes the older groups who gigged around the Black Country. We would copy their techniques, mimic their stage moves and try to sing like them. Kenny and myself both had old motorbikes; he had a knackered 250cc Arial and I had a 1947 250cc BSA, which we would ride around the fields in the hot summer days when we were not rehearsing. I suppose I always had a bit of a rebel in me.

Cosha's older brother Billy ran us around in his old motor car and got us some rehearsal rooms to practice in, so I suppose he took on the role as our first manager. One place we practiced at was a café in Handsworth in Birmingham and it was there when I got my first free vocal lessons by the owner who was a lovely big woman with an even bigger set of lungs; she was a retired opera singer and made a living from training budding young singers.

In the sixties, café and coffee houses became popular in Britain's biggest cities as part of the new wave of popular culture after World War II; suddenly everybody who wanted to be seen as cool was drinking espressos or cappuccinos. And cafés became hang-out spots for young artistic people just like the ones in Paris or San Francisco.

Sadly, our little trio never got off the ground because Cosha's brother had a bad road accident, which killed Billy's wife and her in-laws and we seemed lost without his help so we decided to call it a day.

I learned a lot from my first band experience; for one thing it boosted my confidence and I got to practice as much as possible and show off my growing talents in front of people. I also got to witness other bands in the area after our rehearsals finished. One group from Birmingham I liked was called Denny and The Diplomats with singer Denny Laine; I would watch them on Sunday lunchtime down at our local public house called The Golden Lion. This is where I tried my first alcoholic drink and definitely not my last. Drinking beer for the first time is a weird experience; it doesn't taste all that good yet you have another and another and it becomes an acquired taste.

Watching the growth of Denny's career really inspired me; he's from Tyseley in Birmingham. Denny Laine left the group in 1964 and went on to play for the now legendary band The Moody Blues – another Birmingham band – who had a number one single with a song called "Go Now". For a young musician like I was in 1963, it was encouraging to see how you could be playing in a pub one day and be a big pop star the next. Years later Denny went on to play alongside Paul McCartney in his band Wings and other major acts, including Ginger Baker's Air Force. Denny's former colleagues also had success because The Diplomats featured future members of The Move and Electric Light Orchestra.

1963 was a successful year for rock and roll and pop music in Britain. The Beatles released their debut album »Please Please Me« through EMI. They'd done their training in front of reluctant audiences at dingy clubs (most famously the Star-Club) in Hamburg, Germany and came back to Britain firing on all cylinders, filled with determination and ready to take any kind of criticism. »Please Please Me« is a great record; songs like "Love Me Do", "I Saw Her Standing There" and the title track really struck a chord in Britain's youth who craved for a bit of home grown talent. The Beatles weren't to everybody's tastes but it certainly seemed that every child my age was in awe of them. A similar thing would happen in the nineties with Oasis.

Obviously, there wasn't anything wrong with the American rock and roll records, it's just that we needed other artists in this country besides Cliff Richard and he was just a rip-off

Elvis, anyway. I bet he'd freely admit that now as well. But boy did The Beatles make an impression; their success went global. Cliff Richard's backing band The Shadows with the terrific Hank Marvin were, in fact still are, excellent but The Beatles were fresh, vibrant and uniquely talented. They looked great, sounded even better and they had working class accents. Everybody was used to hearing posh accents on the TV or the radio but The Beatles were authentic Northerners, well, Scousers.

Tommy Steele was another pop star that was similar to Cliff Richard but he's generally acknowledged as the first ever British pop idol. Okay, he tended to cover American songs like "Knee Deep In The Blues" and "Singing The Blues" but Britain had never seen anybody like him before. At the end of the fifties his career was on the slide but he continued to hold down a steady job in the entertainment business.

Before I talk about the Birmingham Beat Boom, it was the Mersey Sound – also known as the Merseybeat – that brought British music to the world's centre stage. From around 1961 to 1965, Liverpool produced many bands of great talent although most of them are little known today. At the time Liverpool had The Beatles, The Searchers, Gerry and The Pacemakers, Cilla Black, The Undertakers, The Swinging Blue Jeans, The Fourmost, Rory Storm and The Hurricanes, Billy J Kramer and The Dakotas and The Big Three. Liverpool appeared to be a hive for great pop music that had R&B, rockabilly and soul influences. Remarkably, a lot of the Merseyside bands had success on the other side of the Atlantic Ocean albeit only temporarily. Before The Beatles, Liverpool was a poor city that was mostly famous for having a sea port but during the time of the famous four's ascent to world domination, Liverpool was suddenly the pop centre of the world. Since the sixties, money has been poured into the city to make it a better looking and more vibrant place. This explosion of pop music in Britain, which travelled over the Atlantic, led to the name The British Invasion. The first British band to have a Number One pop single in the States was The Animals with a cover of the folk song "The House Of The Rising Sun". Eric Burdon is one hell of a great blues singer and even now he's still singing the blues.

Manchester also gave birth to some good bands, including The Hollies, Freddie and The Dreamers and Herman's Hermits. I saw first-hand how all this music exploded in the North of England within a short space of time. It was a great decade and anybody that lived through it will tell you how amazing it was.

I was fortunate enough to have been born just after the Second World War because that meant I could witness the creation and progression of rock and roll.

The great rock and roll stars of the fifties had their glory days behind them. The British bands became the dominant force in the business. Elvis had joined the army in 1960 but when he returned to music he made some dire films which halted his career until he made a big comeback in Las Vegas. Bill Haley and Jerry Lee Lewis were still popular on the live circuit but their creativity in the studio was underwhelming and so their success in the charts declined massively. Carl Perkins was another one who wasn't doing to well; he got himself hooked on booze and drugs. The great Buddy Holly died in 1959 in an airplane accident which also killed his fellow rock and roll passengers Ritchie Valens and The Big Bopper. And then there's Little Richard – the legend behind "Tutti Frutti" and "Long Tall Sally" – who became a preacher and born-again Christian in the late fifties. I've already mentioned the sad death of my idol Eddie Cochran, which had the biggest impact on me as a budding musician.

The Midlands had been lucky enough to have been host to concerts by some of these legends in the fifties and sixties. Gene Vincent had played at the Adelphi Ballroom in West Brom. Jerry Lee Lewis had played at the Birmingham Town Hall. Coventry Theatre had seen Eddie Cochran grace its stage and even Buddy Holly and The Crickets had performed in Longbridge. Sadly, Elvis never visited England, although I've read reports that he briefly touched down in Scotland while the plane he was on was getting refuelled.

Bruno and me sampling a fine alcoholic beverage known as Holdens Golden Glow.

1963 saw me in my first real group that would play to paying audiences and I teamed up with a friend who would be with me in various groups for the next 20 years. He was a big lad and a big musician and his name was Brian Stapenhill but everyone knew him as Bruno; he was in the year below me at school. Most of my school friends were not interested in forming bands and playing live so it came as a surprise to find somebody as eager about it as me. Sure, lots of my peers listened to music, but they didn't want to make music. We swapped records and spoke about music at school but it was clear that I was the most eager music fan.

My parents loved Bruno; he was a good influence on me, not like some of the rogues that I used to hang around with before I got into music. I think Bruno was like an adopted son in my family. Bruno was a big gentle giant with long hair and a thick beard; he looked more like a roadie than a bassist. He was someone you just loved and could never fall out with and he was a fantastic bass player too – one of the best around.

I first heard Bruno practicing on his guitar at the back of my house in Caldwell Street, West Bromwich. He lived practically opposite my back garden and was always playing Hank Marvin and The Shadows instrumentals and I used to think how good he was. When we first met up I couldn't believe it, he had only just left school but he was a burgeoning wizard on guitar. The Shadows were by far his favourite group of the era; he absolutely loved them. They'd formed in 1958 initially as a backing band for Cliff Richard who was Britain's biggest and best looking pop star. Hank Marvin was Bruno's idol and would play such instrumentals as "Apache", "Kon Tiki" and "Wonderful Land".

Bruno and myself decided to form a rock and roll group merging our influences together; Bruno was into pop music of the day while I was into American blues and rhythm and blues. We brought in two other lads to join us in our quest to form a successful band. We hired bass player Brian Powney and it was his brother John who suggested Brian; they lived down the road from me. We also hired Colin Mathews on rhythm guitar and we called ourselves The Medallians; in hindsight it's an ugly name – I can't remember why we chose it in the first place. We looked very smart in our grey trousers and blue blazers with a yellow letter 'M' sewn on to our top pockets. It was the normal thing to do in the sixties, to make band members look identical with the same haircut and wear the same clothes. You see it now with bands like Franz Ferdinand and The Hives – it's all been done before. In hindsight, it looked good but I prefer each member to have their own identity to express their individual personal tastes.

The first booking we ever had was at a neighbour's wedding reception at The Coral Hall, by the All Saints in West Bromwich. Bruno was about 15 years old and I was a bit older. It was a horrible venue; it was like a tin shed but those kinds of cheaply built places were common in those days. It's since been knocked down ... for the better. I don't actually remember anything about the gig except the venue but as time progressed we improved our sound.

We were successful with our very first gigs and our setlist was mainly The Shadows music and we even threw in a couple of pop songs by The Beatles to make us sound good. We branched out when we became more confident and even started to play some Smokestack Lighting and Muddy Waters songs as well as some home grown blues songs.

My old band The Medallians: Colin, me, Brian and Bruno.

It was at this time that John Mayall and The Bluesbreakers began making a name for themselves on the live circuit. Mayall is a Northerner who was inspired by the great American blues artists and wanted to bring those guys over to England.

One gig that I remember was for Jenson Motors whom Colin worked for briefly at their employee's party and we got paid £40 and all the food we could eat. That worked out at £10 each which was nearly a month's wages to me at the time and coming from a working class background I had never seen so much food or even eaten some of it: king prawns and melon was never on our menu at home, it was nearly always fish and chips or a dripping sandwich because mum worked at the local chippy.

"This is brilliant Colin, look at all this great food", I said.

"I know, I can hardly believe my eyes."

Sadly, The Medallians didn't last very long and I eventually sacked both the new players for not taking the band seriously enough. I later found out that Brian Powney joined a band called Herbies People as the keyboardist. They were one of the best Black Country bands that came from Dudley/Bilston area. In '65, they played London's Albert Hall and signed with CBS but never got their just rewards like a lot of bands. I didn't know he played keyboards so I was totally shocked when I found out.

Bruno was with me all the way and was as eager and passionate as me about taking a music career seriously. It wasn't just about making money, it was about making music that people would remember and because neither of us wanted to be stuck in a dull nine to five job, we worked tirelessly to become good musicians and to make a name for ourselves.

After Bruno and myself got rid of Colin and Brian for being lazy, a mutual friend of ours named Ken Ford introduced us to a guitarist called Albert "Hoggy" Hinton who was a bit of a Mod and wouldn't have looked out of place in The Small Faces. Christ, at that time we needed somebody who would take the band seriously enough to want to live off rations and literally starve for the music. The three of us got on very well together and decided to stay as a trio for the time being to see how things worked out, so Bruno swapped his lead guitar for a six-string Futurama bass and bought an enormous Park speaker cab, which contained two 18-inch speakers.

I remember saying to Bruno at the time: "How the fucking hell are we going to transport that?!"

Always an optimist, Bruno said: "Don't worry, we will think of something."

He was a natural bass player and this is where his future lay. From early on, I would handle some of the vocals as I fancied myself more of a singer than a drummer; I eventually took over all the vocals as well as the drumming. We called ourselves The Reaction and began playing straight away. Years later, I found out that Queen drummer Roger Taylor was also in a sixties band called The Reaction in the West Country.

> *Ken and I obviously go way back; we still keep in touch occasionally and he would like to add a few words.*
> Ken Ford (childhood friend & manager): "I worked with Albert Hinton at Robinson Brothers as an apprentice electrician in the mid-sixties; he was playing once a week at the British Legion in West Bromwich with some of his friends. I don't remember but I may have been the link between Al and Bruno to form The Reaction. They played covers to perfection. I got them a Friday night residency at the Old Grand pub in Walsall. The management/agent for the pub was named Sid and the barman was a middle-aged man named Ted who also sold condoms behind the bar. The band used to get a lift to the gigs from either Tom from Friar Park in his old Morris J2 Mini bus or Bill Carter from Tipton. The band later bought their own Bedford van and a friend named David Dowd drove it for them."

I don't remember my parents giving The Reaction much of a chance although my mates loved the band and after some strenuous rehearsals at a pub in West Bromwich town centre we built up something of a following wherever we played. The enthusiasm from the audience members gave us the kickstart we needed.

After a few months performing together as The Reaction we decided to get ourselves a manager and asked our friend Ken Ford if he would be interested in the job. Ken was an electrician by trade which was very handy and the first thing he did, was build us a long cabinet which contained different coloured flashing lights and we thought we were the bee's knees because no other local groups had anything like it. It made us feel important, like we were the most popular group in West Brom.

As we entered 1964 at the slow pace of a snail, we decided to expand and find some more serious players to join us and the first player to join was Brian "Bingy" Fieldhouse. Brian was introduced to me by my life long friend big Archie Cole. Brian was something of a local hero on guitar; he could play anything by the best guitarists of the day. He came from a band called The Hellstones and was the owner of a very handsome Burns Marvin. In fact, years later that particular guitar was discovered to be the seventh one in an assembly line made especially for the great Hank Marvin himself by Jim Burns and Jack Golder who took Hank's own specifications for the model. As we all know, in the end, Hank opted for a Fender Stratocaster endorsement. This guitar of Bingy's was to become very collectable and is now on display at a Hard Rock Café; they won a bid for it at an auction run by Sotheby's or Christie's, one of the big auction companies. It was thanks to the group's lifelong fan and friend Alan Grosvenor that the guitar ended up on public display.

After joining us, it was Bingy who said I was a better vocalist than drummer and deep down I knew this was true. He suggested that I should swap my sticks for the mic so I did and we brought in another drummer who was an old friend of Bingy's named Lawrence "Lossa" Farley from another local group called The What Four. This was great for me because it gave me the chance to develop my vocals.

From that point onwards we had become a five-piece act and were sounding better every time we played. So with an amended line-up we basically gigged, rehearsed and tried tirelessly to promote ourselves in the West Midlands. It was hard but the success of local groups from Birmingham and surrounding areas really inspired us.

"This is what we need", I said to Bruno one day. "We need a hit single, look at all the other bands out there. They're on the radio. We need to start making our own material."

1964 was a better year for us and for the British music scene in general which prospered like a flower during spring time. And in Birmingham, the music scene was simply awesome because there were bands everywhere. I remember a music magazine called the Midland Beat, which was basically a copy of Bill Harry's Mersey Beat. Midland Beat was a great magazine because it printed reviews, gig listings and advertisements for those who wanted to hook up with other musicians in the area. Some of my bands got minimal amounts of local press, nothing big, just a few lines, but it all helps. But there were other bands who got loads of free local press. I would buy the weekly music papers Melody Maker and New Musical Express and The Beat Instrumental, which was a monthly magazine. I still have about 20 of those stored away somewhere in my cupboard at home. Melody Maker had the best music writers in Britain and it was always great to read about bands from the Midlands who had hit records.

I remember that a Birmingham band called The Applejacks were signed to Decca Records and were at some point in '64 in the Top Ten charts for 13 weeks peaking at Number Seven with a song called "Tell Me When". The Applejacks came from Solihill and although they befriended The Beatles and had a Top 20 single, their success didn't last after the release of their self-titled debut album in 1964. But it was better than nothing. The group recorded a song written by Lennon/McCartney called "Like Dreamers Do" and it reached Number 20 in the UK pop charts.

I wanted us to have that kind of success, an authentic rags to riches story but obviously with long lasting effects. I also recall an album released in '64 called »Brum Beat«. Dial Records were clever releasing a compilation record of eleven of Birmingham's best bands, including The Fortunes and The Renegades. It capitalised on the local beat scene whilst also promoting the best bands in the area. It was a brilliant collection and might be worth a few pounds now.

A band down south named The Kinks released a single called "You Really Got Me" and I remember when I first heard that opening electric riff – wow! Now that riff was really something special! It's often been said that "You Really Got Me" laid down the blueprint for what we now know as heavy metal; even Van Halen covered it. I think Ray Davies is one of this country's finest songwriters; he's a songwriting genius. The Kinks quickly became a great rock and roll band; their self-titled debut album features great tunes like "Cadillac", "Bald Headed Woman" and a rousing version of Chuck Berry's "Too Much Monkey Business". »Kinda Kinks« is another great rock and roll album and so is »The Kink Kontroversy«.

The Kinks quickly become one of Britain's top bands; along with The Beatles, The Who and The Rolling Stones they dominated the American music market in the mid-sixties. And like every other desperate kid I started to mimic myself on some of those bands.

In early 1965, Bingy suggested we change our name and he came up with The Bitta Sweet, which we all really liked. And we thought it was a good idea to try another name. The Bitta Sweet was the same line-up as The Reaction: me on vocals, Bruno on bass, Albert Hinton and

One of my old bands The Bitta Sweet: Bruno, me, Bingy and Albert. This was taken in Birmingham City Centre.

Brian Fieldhouse on guitars and Lawrence Farley on drums. Our image was a bit of a mix of everything that was happening at the time: Albert was a Mod and dressed in trendy clothes and had a spikey haircut and big sideburns. Brian was an old Rocker who couldn't change his style to go with the times. Bruno dressed like me – a bit of a Mod and a Rocker. Lawrence was always dressed immaculately with a smart haircut to match his attire. He eventually ended up as a hairstylist and owned his own shop. Sadly, he died in 2006 from a massive heart attack. I kept in touch with him over the years, so his early death was a major shock to me.

We were still in jobs so it was difficult to arrange time for practicing and playing live; to be truthful, looking back at those years I don't know how we did it. It was bloody hard work doing a day job and then running home for some food before meeting up with Bruno and the lads to play a gig or rehearse. It's not the gig that's tiring, it's everything that leads up to it: getting the equipment over to the venue, setting everything up, doing a quick soundcheck (if you were lucky enough!) and then just hanging around waiting to play. That can be the worst part; waiting for the gig is just so boring and like all good rock and rollers we'd drink booze before we'd go on stage and sometimes we'd drink a little too much. I don't think I ever went onstage absolutely pissed but definitely a little tipsy. I still like a pint before I go on stage; it's good for the nerves ... at least that's what I keep telling myself.

By now our manager Ken got us booked with a series of gigs at Mary (also known as Ma) Regan's famous Plaza Ballroom in High Street, Old Hill, after we had successfully passed her audition on my birthday. The Plaza Ballroom was a very famous venue: The Beatles, The Rolling Stones and The Animals played there. The Plaza Ballroom even played host to gigs by the great Bill Haley and Jerry Lee Lewis. Sadly, Ma Regan died in March, 2007, aged 94. As a sign of respect, the Plaza Ballroom (now known as a Bingo & Social Club) was temporarily closed.

Our music got a little bit more adventurous and we changed our setlist to songs by The Yardbirds. The heavier bands were my main influences. From the mid-sixties onwards, rhythm and blues in Britain was getting heavier and louder. The Yardbirds were one of our earliest musical influences; they started out as early as 1962 but didn't appear live under The Yardbirds moniker until September 1963. Over the next few years they attracted some of the greatest guitar players around like Eric Clapton, Jeff Beck and Jimmy Page. Like me, all these guys were born in the forties and I couldn't believe they'd had so much success so soon. Clearly, they're more talented than me but that didn't stop me from feeling envious.

We carried on playing at the Old Grand until September 1965. I found that we were building up quite a name for ourselves in West Bromwich. Other gigs I remember playing were the YWCA in Walsall, The Ritz in Kingsheath, The 64 Club at Stone Cross, The Rink Ballroom in Birmingham and Swadlingcote in Derbyshire. We also played at the Silver Blades ice rink in Birmingham, which was more than a little strange because we played to the audience as they ice skated around the rink while we performed in the 'Search For Sound' competition. We did get through to the next round though. I remember we couldn't get Bruno's bass amp through the main door because it was too bloody big, so we had to take it around the side door of the venue and slide it across the ice; the four of us had to lift the bloody thing up onto the stage. He was just a little pissed off later when our roadie broke the neck off his bass guitar while loading the gear into the back of the van after the gig.

"I don't believe this, my dad is gonna kill me", he balled.

The band offered to pool some money together and buy him another one but he declined the offer; instead, the next day he went to Jones & Crosslands music shop in town with his dad, Tom Stapenhill, to sign for a new one. Money was very tight in those days so he couldn't afford to buy a new one in full, opting to pay instead with monthly instalments. He bought a lovely brand new Fender Precision for £85.00 and he still plays it to this very day.

We also played a gig at the Lodge Road Youth Centre after it had just had some sound-proofing done because the local neighbours complained about the noise; we were the test for its strength. We played for half an hour before a police inspector arrived in his black car and ordered us to stop playing. Nowadays, concert venues are like fortified temples to stop the sound from disturbing local neighbourhoods but back then the smaller venues were not quite as powerfully built.

Ken Ford recently found a setlist from when we played at the Gala Hall for a fee of £10.00 alongside the Mac Thomas Orchestra. Looking through my archives I have noted that throughout the year The Bitta Sweet played gigs at The Grant Hall, The Ritz, the Conegre Youth Centre, The Plaza in Handsworth, The Plaza in Old Hill (as support to Heinz and The Wildboys) and the Hall Green Civil Service Club. I remember playing The Plaza in Old Hill in Sandwell because the venue had a revolving stage, which was quite a good gimmick in those days. The venues we played were quite big places actually, much better than playing in pubs and tiny social clubs with unresponsive audiences.

By now, we were heading toward the end of 1965 and around this time a Birmingham pop group was formed called Locomotive and featured a friend of ours on guitar named Joe Ellis who hailed from Friar Park. It seemed that every band around me was becoming successful except ours. Between 1966 and 1970, Locomotive featured an array of talented musicians including Chris Wood of Sounds Of Blue, which later became Chicken Shack. The band was formed by jazz trumpeter Jim Simpson who was a photographer for the Midland Beat; he would later play a major part in the Birmingham music scene with his club residency Henry's Blues House at The Crown pub on the corner of Station Street and Hill Street in Birmingham. Through Jim's love of jazz, Locomotive was initially called The Kansas City Seven but in Birmingham in the mid-sixties that name would hardly have given them a hit single.

Locomotive played extensively around Britain during the sixties and in 1968 they charted at Number 25 with the hit single "Rudi's In Love". It was their only hit record. Jim Simpson left the band not long after to go into management and promotion. Years later, Simpson was noted for forming the blues record label Big Bear Records but before that there was something else he was more famous for: discovering and managing Black Sabbath but more on that later. Locomotive released their only album in 1970 called »We Are Everything You See« but because of their constant image changes (were they a jazz, pop or progressive band?) the album flopped.

Also in the mid-sixties another Birmingham band called The Fortunes had a Number One hit with the unforgettable vocal harmonies of "You Got Your Troubles" and they also scored hits with brilliant songs like "Here It Comes Again" and "Here Comes That Rainy Day Feeling Again" and in 1966 with "Golden Ring". They were a great pop group and "You Got Your Troubles" was also a big hit in the States, something which every British band is in search of. These guys formed after the highly-lauded Merseybeat era and considering Americans seemed to love us Brits their career sky rocketed after signing to Decca Records in '63. Their second single "Caroline" was another favourite track of mine. (During the writing of this book, Rod Allen, singer of The Fortunes, passed away from liver cancer in January, 2008. Apart from The Fortunes' hits, his voice was famous for Coca Cola's jingle "It's The Real Thing". He was a very talented man and will be missed by many).

I also kept my eye on another Beat band, this time from Rugby in Warwickshire. In 1965, a group called Pinkerton's Assorted Colours had been signed to The Fortunes' manager Reg Calvert who got them a deal with Decca Records; they were originally called The Liberators which I think is actually a better name. Pinkerton's Assorted Colours was a good group and in '65 they charted at Number Eight with their first single "Mirror Mirror" which was penned by Tony Newman. The following year they released the single "Don't Stop Loving Me Baby". The group featured Samuel "Pinkerton" Kempe (autoharp/vocals), Tony Newman (guitar), Tom Long (guitar) and Barrie Bernard (bass guitar). On drums was the future Trapeze and Judas Priest sticksman Dave Holland; I'd never have predicted that one day I would end up working with Dave Holland. It's funny how things like that work out in life. Pinkerton's Assorted Colours didn't have much success after the third single "Magic Rocking Horse" and they even changed their name again to Flying Machine. Like many bands of the era, their success was brief and they also faded into obscurity.

On a personal front, I really don't know where The Bitta Sweet's music lay at this particular time but it must have leaned towards more of a modern pop/rock and roll vibe akin to The Shadows, which was Bruno's idea.

It was apparent that only two distinctly different youth movements appeared in the mid-sixties: they were called the Mods and the Rockers. I have a picture of me when I was 16 years old; I'm wearing a collarless Beatle jacket, Drainpipe trousers and Winklepicker shoes with a Teddy Boy haircut, but I had long hair so I was a bit of a rocker and roller at heart. A Teddy Boy, by the way, was a well dressed young man who took influences from the English Edwardian era. To begin with, the Teddy Boy subculture started in London but drifted up to Birmingham and the rest of the country throughout the fifties. The scene really came to light in the sixties during the reign of the Mods and Rockers with many Teddy Boy's becoming Rockers. It sounds complicated now, but in those days the two sides hated each other with a passion. I guess like most teenagers I was still trying to find a comfortable identity for myself so I dressed myself using different influences.

1964-65 saw serious action between both groups; it wasn't exactly fun and games. The Rockers dressed in outdated American influenced attire with leather biker jackets which made them look masculine but quite threatening. They listened to American fifties style music by people like Gene Vincent, Elvis Presley, Jerry Lee Lewis and Eddie Cochran.

The Mods, however, were slick and kitted out in suits and expensive designer coats designed and made by posh tailors in London's West End. They rode scooters and the type of music they were into came from groups like The Who, The Yardbirds and The Small

Faces. The Mods liked American blues, rhythm and blues and a bit of soul. The Mods didn't seem to have any conscience: they would sew fishhooks into the back of their coat lapels as a way of intimidating the Rockers. During fights, they would use the fishhooks as weapons which would often led to severe injuries. They'd even cut the fingers of any Rocker that grabbed hold of them during their violent gatherings. It was really serious stuff which got way out of hand; these days I suppose you could liken it to Goths and Chavs and how they hate each other but it was much more threatening in the sixties.

Large numbers of fans from both hugely popular movements descended on southern English seaside resorts like Margate in Kent and Brighton on the Sussex coast over the English bank holidays and trouble was always inevitable. I remember watching on the television in 1964 when the riot broke out between the Mods and the Rockers on Brighton beach; the police were there but it didn't look as though they could control the situation. It seemed a long way away from my life in West Brom were I could comfortably sit back and watch it all happen from afar. But after just two or three years, around 1966, the fuss over these movements died away and a new uprising of groups appeared, namely the violent skinheads and the peace loving hippies. I didn't belong in any group which is just as well because our music was an odd mix of sounds; I was influenced by Eddie Cochran as much as I was by The Who. Speaking of The Who, they made a brilliant film in the late seventies called »Quadrophenia« which dramatized the conflicts between the Mods and the Rockers during the 1960s; they also made an album called »Quadrophenia« in 1973. The Who have always been a bloody brilliant band and even though Keith Moon and John Entwistle are no longer with us, Roger Daltrey and Pete Townshend still continue to record and tour under the band's name. The original line-up was one of those rare bands were each member was just as talented as the other. Pete Townshend was a nutcase but a uniquely brilliant guitarist and singer-songwriter. He was and still is the real brains behind the band and Daltrey is surely one of the greatest rock front men of all time. I really admired Entwistle and Moon because as a rhythm section they were just so tight and powerful. Listening to Entwistle's bass line through "My Generation" for the first time is something I've never forgotten. Moon was a crazy bloke but an amazing drummer and a great personality which aided the band.

While local bands like The Move, The Fortunes, Listen and The N' Betweens gigged and released singles, my band, The Bitta Sweet, was playing comfortably in the West Midlands but I really wanted us to cut a record, to make a name for ourselves by appearing on TV and in big music magazines like Melody Maker. Well, that's what I always wanted, but with The Bitta Sweet I felt we had a strong connection that could have gotten us far.

I have often thought that The Bitta Sweet had folded by 1965 but I have only recently found some archives that suggest we actually carried on playing right through into 1967, which came as a major surprise to me.

Let me explain: for years I thought The Reaction was formed and folded in 1963 (which is correct) and The Bitta Sweet, which was merely an expansion of The Reaction, folded in '65. I was wrong. So much happened in the sixties that it was hard to keep track. Jesus, I can barely remember what I did last year, let alone in the sixties when I was smoking pot and drinking too much beer.

It came as a real surprise to find some documents and photos during my research for this book which state that The Bitta Sweet gigged in 1966 and 1967.

Another old picture of The Bitta Sweet

Let me tell you a few interesting things happened in '66.

1966 was a lively year full of great sounds, fancy haircuts and flashy clothes. The »Ready Steady Go!« pop show finished at some point during '66, which was a crying shame. »Ready Steady Go!« was the main source of music news on British television and it was actually one of our first ever music TV programmes. I remember when it was first aired in the early sixties; it was like nothing you'd ever seen before on the box. Before that, we'd learned about new bands through word of mouth, on the radio and in the papers, so to actually see bands on TV was wonderful. Television has had such a major impact on the way popular music reaches the masses. As I've said, it's such a shame that the TV replaced the radio as the main source of entertainment and news; the state of radio has changed massively since I was a boy. I used to listen to the radio (we used to call it the wireless) all the time, but how many kids these days listen to the radio? Probably very few ...

»Ready Steady Go!« didn't last long though, about three years, but I did get to see The Beatles special which featured one of my favourite tracks "Can't Buy Me Love". »Ready Steady Go!« featured some of the very best artists of the day including my personal favourites: The Who, Them, The Kinks, The Rolling Stones, The Animals and Jerry Lee Lewis. It was later replaced by »Top Of The Pops« which has now attained cult status after it was axed in 2006, which was another crying shame.

The Bitta Sweet was going strong after more than a year together but it is difficult to recall all the exact details. I know that around this time we started to play alongside big name stars like David Bowie, Cat Stevens, Dave Dee, Dozy, Beaky, Mick and Titch (try saying that when you're drunk) and Long John Baldry and The Steampacket, which featured a young Elton John on keyboards and a certain Rod Stewart on backing vocals/harmonica. The Steampacket had supported The Rolling Stones on a UK tour in '65 and made quite an impression on the audiences. Typically, there was a cock-up with their contract and an album was never recorded. Elton John began making a name for himself in a mid-sixties outfit called Bluesology, and before playing support and performing with Long John Baldry, they supported such American legends as Patti LaBelle and The Isley Brothers. Before Rod Stewart got himself trapped in the late seventies' disco nonsense of "Do You Think I'm Sexy?" and the recent »Great American Songbooks«, he was a really great British blues singer and somebody I really admired. He's a great harmonica player too.

Opening for those bands was a great experience for us and sometimes we would open up for one group at the Old Hill Plaza and finish the night with another set at the Rookery Road Plaza in Handsworth if another act didn't turn up. After playing with Long John Baldry at one of the shows, Rod Stewart and myself had a drink and a chat in the bar and he told me he had been busking around Europe before going back to London hoping for a big break. He was spotted by Long John Baldry whilst busking. Baldry asked him to go to an audition as he was looking for new backing singers and he gave him the job. Sometime later, I was watching TV and spotted him in The Faces; I recognized him instantly and thought how good he was. On the other hand, Elton asked Ken, our manager, if he wanted to go back to his room for a drink but Ken declined the offer.

Out of the hundreds of many local groups that had started life earlier in the Birmingham Beat Boom only a handful had survived, and out of those players that were left you sensed that there could be a few stars in the making. Let's not forget some of the lesser known bands of that era: The Vikings, Pat Wayne and The Deltas, The Jaguars (with Dave Mason), Gerry Day and The Dukes, The Cutaways, Highwaymen, The Stringbeats, The Nomads and The Sundowners.

A favourite of mine was The Crawdaddies with the now revered bassist Dave Pegg. He never made it into The Uglys with Steve Gibbons because he failed the audition but he did go onto join Fairport Convention and even Jethro Tull for a spell in the eighties. It's still great to see him in Fairport Convention.

1966 saw a Birmingham band called The Move making quite an impression on the local Beat scene. I was beginning to lose count of the amount of bands that were coming out of the Midlands. The Move formed in '65 out of the ashes of groups like The Nightriders and The Vikings. The Move featured Carl Wayne, Bev Bevan, Ace Kefford, Trevor Burton and Roy Wood. To quickly get them noticed and gain lots of free publicity, they smashed up TV sets on stage with sledgehammers, which worked because they eventually got a residency at London's famous Marquee Club.

The Move's first single "Night Of Fear" hit the British charts in early 1967 and over the next five years they had 20 chart hits, one of them made it into the pop history pages because DJ Tony Blackburn picked their hit single "Flowers In The Rain" as the first record to be played on Radio One. This song also made history in another way too when their manager, Tony Secunda, defamed the character of the then Labour Prime Minister Harold Wilson on a promotional postcard without his knowledge. This landed them in court and Harold Wilson was awarded all the royalties from the "Flowers In The Rain" single to be allocated to charities of his choice, a ruling that is still in place today. After members of The Move went their separate ways, Roy Wood went on to co-found Electric Light Orchestra with Jeff Lynne and Bev Bevan but he left due to friction within the band. He missed out on that because ELO went on to have massive commercial success with singles like "Strange Magic" and "Evil Woman".

After leaving ELO, Wood formed another successful band called Wizzard, which churned out hit after hit but they're mostly remembered for the smash hit single "I Wish It Could Be Christmas Everyday" which reached Number Four in the UK charts in 1973. Wizzard, like Slade, had a lot more talent than people gave them credit for and they certainly deserved much more attention for the rest of their music. (Note to future bands: don't release a Christmas single). Wizzard had such hits as "Angel Fingers" and "See My Baby Jive", both of which went to Number One. Roy Wood is undoubtedly a rock legend and one of the most talented musicians to come out of the Midlands. I do think Roy Wood is one of the great unsung heroes of British rock.

Indeed, it was all happening in the Black Country …

In 1966, two other local groups recorded the same song called "You Better Run" by the American group The Young Rascals but neither had a hit with it: one version was by The

N' Betweens from Wolverhampton and the other was by the Walsall based group Listen that featured lead guitarist John Crutchley, bassist Geoff Thompson and drummer Roger Beamer, and a certain singer from West Brom named Robert Plant. Although unsuccessful, Planty had been in other local bands such as Delta Blues Band, Sounds Of Blue, The Crawling King Snakes and the Tennessee Teens.

Despite being signed to the big American label CBS, Listen had little if any success although they made a name for themselves in Birmingham playing at venues such as the Plaza Ballroom. Toward the end of 1966, Planty left Listen and joined The Band Of Joy, which was formed by a Stourbridge guitarist named Vernon Perara, formally of The Stringbeats.

They were making a name for themselves in the region and Plant was a welcome addition to the fold. The Band Of Joy's main area of interest was the West Coast sounds of America, stuff like Love and Buffalo Springfield. Beginning in the early sixties, the hippy scene was mostly prominent in San Francisco before it spread around the world and eventually reached Britain. In 1969, the Woodstock festival was attended by 500,000 people and it was a great movement to be part of. Planty was heavily involved in the West Coast bands; personally, I only like the more electric stuff. I wasn't really keen on Crosby, Stills & Nash and Joni Mitchell; I wanted loud guitars that produced great riffs, bluesy vocals and pulsating melodies.

The Band of Joy: Chris Brown, Kevin Gammond, John Bonham (back) and Paul Lockey. Robert Plant is on the far right looking deep in thought.

Confusingly, Planty fronted the band through three different versions from 1966 to 1968. Moving into the seventies, the band went through a few line-ups but the more popular version (Plant's third line-up) featured singer Robert Plant, John Bonham on drums, Chris Brown on keyboards, guitarist and singer Kevin Gammond and bassist Paul Lockey.

I would often see Planty quite a bit around town; he was born in West Bromwich but later moved to Kidderminster. He moved back home when courting his girlfriend Maureen, who lived in Trinity Road at the top end of town. He was a nice guy but eccentric. Until he spoke, you wouldn't have thought he was born in the Black Country … maybe Paris or San Francisco. He was definitely a bohemian, intelligent and artistic.

Robert Plant and myself both played on the same bill in 1967 at a well-known local venue called the Adelphi Ballroom, which was originally called The Palais Dedance, situated in New Street, in the centre of West Bromwich. John Bonham was on drums and they only had a small Marshall P.A and a cheap mic so he asked if he could borrow mine and I told him to "fuck off." Okay, I'm just kidding – I let him borrow it.

The night I played on the same bill with Robert Plant was also unforgettable but for other reasons because things didn't quite go to plan for us. The Adelphi Ballroom had a revolving stage and after we had finished our set, it broke down so we all had to pedal it around. The audience were in stitches laughing at us pushing this big heavy stage around; we must have looked more like a comedy act from some silent film with Charlie Chaplin than a modern rock and roll band.

"I can't believe this is happening", Bruno said.

"Neither can I. Let's just get it over and done with and then get drunk."

Bruno decided to move off the grand piano to make it a bit lighter but one of the legs broke off and it toppled over off the side of the stage and we all fell about laughing at ourselves. It didn't put Planty off though and his band went on to play a great set.

The Adelphi Ballroom was famous in the Midlands; it was owned by John Gordon and managed by a guy called John Singer who was not unlike Freddy Garrity from Freddy and The Dreamers group. He was a small thin guy and wore thick black-rimmed glasses, an Italian cut suit and winkle picker shoes. He certainly didn't look like one of the locals; he was the proper managerial type: self-important and confident.

At this point our setlist was a mix of stuff. If I remember correctly, we played some familiar tunes like "The Night Of Fear" by The Move, "Rack My Mind" by The Yardbirds and a couple of songs by The Who, probably my favourite band of the era. The setlist was: "The Nazz Are Blue", "Come See Me", "I Feel Good", "The Night Of Fear", "The Kids Are Alright", "Barefootin'", "Ride Your Pony", "N.S.U.", "Rack My Mind", "It's Not True", "Everything's Alright", "Ready Steady Let's Go", "Head Over Heels", "La. La. La. Lies", "You Must Believe In Me" and "Stepping Stone".

All the local lads hung out at the Adelphi Ballroom to listen to the live bands, the records that DJ Barmy Barry played and to check out the local talent (i.e. girls). As the nights wore on and a few beers were drank, there was nearly always a fight or two that broke out in the audience but they were quickly dealt with and the troublemakers were shown the door by the two big burly bouncers named Charlie Leadbetter and Jimmy McCauley.

If I wasn't gigging myself I would go there whenever I could to listen to some of the groups that played there. The Beatles played at the Adelphi Ballroom in 1962 but unfortunately I missed them. I never got to see The Beatles live; that's one of my biggest regrets. I did get to see The Ugly's that featured Steve Gibbons on vocals; he later had a hit single with the song "Tulane".

I also saw The Idle Race, which featured Jeff Lynne who, as I've said, went on to form the sensational progressive rock group ELO. I remember hearing »The Birthday Party« by The Idle Race and was very impressed by it. I also saw the great local outfit The Spencer Davies Group; they'd formed in 1963 when Spencer Davis hired singer and organist Steve Winwood and his brother the bassist Muff Winwood. Steve still has one of the greatest soul voices this country has ever produced, perhaps the best. In the sixties, they had a stream of hits most famously "Keep On Running", "Somebody Help Me", "Gimmie Some Lovin'" and "I'm A Man". Steve went on to feature in other groups like Traffic, Go and Blind Faith as well as successful solo work while Muff moved in to the business side of the music industry working in A&R and also as a record producer.

At the Adelphi, I also saw The N' Betweens who later became Slade under the direction of their manager, former bassist of The Animals, Chas Chandler. Slade were in a league of their own. It has often been said that Robert Plant had been considered for the role as singer but it went to their guitarist Noddy Holder. Members of The N' Between's didn't see Planty as a worthwhile frontman. Boy were they wrong. It worked out for the best because Noddy was a brilliant frontman as well but entirely different from Robert. What both singers have in common is their down-to-earth working class personality which never disappeared even when they hit the big time.

Slade are known for their raucous hit singles but they've made some great ballads over the years like "Far Far Away". They never really made it big in America but when the heavy metal band Quiet Riot released a cover of "Cum On Feel The Noize" in the early eighties, they must have got a big cheque in royalties. Quiet Riot also covered "Mama Weer All Crazee Now" which hit the Number One spot for Slade in 1972. Slade were pioneers of glam rock along with T-Rex, Suzi Quatro, David Bowie, Queen and The Sweet. Sadly, Slade didn't have much luck in the States but at least they're loved on our shores.

I also saw The Who and Cream at the Adelphi Ballroom and I mustn't forget to say that I saw Pink Floyd with Syd Barrett, who played there in February, 1967. That was the first time I saw Pink Floyd live; they were simply amazing to watch and their music was incredible, like nothing I'd heard before … ever. Bruno was with me and he was utterly amazed too. They draped white sheets of cloth over their sound equipment and used a projector to create effects. Obviously, the lights were dimmed in the ballroom so the projector show was quite surreal. They had some great songs like "Interstellar Overdrive". To my mind, Syd Barrett was a true artist and something of a genius on drugs.

I was gigging myself with The Bitta Sweet the night Cream played at the Adelphi Ballroom in '67. Luckily for me it was just a local gig and as soon as we had finished our set and loaded up the van, Bruno and myself dashed over there to get a front stage view of them. It was an all night gig and Cream were due on stage at about midnight. You can't find this Cream gig listed in their old gig lists because they have it down as Smethwick Baths but John Singer persuaded them to play two gigs that night for the right money and they obliged. It was not uncommon for bands to play two gigs in one day, nowadays bands are far too pampered to commit to something like that.

When we arrived we barged our way to the front of the stage, through the waiting audience. The band playing before them was The Band Of Joy featuring Robert Plant and Vernon Perara, possibly with Mick Reeves, Peter Robinson and Chris Brown. Anyway, I'm pretty sure it was the second version of the band that played that evening. They were jamming away at some old twelve bar blues song and it sounded great. It was one of the best things I'd ever heard. The sheer feeling and depth of their talent was on full display.

Anyway, when Cream finally came onto play it was about half one in the morning and Ginger Baker looked awful and had to be helped onto his drum stool. They kicked off their set with Ginger's opening drum passage to the song "N.S.U" and they sounded absolutely awesome. There has never been a band like them; their ability to play such technical solos and to jam for so long was utterly mesmerising. Obviously, they were all working in London either as session musicians or in other bands, so when they actually came together to form what is perhaps the ultimate supergroup, the results were stupendous. You'd never get a band like that today. It was because of Cream that other established musicians started to form supergroups in the 1970s and onwards; it's a great commercial idea if the chemistry is right.

I stood right in front of Eric Clapton and he never sounded or played better, it was a night Bruno and myself would never forget. Cream didn't last long and like every other fan of theirs I was disappointed they called it a day after just three years. Each of them – Eric Clapton, Jack Bruce and Ginger Baker – were (still are) so uniquely talented that it was almost inevitably their egos would clash. Their second album »Disraeli Gears« was released the year I saw them play and I remember hearing some of those songs played live such as "Strange Brew" and "Sunshine Of Your Love". Their reunion a couple of years ago wasn't quite the same; they still sounded excellent but through time they lost the electric magnetism and thirst to play for hours that made them so great in '67. I was absolutely gutted when Cream broke up in 1968; they were my absolute favourite band (and Bruno's too). They fused together rock/blues and jazz like no other band had done before or since come to think of it.

There were other venues – whether they be clubs, pubs or actual music venues – in the Midlands that created strong reputations because they hosted live music nights. Here are just some of them: King's Head pub, Yates's Wine Lodge, Rubery Social Club, Golden Eagle pub, Star Coffee Bar, Digbeth Civic Hall, Penthouse Club, Grotto Club on Bromsgove Street, Cecilia Coffee Bar in Edgbaston and even Kidderminster Town Hall. In fact, it wasn't too long ago that Robert Plant formed a new version of his 1950s covers band The Honeydrippers to play two gigs at Kiddminster Town Hall. Clearly, there were lots of places that played live music and it was great for local bands. Predictably, the Birmingham Beat scene had imploded by the end of the swinging sixties. I very much doubt something like that will ever happen again in my neck of the woods.

The sixties was a cultural revolution as much as a musical one: in France film directors like Jean Luc Goddard changed the face of cinema and in America novelists like Allen Ginsberg and William Burroughs became cult icons through their crazy style of writing. It was cool to be heard talking about French films or American novels. Popular culture had its head turned upside down.

The Bitta Sweet actually split up in 1967 when Hoggy decided to get married and leave us for a new life in sunny Australia. I wasn't bitter about it – no pun intended – but I was a bit upset because we had a good band. He still lives in Oz and gigs in a band called The Renegades.

I was still working as a mechanic at a small local company. I stuck at it for four years in total. I've no idea how much I earned but I know it wasn't much – I could barley afford new clothes. I just about managed to give my parents a bit of money each week for food and to add toward the bills. If I did have any money left to spend, it all went on records. I had amassed a huge record collection, most of which I still have at home; stuff like Hendrix, Clapton and John Mayall. Records were reasonably priced unlike today's CD's; also in those days artists would release singles that did not feature on the album so you had to buy the album and the single to collect an artists complete catalogue.

Well, because I owned some of his records, it seems more than appropriate at this point to mention Jimi Hendrix who is an inspiration to millions, including Kenny Downing and myself. »Are You Experienced?« was issued in the UK in '67. Aided by his manager Chas Chandler, Hendrix came over to the UK in 1966 on the strength of a song called "Hey Joe", a cover of an obscure folk song. Through his technical brilliance, Hendrix wooed British guitarists like Eric Clapton, Jeff Beck and Pete Townshend. Like Clapton and his peers, Hendrix founded his career on covers of old blues classics like "Rock Me Baby" by B.B. King. Hendrix got a band together whilst in the UK – where he remained until his premature death – and called it The Jimi Hendrix Experience.

Like most budding professional rock singers I was in awe of Hendrix. I bought »Are You Experienced?« and played it constantly. You can't deny the quality of songs like "Foxy Lady", "Fire" and "Third Stone From The Sun". Those songs have such profound qualities and an unnerving amount of electric magnetism and that is what makes damn good music.

After about three years of fronting bands I became much more confident; I started to play guitar and write my own songs. My lyrics tended to be filled with dreamy images and fantasy ideas; you needed to have some kind of imaginary release in a town filled with coal mines, factories and shops. I sold one of my first songs for £25, which was a lot of money in the sixties, and I swapped another song for a Les Paul shaped Hofner guitar; it wasn't exactly a big business transaction but it was a start. Bruno and myself wrote one song together called "Sugar Tree Park", which got recorded on the Fontana Record label by a top local band called The Montanas, featuring singer John Jones and guitarist/keyboardist Terry Rowley. In 1969, they would form Trapeze with Glenn Hughes and Dave Holland, however, they soon returned to The Montana's leaving Trapeze as a hard rock trio.

The great thing about being in a rock and roll band is that the image attracts women; I read somewhere that the only reason why Lemmy joined a band was for the chicks. I didn't have a steady girlfriend as such; I just had plenty of one night stands. It was the swinging sixties and even in Midlands rock and roll fans were enjoying the liberal ideas of the decade – pot, sex and music.

The most important musicians in the British Blues Boom (as it has since been called) of the sixties was undoubtedly John Mayall, Long John Baldry, Alexis Korner and Cyril Davies. Although he's largely unknown these days it was Korner, especially, who helped the careers of some of Britain's greatest musicians and singers; namely, Jack Bruce, Robert Plant, Graham Bond and even The Rolling Stones. Liverpool and Birmingham spawned lots of bands in the earlier sixties but toward the end of the decade it was London that became the main city for music; many of those London musicians have since become legendary. The Animals travelled down to London from the North East and Southern bands like The Yardbirds, The Who, Cream and The Rolling Stones made earth shattering music.

It was a great time for blues music but slightly ironic that it took us British folk to make American blues popular. We even made the blues acceptable in America; because of segregation most white people didn't listen to blues music until bands like The Who and guitarists like Eric Clapton and John Mayall changed all that. This meant that many of the great blues players underwent career revivals and travelled to England to play shows at places like the Marquee in London.

I remember reading about the American Negro Blues Festival that was held in Croydon in 1963, hosted by Chris Barber. On the bill were all the greats like Muddy Waters, Big Joe Williams, Sonny Boy Williamson, Memphis Slim and Willie Dixon. Sleepy John Estes and Buddy Guy also played at festivals in London. They'd come from America to Britain and it was here that they were treated like royalty. And all that happened because of the British Blues Boom.

Some of the great blues masters even came to the Midlands: John Lee Hooker, Memphis Slim and Sonny Boy Williamson played separate gigs at the Whiskey A Go Go, which was a former dance hall above a gentleman's clothes store in Navigation Street.

I also read a story somewhere that a young Robert Plant got to meet Sonny Boy Williamson backstage after one of his gigs in Birmingham. Lightin' Hopkins also visited the UK in the sixties and the great B.B. King is still playing live to this very day; he played his penultimate tour of Britain with Gary Moore in 2006. Unfortunately, I never got to see any of those great US blues masters because I was often gigging myself but I did read about them in the music press. The only blues players I did see were people like Peter Green and Eric Clapton whenever they came to Birmingham. I saw Peter Green with the John Mayall Blues Band at the Lafayette Club in the centre of Wolverhampton in the seventies and it was a great gig. Peter Green was a brilliant blues guitarist and proved to become a brilliant songwriter too after he left Fleetwood Mac. Also on the bill that night was the excellent band Colosseum.

My old mate and former Blue Condition and Lion band mate Pete Boot.

1967 and 1968 saw Bruno and myself going through different line-ups of bands ... yet again. You'd think that throughout those years when we formed several bands we'd argue a lot; after all, bands argue all the time. They're famous for it. Well, to be truthful, I don't remember one argument between Bruno and myself. Honest. We never fell out over anything and are still friends to this very day. Perhaps the only thing we did argue about was who's going to buy the next round of pints.

One group was called Blue Condition and featured Pete Boot on drums. At first we couldn't decide on a name; weeks went by where we brainstormed but still couldn't find something suitable. In the end our band name actually came from the Cream song "Blue Condition" from their brilliant 1967 album »Disraeli Gears«. Released in November, it was their second album and boy did it blow me away. Basically, we wanted to make a heavy blues band in the tradition of Cream and thought the name Blue Condition would be a nice touch.

I remember one cold night in late 1967 when Pete was practising in the upstairs room of his parents' café – called The Spot Café – in Darlaston; Bruno and myself went round to his place to ask Pete if he would like to audition for us. We hadn't come up with a name at that point; we just had plans to form yet another band together with a new drummer and guitarist. We'd heard of Pete through word of mouth and thought he would be up for the job. I've never forgotten the look on Pete's face when he answered the door. Bruno and myself are big guys and as it was dark he thought we were a couple of heavies.

Pete's tastes in music tended to be more pop-orientated. When Pete first auditioned for us he was good and loud but played very rigid and the skins on his drums were very tight so I lent him one of my Cream albums, »Disraeli Gears«, and told him to listen to Ginger Baker's style and sound which is what we were looking for. Ginger is a great drummer with lots of jazz and blues influences in his sound; in fact, I read somewhere that he hates being referred to as a rock drummer. His live improvisations were outstanding during the Cream years. Anyway, after some discussion and plenty of jamming sessions he accepted our offer.

The next week, when we rehearsed, he sounded much better and years later he became one of our great British drummers and even influenced Budgie's sound when he played on their »In For The Kill« world wide hit album. Perhaps just as important as being a talented and eager drummer Pete owned the band's van – a Ford Thames.

We had a guy called Dave Goodman on guitar and he was quite good, very bluesy. He was a nice but quiet guy. We were both influenced by bands like Cream, The Who, The Rolling Stones and The Yardbirds. Pink Floyd were also coming on the scene with albums like »The Piper At The Gates Of Dawn«. Floyd were progressive and quite heavy and I liked that. It was always about listening to the next thing that was happening and taking ideas and influences from them, and seeing how they control audiences at gigs, watching them play, and learning from them.

We weren't a band that was focused heavily on the whole drugs and drink image; I mean, I enjoyed the odd joint and Bruno loved his beer but it never distracted us from the music. Everybody was smoking pot in those days because it makes you feel good and it doesn't kill you like the harder drugs which I never, ever touched. It was a hard life and guys like me needed something to relax us. Sex can be tiring but sitting back and smoking a joint is effortless.

From the end of '67 into 1968, all we did was practice and play live as much as possible.

One day the lot of us travelled down to Romford in Essex to audition for Ron King. At the time Ron also handled Amen Corner and Andy Fainweather who later went on to work with Budgie and Eric Clapton.

Suffice to say the audition didn't exactly go according to plan. The hall where the audition was held was near a market stall so we had to carry all of our gear through the fruit and veg stalls; it wasn't exactly a continental market. I remember seeing cabbage stuck down drains and unwashed fruit on the ground.

When we finally got there we were told to play in one corner of the hall and play just three songs. After opening with a Hendrix song one of Bruno's strings snapped on his bass and because we were tired from the travelling we didn't play too good.

"I can't bloody believe this", I heard Bruno say under his breath. "All this hassle and we sound crap."

After we finished there was a deadening silence, which was broken by Ron's bad temper. He shouted at us in a thick cockney accent: "You're too fucking progressive!"

"Are we?"

"Yes, you fucking are!"

"I didn't think we were heavy enough", I said.

Having said that, he did offer us advice on how to make it in the music business and even though we weren't the right band for him he was sincere.

"You've got to concentrate on your image and tighten your sound", he said.

Unfortunately, Blue Condition didn't last very long; perhaps we gigged for about six months and lasted maybe a year in total. We split up at some point in early 1968. We did manage to play together at venues like The Ship & Rainbow in Wolverhampton. I can't really remember why we split up; I guess it just didn't work out. Maybe we didn't go in the direction I wanted us to go in? That's what happens with bands – conflict of interests. I don't know what happened to Dave after the Blue Condition folded but Pete went onto join a band called The Extreem. I can tell you that Blue Condition was the true predecessor to Judas Priest and by far the heaviest band I'd been in prior to Priest.

One of my pre-Judas Priest bands The Sugar Stack: John Partridge, me, Bruno, Mick Reeves and Jeff Furnival.

In 1968, Bruno and myself joined another local group called Sugar Stack (don't ask me where the name came from, I know it's crap) but this group barely lasted a few months even though they had been together since my time in The Bitta Sweet.

Here's another cause of debate between me and my friend Bruno: I'd often thought that Blue Condition came after Sugar Stack but some photos I found in preparation for this book contradict my initial thoughts. Hell, the sixties was a busy period for me! So many bands and too many dates have confused my mental timeline over the years.

Sugar Stack actually existed before we joined; it was a very good band that featured Jeff Furnival and Mick Reeves on guitar and John Partridge on drums. They'd heard that The Bitta Sweet and Blue Condition had spilt up and asked us to join them; with nothing else on the cards we enthusiastically said YES.

Mick played a lovely Gibson twin-neck guitar similar to the one Jimmy Page of Led Zeppelin made famous in the seventies when Zeppelin became the biggest rock band on earth, and John owned a double bass drum kit and was a great imitator of Ginger Baker's style and sound. Mick and John where forever falling out over the band's music. They were a great couple of characters and like children in the school playground they were always arguing and making friends again in the next breath. One time we pulled up at a petrol station to fill the tank up and we all put together to buy the fuel, except Mick who said he didn't have any money. So Mick and John started yet another row over this. It was in the times when a forecourt attendant would come out to you and fill your tank up for you, and you paid them there and then. At this station it happened to be a young, good looking girl. She stood there waiting to see how much petrol we wanted when all of a sudden the van door opened and out fell John and Mick who were fighting like dogs. They rolled on the forecourt, punching and kicking each other. The young lass screamed and ran off; I have never laughed so much in all my life. They later made friends again and off we went to our next gig with John having a black eye and Mick with a swollen lip.

I thought this group was great fun to be with and they were all very good musicians and we all worked very hard on the road. Jeff had the idea of having two different setlists: one was commercial pop and the other was heavy blues rock music. This band kept us on the road with plenty of work although Bruno, John and myself, preferred playing the latter stuff rather than light pop music. I mean, my favourite music was Cream, Hendrix, and Peter Green so I always wanted to play blues rock and didn't really enjoy the pop side of the band although I understood why Jeff and Mick wanted to go down that road ... money!

One night we would be at a rock venue with the amps cranked up and the next night we would be playing Tamla-Motown at some random town hall or a low-key venue. It was a very odd mix of material which myself and Bruno didn't always agree with.

"I hate this motown-pop shit. I wanna play rock and roll. I wanna play it loud!" I angrily said to Bruno one evening after a gig.

"I know mate, it's all bollocks."

Our agency was based south of Birmingham in Evesham and we played a lot of gigs around that area like Stow, Tewkesbury and Worcester. One gig I remember was for a private party for the BBC and the theme was a Roman one so everyone was wearing togas and laurel crowns, we had some great fun that night.

I have some fantastic memories of this band and playing in working men's clubs and public houses was great fun. Other gigs I can recall playing where at The Hen and Chickens on the Wolverhampton Road, The Belfry Golf Club, Birmingham City Football Club, The Connaught Hotel, The Ship and Rainbow and The 64 Club, to name a few.

When Sugar Stack disbanded Mick went on to join a group called Possessed, which featured local guitarist Vernon Perara who as I've already said once played alongside Robert Plant. Sadly, both Reeves and Perara were killed in a motorway accident when returning from a gig up North in Carlisle. This terrible accident made headline news and everyone who knew them was deeply shocked and saddened by this tragedy. I didn't go to their funeral but Pete was asked to go and salvage anything from the wreckage, which was a job I did not want to do. Close family and friends arrange reunion/memorial gigs every now and again and I'm also asked to attend which I do.

Geoff later married a girl called Sandra from Tewkesbury and ended up in a pop band called Design.

I decided to take a breather and ponder my next move. By this point I was getting really tired of the whole music scene. It seemed that nothing good was happening despite all my hard work and efforts. But then I'd wake up early and go to work and really hate it. I decided that I would rather carry on gigging in the hope that I'd make it big then continue to work in a depressing job with no ambition.

At some point towards the end of 1968 Bruno and myself formed a group, which I first called Halfbreed but then changed to The Chapters Of Life.

Our management didn't like either name very much; they didn't think we would be a marketable band so they made us change it. It was the Nita Anderson Agency in Wolverhampton who took care of us and they're still going strong after 50 years of business. She put a guy named Jimmy Powell in charge of young bands. Jimmy had just started working for her and prior to that he was a singer with a sixties band called The Dimensions. Basically, he didn't like the name we were going to call ourselves and said we should use a short name that people would remember and he came up with 'Jug' which had a double meaning: a jug is what old blues bands used to blow into to make a sound but it is also a term that some people used to call jail. Either way it was fucking shit; I thought it made us sound outdated. But what the heck, as long as we were getting gigs from them I didn't care.

I had no option but to agree with them really. When you're a young and relatively inexperienced band sometimes you have to bite the bullet and do whatever your management says. Managers can be wrong as well but we didn't want to argue, we just wanted to play.

This band featured Barry Civil and John Perry on guitars, and his brother Jim on drums. We played a style of electric blues rock and again, our main influences were Cream and The Jimi Hendrix Experience. They were two of my favourite groups and both bands seemed to play louder and more exciting music than anyone else around at the time. Our agency wanted to model us on that image, bands like Ten Years After and Love Sculpture. Ten Years After were a top blues rock band from Nottingham; their self-titled debut album was released in 1967 on the Decca owned label Deram. I liked Ten Years After but it wasn't necessarily the direction I wanted us to go in.

Barry Civic — Lead guitar
Jim Perry — Drums
Bruno Stapenhill — Bass Guitar
Al Atkins — Vocals/Harmonica
John Perry — Rhythm Guitar

A cool picture of a band I was in just before Judas Priest called Jug Blues Band.

The Jug Blues Band was a very good group in my opinion but the hunger to make the big time was always there with me. If I thought there was an easier route I would have took it. One night after playing a gig at the Wolverhampton Civic Hall with local lads Slade and the progressive rock band Spooky Tooth (hailing from the South, Spooky Tooth wrote a song called "Better By You, Better Than Me" for their 1969 album »Spooky Two«. The song was covered by Judas Priest and has a slightly controversial history), I was later approached backstage by Adrian Ingram – who was one of the best guitarists around at the time – to sing with his new band called Evolution.

Evolution had arranged to play a three to four month tour of Morocco. Admittedly, it was very tempting so I said yes. But after a week or so, I ran into management problems with Jim Simpson and I decided to leave the band. Basically, they wanted me to drive the tour bus around Morocco, which I thought was an insult and I told Simpson to stick it.

"There's no fucking way I'm doing that", I shouted. "I'm a fucking singer, not a dog's body for your fucking band."

Simpson also asked me to sing in The Bakerloo Blues Line – the band that he managed – but I declined; they later changed their name to Hannibal. Adrian Ingram is now one of Britain's top jazz guitarists and Jim Simpson runs the respected label, Big Bear Records.

I've read that both Simpson and Ingram don't remember me (probably because of my long hair and scraggily beard) but I can assure you that I was in Evolution albeit temporarily and Simpson did ask me to sing in The Bakerloo Blues Line.

After my split with Evolution I wanted to go back to The Jug Blues Band, but even though I was a founding member, they told me they didn't want me anymore because I went off with another band.

"Fair enough lads, I understand", I said, genuinely.

I firmly believe that in the cut-throat world of rock and roll you should take any opportunity that lands on your doorstep even if it means pissing off a few people. I was given an opportunity to work with two talented local people and I took it. Even though it didn't work out, if I had not joined Evolution it would have plagued me for the rest of my life. Who knows what can happen, you have to do what your gut tells you to.

It wasn't long after I left that The Jug Blues Band decided to split up anyway, so I ended up with no band at all. Hell, we all make mistakes. I think the band lasted about a year.

The annoying thing is I wrote a song with Barry Civil during my tenure in The Jug Blues Band which was to be put onto a demo, however, because I left, they never bothered with it. But a year later, Barry teamed up with Pete Boot's band The Extreem and they played the song in their live set and eventually recorded it. The song was called "Out Of The Sky" and was recorded at Decca Records in London in 1969 for an album also called »Out Of The Sky«. It was re-released, I think, in 2003 by Japanese independent label Birdman Records. The lyrics are shite but the music side of the song was good. I must have been smoking pot; I don't know what the bloody hell I was rambling about. I wrote so many songs back then that I just didn't realise what I was saying. I think I was in such a desperate rush to make it big that I hurried the song writing process. I have since slowed down considerably.

"Out Of The Sky"
(Atkins/Civil 1968)

You hear the people laughing
You see the people falling in love
I see the people crying
Falling angels from above

Life is a clockwork circus
Women are lions to be tamed
Magazines filling your head with war
And nobody is to be blamed

And from out of the sky came the sun
And from out of the sky came the sun

Working all day 'till the day you die
Life is a waste of time
Try taking the road that will make you high
And let life pass you by

And from out of the sky came the sun
And from out of the sky came the sun

One killer club, which opened in 1968, was called Mothers. Based on Erdington High Street, it was one of the Midlands most famous music venues that played host to some of the country's most talented and interesting bands. America's Billboard magazine once classed Mothers as a famous rock venue, one of the best in the world.

> *Rob Halford speaking to the Daily Telegraph on March 19 2005:* "We would all go to Mothers club in Erdington. I saw Pink Floyd, Deep Purple, Zeppelin and a ton of other bands there. That's were you really got your inspirations from. The feeling was why should it all happen in London?"

Mothers was originally called the Carlton Ballroom and uncontroversial, less dangerous artists like Billy Fury appeared there but then it had a name change and turned into a progressive rock venue. It actually became the first progressive rock club in the UK outside of London.

It was on the top floor of a building above a furniture shop.

After the name change, it was a great place to see lots of top bands and was always packed, which could have got the management into serious trouble for breaking fire regulations ... if there had been any! You had to go upstairs where there was a bar to your left; then you entered a large room with wooden beams going up to the ceiling at either side, which you could climb up to sit on and watch your favourite bands on the big stage. It was very hot, smoky and sweaty but with a cold pint in one hand and a cigarette in the other, you'd soon lose any feelings of discomfort.

The bands didn't need dry ice or smoke screens back then because everyone smoked cigarettes and anything else they could get their hands on too, and it created a vibrant atmosphere. I can't remember the ticket prices for Mothers but it wouldn't have been a lot, probably the price of a beer.

The late John Peel, the most respect broadcaster in the UK, was the resident DJ; he always raved about the place.

> *John Peel was quoted in »The Home Of Good Sounds (1968-1971)« by Kevin Duffy:* "Mothers was one of the best nightclubs in Britain of its time."

Loads of great bands played at Mothers, including Fleetwood Mac, Free, the great rock band Traffic featuring Steve Winwood, The Who, Black Sabbath, Steppenwolf, Nice, Tyrannosaurus Rex, Family, Taste and Roy Harper.

I'd often go round a friend's house and say: "Wanna go down to Mothers tonight and see who's playing?" So it was like going to the cinema because there was a band on every day and it was great. You just don't get that these days.

I went to see Jeff Beck, one of my favourite guitarists, twice at Mothers but both times he never turned up for the gig! Beck was a temperamental figure, most artists with a great talent usually are but I was bloody annoyed that he never played at Mothers after I'd bought a ticket. I didn't care about the money because I got a refund; I just wanted to see one of England's greatest guitarists. I was a huge fan of The Jeff Beck Group and their two albums »Truth« and »Beck-ola«.

I once saw Stan Webb's Chicken Shack at Mothers. Chicken Shack was a great blues band that featured bassist Andy Sylvester, drummer Alan Morley and keyboardist Christine Perfect. I remember that Perfect walked off the stage after the first song complaining that the house upright piano was too out of tune so she couldn't play properly. She actually lived in Birmingham for a few years because she studied at the city's college. She left Chicken Shack in '69 to join Fleetwood Mac after hooking up with the great British bassist John McVie. She's certainly done alright for herself since then.

I attended two great gigs at Mothers in 1969; one was on April 27 to see Pink Floyd when they recorded part of their legendary »Ummagumma« double live album. I'd seen them a couple of years before at the Adelphi Ballroom with Syd Barrett but this was something different because he was no longer in the band having been fired in '68. Floyd had begun to make a name for themselves as a weird, arty progressive rock band. There wasn't a band like them at the time so it was a spectacle to go to one of their gigs.

I can say that I'm part of Pink Floyd's history because I was there when they recorded part of their famed double album; it's the first disc that features songs from the gig that I went to while the second half was recorded during a gig they played in Manchester at the College of Commerce. The album was a huge hit and I remember telling my mates that I went to that gig! And yes, they were jealous.

"Jesus Christ, Al, why didn't you tell us you where going to see the Floyd? I would have gone."

From what I can remember; the evening was pure psychedelic prog rock. I should have taken some LSD that night and it would have been an even wilder trip, like something from a crazy cult novel by Hunter S. Thompson. To be honest, I can't remember enough about the show to go into fine detail. I do recall that it seemed to go on forever. I don't think the setlist was any different from their usual gigs but it was the experience of watching them perform (as opposed to listening to them) which really made an effect on me. I do remember them playing the only song I knew at the time which was Syd Barrett's "Astronomy Domine" but it was a long time ago and too much has happened in my life to remember everything that happened in the late sixties.

The band didn't seem the same without Barrett although Dave Gilmour was a better guitarist. Barrett lost himself in a haze of psychedelic drugs; he took LSD and his personality and attitude completely changed with all the drugs he was consuming. After I heard Barrett was sacked from the band I remember thinking, I'm glad I got the chance to see him perform with Floyd because I'll never get another chance. The band continued without him and went on to achieve greater success. Dave Gilmour is a wizard on guitar and watching him play at Mothers was mesmerising. I wish I could go back and capture that moment again ...

The other gig was Led Zeppelin who played a monster set on Saturday, March 22; they were supported by Mick Abraham's Blodwyn Pig and were paid a grand fee of £75, which was pretty damn good in those days.

To be honest, I can't remember what they played in their setlist on the night but it was probably songs from their first album. Their self-titled debut album features some cracking rock songs like "Communication Breakdown" and "Good Times Bad Times". I can tell you that they were simply brilliant on stage; I just sensed on the night that I was witnessing something very special. They had this brilliant blues-rock sound like my favourite band Cream but it leaned more to the rock side with a much heavier sound. I think Clapton went to see Zeppelin at a gig in England but thought they were too loud.

Having seen Planty sing in the past in various blues jams and also appearing alongside him and his outfit The Band Of Joy, I couldn't believe his transformation since teaming up with Jimmy Page; he had gone from being a fairly good blues singer into a fully-fledged rock icon overnight. Although I have to say that John Bonham was the worst for wear that night, but he still played out of his skin until the encore number when he was simply too pissed to play; Ron Berg – the drummer with Blodwyn Pig – stepped in to play his part. What a night!

Bruno and myself had many a good time at Mothers with a bottle of Newcastle Brown Ale in one hand and a joint in the other but we're always a little envious that we weren't up on stage playing too. It was a crying shame when the place closed down in 1971; more than 400 bands played at Mothers, including some of the greatest bands of all time.

Mothers wasn't the only great club in the Midlands. Jim Simpson opened another famous club in the sixties called Henry's Blues House; it was based in the centre of Birmingham above a pub called The Crown, situated on the corner of Hill Street and Station Street. The Crown public house used to host band nights on the ground floor but then Jim Simpson shrewdly rented the first floor for his own jam nights. Apparently, Henry's was named after an Afghan hound. For a couple of years Simpson ran a Henry's Blue House in Worcester but the real blues rock boom was in Birmingham.

Simpson brought lots of great blues players over to the Midlands like Champion Jack Dupree and Arthur "Big Boy" Crudup. Sadly, I didn't manage to catch the greats like "Big Boy" Crudup; he was the guy who wrote "That's All Right Mama" which Elvis covered and made universally famous. Crudup was a great delta blues guitarist and singer. Jack Dupree, on the other hand, was a blues pianist who brought his boogie-woogie style of piano playing over to the UK in the sixties. He performed with some of my favourite guitarists, including Eric Clapton and John Mayall. Believe it or not, the guy who hailed from the south of American ended up living in Halifax in the seventies and eighties after meeting a local woman.

Home grown bands like Status Quo and Irish rockers Taste (with Rory Gallagher) also performed at Henry's Blues House. Other names to drop by at Henry's included John Bonham, Spencer Davis, Jeremy Spencer and Cozy Powell.

The bands weren't paid a lot of money; top bands probably got paid around £30-£35 while most other bands got around £15. That's per band, not per person so it wasn't a get deal of cash. In '68 and '69 the likes of Zeppelin could ask for up to £100 and then their fees sky rocketed when they became a top selling rock band.

Prior to joining Led Zeppelin, Robert Plant would always be found at Henry's Blues House jamming with one blues band or another. It wasn't long after the opening of Henry's that Plant joined The New Yardbirds with Jimmy Page, soon to become Led Zeppelin. In fact, Led Zeppelin was an early band to perform at Henry's Blues House.

Jim Simpson booked a Birmingham band called Earth to play support to Ten Years After. Earth was greeted positively by the audience even though they where there to see Ten Years After and not some unknown group of misfits. And after seeing the audience's response to them, Simpson asked if he could be their manager as he already managed two other Birmingham bands: The Bakerloo Blues Line and Tea and Symphony.

After agreeing to his request, he sent the band on a tour of Germany and one of the venues was based in Hamburg called the Star-Club, which The Beatles had previously made famous. The audiences loved this energetic band from Birmingham who churned out blues hits and rock and roll standards like "Blue Suede Shoes". Like Cream, Sabbath would im-

The legendary Birmingham heavy metal band Black Sabbath 1968 (still named Earth at this time): Geezer Butler, Ozzy, Tony Iommi and Bill Ward.

provise and jam for as long as they could although they were mostly given sets lasting less than an hour.

At this time, there was another group called Earth and to avoid any confusion Jim asked them to come up with another name. Their bass guitarist Geezer Butler came up with Black Sabbath, nicked from a Boris Karloff horror movie. Created in 1968, Black Sabbath are now universally known as 'The inventors of heavy metal.' The band featured Ozzy Osbourne (vocals), Tony Iommi (guitar), Bill Ward (drums) and Geezer Butler (bass). These days it's difficult to tell who the hell is actually in Black Sabbath but the original line-up has become legendary.

There were some bands that I missed like Black Sabbath because I was usually playing a gig with my own band on a weekend, but the decade was a very exciting time in music either to play in your own band or to watch on stage or just on the television.

A band I witnessed on the TV in '68 was The Crazy World Of Arthur Brown. A lot of weird things happened in the music industry at the end of the sixties but they were a band that really stood out. In the seventies, America would have Alice Cooper and Kiss but we had Arthur Brown. I nearly shit myself when this lunatic with his head on fire came on the television screen singing, "I am the God of hell fire". What a great character he was and he ended up with a Number One hit single and album. I remember hearing their debut album at the time it was released ... Jesus, what a trip! In 1975, his band signed to Gull Records; the company that had signed Judas Priest in '74.

I had the chance to see Arthur Brown at Mothers in '69. One of my favourite local vocalists was Jess Roden from Kidderminster and I even saw him perform with Arthur Brown. You may not have heard of Jess Roden because he never achieved big success. One of Jess's first bands in the early sixties was with Robert Plant's guitarist Kevyn Gammond and I think he influenced both Planty and myself with his soulful-bluesy vocal style. In 1970, he formed the country rock band Bronco, which went through various line-up changes over the three years they were together; members included the great Midlands guitarist Robbie Blunt, Kevyn Gammond and also Ian Hunter (from Mott The Hoople). Bronco only made two albums. Roden later went on to form The Butts Band with two players from The Doors. I have to go on about him because he was another one of those casualties of music who did not make it as big as he should have done.

So there you have it; my life before Judas Priest. I'd seen lots of great bands perform live on stage, including Ten Years After, Jethro Tull, Cream, The Who, Deep Purple and Led Zeppelin; and I was part of an era that changed the course of popular culture. I was born at the right time: I grew up listening to great rock and roll artists like Elvis and Chuck Berry. I bought The Beatles first single on its original release and from my home in West Bromwich I witnessed the rise of The Beatles on a global scale. I was fortunate enough to have watched the early years of great bands like Led Zeppelin and Black Sabbath. I was part of an era that will probably never be copied or equalled.

I was in quite a few bands myself and although nothing became of those bands I made lots of great friends and enjoyed myself more than I could ever have imagined. I didn't make much money but it wasn't about the cash, it was about the music. Christ, I didn't make any money in the sixties and nor did Bruno; we were both living with our parents. Sometimes my parents got annoyed when I would come home late from a gig and wake them up past midnight. There was one night when I came home late and completely stoned out of my head. I can't remember a lot for obvious reasons but apparently I walked up stairs and instead of going left into my bedroom, I turned right into my parent's bedroom. I then turned right again and walked into their big double wardrobe, shut the door behind me, took a leak, then turned around, walked a few footsteps and fell on top of my parents who were lying in bed.

For me personally, and many others like me, the sixties were all about rock and roll and to a certain extent – sex and drugs. If you asked me now: would I have done anything differently? My answer would be a definite NO. I had a bloody good time back then and don't regret a damn thing.

The sixties was a hell of a ride. But my tales of that decade are not quite over yet; there was another band that formed in 1969 and like Zeppelin and Sabbath they would make history. Blue Condition and The Jug Blues Band, especially, provided a catalyst for what was to come: a heavy blues band that merged all my influences together and was set to destroy the Midlands.

And so it is time to reminisce about the dawn of the Metal Gods ... cue the music.

Chapter 3
The Ballad Of Al Atkins & Judas Priest (1969-1973)

Led Zeppelin released their self-titled debut album in March, 1969 on Atlantic Records. They had gotten a unique deal with the American label that had some great names on their books like Aretha Franklin and Ray Charles. I'll never forget hearing »Led Zeppelin« for the first time; they had taken American blues to a whole new level of meaning with songs like "Dazed And Confused" and "You Shook Me". My fellow Black Country men Robert Plant and John Bonham certainly did themselves proud. They released their second album in October to better acclaim and higher sales. Two albums in one year from an unknown band was unbelievable! I wish I was in their shoes! Their success gave me impetus to continue with another project.

After my tenure in The Jug Blues Band, 1969 saw me feeling depressed with no money to my name and just the old clothes on my back. If I didn't have family to rely on, I'm sure I would have been homeless. I had become the proverbial black sheep of the family but after the dust had settled I went round to Bruno's and asked him to join up with me again. I don't know why he stood by me through the years; his loyalty showed no bounds. I felt that I had let him down badly by walking out on him and The Jug Blues Band after we had worked so hard together but he forgave me and we both set about forming another band … yet again.

After some thought we decided to use the best musicians from our old line-ups: Johnny Perry (guitar) from The Jug Blues Band and John Partridge on drums from Sugar Stack. It was kind of like a mini local super group. It was a great idea and for the first time in a few years, I was really excited about being in a new band. We'd all been around the block as it were, and so we shared similar ideas.

As a four-piece we started rehearsing straight away and I must say this line-up sounded really exciting, and it wasn't long before we had got a set of songs for our first gig. All we had to do was choose a name for ourselves.

Johnny Perry and myself had become good friends in our last group so we hit it off straight away; he was just 17 years of age and reminded me a lot in looks and playing of a young Gary Moore who was then in Skid Row.

Johnny and myself would stay up most nights after rehearsals drinking beer and smoking pot until the early hours talking about girls, drugs and, of course, our main passion – music. When he had to take his first driving test, he asked me to go with him as his qualified driver, knowing I hadn't even got a license; since my disqualification some years earlier I never bothered about driving again. When the test instructor asked to see my license, I just told him I had forgotten to bring it with me and he just shrugged his shoulders and shook his head in disbelief, this wasn't a very good start to the day.

The test was taken at Wednesbury town centre on a cold rainy day and John took the test in our old Commer van that we used to carry our musical equipment around in. The van had a few mechanical problems with it: the nearside door would never lock properly

K.K. Downing looking like an iconic metal riff-meister.

unless you knew how to do it and it had no seatbelts fitted, which were not compulsory in those days. Anyway, they both jumped in and set off for the test kangarooing up the road with fumes pumping out the exhaust pipe; and yes, you've guessed it, there was a technical hitch. When they took the first right hand corner, the door flew open and the instructor fell out into the wet road and all his paperwork blew away down the street! Luckily, he was only shook up by his ordeal but needless to say John didn't pass his test.

"I can't believe that just happened", said John. "Of all the bloody things, I just can't believe it."

We laughed about it all the way home and I still have to laugh now when I think back.

One night after a drinking session at the local pub with some friends in which we all seemed to be in a party mood laughing and fooling around, things turned ugly. John dropped me off at home as usual and said he may see me later for a beer and a chat after he had dropped off his girlfriend Dianne but he never showed up, so I retired to bed for an early night's sleep. We'd been rehearsing as well so I was knackered.

In the early hours of the next morning there was a loud knock on my front door, and when I answered it there were two policemen standing there. I thought they had finally caught up with me and my drug taking and I was ready to bolt through the back door when one of them asked me if I knew of a certain John Perry.

"Yes, I know John. Why? What's wrong?"

They said they had got my name and address from a little black diary out of his pocket and at first I thought he had got busted or something, but they told me to sit down. Only they had got some bad news to tell me.

"I'm afraid we've got some bad news. There's been an accident", one of them said.

I felt sick to my stomach when they told me John had been killed in a tragic road accident. They said no one else had been involved in the crash and apparently a witness who saw it said he drove down a very steep hill on the Newton Road at high speed and ploughed into a telephone box, which was situated at the bottom. It was on September 2nd, 1969. It's a date I will always remember. His death certificate stated that he died of a fractured skull and haemorrhaging; they said it was suicide and he took his own life whilst of a temporary unbalanced mind.

I still can't believe it to this day but I do know something: it was a very sad loss to his family, his friends and to music because, personally, I thought he had a great future ahead of him. It was a deep emotional tragedy to me which I have to live with for the rest of my life. Again and again I keep thinking: "Why did he do it?"

I went round to Bruno's the following day and broke the tragic news to him and John Partridge and the three of us just sat around in total shock. His brother Jim (drummer with The Jug Blues Band) came round with tears in his eyes to collect John's guitar and practice amp from Bruno's and not a word was spoken between us. Complete silence.

After his funeral the next week, we discussed what we were going to do with the band and we all decided to carry on straight away because we felt that's what John would have wanted us to do rather than sitting about mourning his death, so we started afresh by advertising for a new guitarist and saying we would dedicate this next group as 'Just For John …'

The auditions took place in September. One of the first guitarists that turned up at Bruno's living room for the audition sessions was a cocky but good-looking lad named Kenneth Downing who at that time hadn't adopted the K.K. nickname and was just 17 years old. If

Ernie Chataway and me meeting again in 2006. We hadn't seen each other in many years.

truth be told he lacked experience at the time despite having firm belief in himself. He hadn't been playing guitar for long and his lack of talent showed on the day; he'd only played an amplifier a few times for the audition so he wasn't prepared at all. He started playing guitar at 16 on an acoustic before picking up a Rickenbacker a year later, so not long before the audition for Judas Priest Mark I.

In the audition, he played really poor versions of Hendrix and Cream. When we asked him to run through a twelve-bar jam, we just couldn't tell what he was playing on his Gibson Junior, which he had just bought. I'm not convinced he even knew what a twelve-bar jam is! His Dallas amp was turned up full and his wah wah pedal was going ten to the dozen so he ended up not getting the job. But with his long blonde hair, his good looks, his enthusiasm and eagerness to get up and play it, left a mark with me which I would remember in the not so distant future. He just needed more training.

The guy who did get the gig was a Marc Bolan look-alike named Ernest Chataway, Ernie to his mates. He was also young but a natural musician and could play guitar, keyboards and harmonica really well. His influences were people like Jeff Beck, Peter Green, Eric Clapton and Gary Moore. He came from a rough area of Winson Green in Birmingham; in fact, he lived just around the corner from Winson Green Prison. When we asked him to show us what he could play he belted out "Wood Choppers Ball" by Ten Years After on his Gibson 335 and that was enough for Bruno to plug in and me to get behind the drums and jam for the next half an hour. We just seemed to gel together, it seemed perfect. We could not have asked for a better guitarist. We told Ernie about Johnny's death and his was a little spooked but got over it enough to accept our invitation in the band and so we started rehearsing at Brunos' house in Stone Cross, West Bromwich. Bruno's folks were really helpful when it came to offering us rehearsal space. I mean, how many parents would put up with a rock and roll band in their house?! I guess his mum and dad thought it was better to be making a noise at home than causing trouble on the streets of West Brom. Kids need a release of some sort; we took music while others commit crimes. I can tell you one thing: as long as we could make music we would not cause any trouble.

Ernie had been signed to the Birmingham company Randells Replacement Agency, which looked for work for unemployed musicians. He told us that he had previously played in a group from the city but they had split up; they had all met through Randells. Apparently, it was a good company to have as your support system. Ernie had also played with another group from Birmingham who had really impressed him. He never stopped raving about them, saying how good they were and that one day they would make it big. This band was called Earth but had since changed their name to Black Sabbath, but seeing as I have already spoken about this band I'll move on. I will say that we all liked the sound of the name Black Sabbath so decided it would be a good idea to search for something in the same vein, you know, something catchy and memorable.

The next morning Bruno came round to my house really exited, shouting: "I've got a brilliant name for the band! How about Judas Priest?!"

"Judas Priest! What the bloody hell is that?" I said.

"Don't you like Bob Dylan, Al?" he replied.

"Well, not really."

Bruno said that he had been listening to one of his Bob Dylan albums the night before; an album called »John Wesley Harding« and a track came on titled "The Ballad Of Frankie Lee And Judas Priest".

"Okay, we'll give it a go. It's better than other names we've had anyway", I said.

And so I agreed to use the Judas Priest name and so did the rest of the band when we told them later. In the States, the name was used as an expletive, so we knew it was always going to get a reaction every time we used it and that's the best band name you can get. Just like Black Sabbath.

When we told everybody about the Judas Priest name there were a lot of sceptics who didn't like it at all. They asked all sorts of annoying questions which really pissed me off.

"You will get nowhere with a name like that …"

"What a bloody strange name!"

"The Christians won't like that at all …"

"What do your mum and dad thing about that?"

This was exactly the reaction we wanted and we new people wouldn't forget it. It's better to have a name like Judas Priest that will cause debate and controversy than a name like The Medallians, which is frankly a load of crap.

So now the seed was planted but like the great oak tree it would take a long time to reach its maximum height, and it was never going to be plain sailing either, especially for four long-haired lads with their arses hanging out of their trousers, no jobs, no money and no transport to call their own. We weren't afraid of hard work but like all young and up-starting bands we needed a confidence boost.

But one thing we never lacked was dedication and determination to make it in the music world and it wasn't long before we started working on the setlist with our new guitarist Ernie. Despite our love of the blues, we actually classed ourselves as a progressive blues rock band and played covers of songs by American groups like Quicksilver Messenger Service, Spirit and the British band Quatermass. I'd also got us to play some of my own songs. I'd been writing for a while now and felt more mature although I'd write some absolute rubbish when I was spaced out on dope.

We were all in our early 20's apart from Ernie who was 17 and we had all gained a fair bit of experience playing live over the years, so it didn't take long for us to tighten our sound and feel at ease with each other on stage and we started to go down well with the audiences.

My friend, the roadie John "Magnet" Ward.

We took on a road manager by the name of John "Magnet" Ward who had got his own transport, which we desperately needed if we were to travel to gigs away from home. Bruno and myself were always lucky when it came to transport because with each band we knew somebody who had a van and would work for us for little or no money. Although we would try to buy our roadies as many pints of ale as we could afford but not before a gig; we didn't want to get the roadies pissed or we'd never make it to the stage.

After weeks spent rehearsing and jamming to old blues tunes, we thought we were good enough to have some management behind us. We advertised in our local newspaper saying that we've got a band together and had played some gigs (which we hadn't … yet) and were really in need of a good manager. A guy called Alan Eade from Ace Management came to our rescue. Alan Eade was a really nice guy who managed several bands; he was probably in his late 30's at the time and was always smart and well-dressed. He had a nice private house in Cheslyn Hay with a beautiful wife. He had an ex-policeman side-kick who worked with him and in his teens he had played in bands himself. Almost immediately, Alan had booked us to go into the studio to record two songs which I had written and he liked the sound of. I had written the lyrics just weeks before; one was called "Good Time Woman", which sounded very much like a pop song, and the other one was a slow bluesy number called "We'll Stay Together", which was more like a Cream song but with vocal harmonies. Those demos only took a few hours to record and I remember that Ernie played brilliantly on both tracks; he was a real guitar wiz.

After recording my two songs, Alan sent them off to several record companies he thought might be interested and we got a good response from two of them who happened to be Harvest Records (owned by EMI) and Immediate, an independent label owned by former Rolling Stones manager Andrew Loog Oldham. Both companies requested to see us play live and both companies had a reputation for taking risks with arty English rock bands.

Unfortunately, I never got to meet Mr. Oldham although when you put his reputation in consideration I would probably have felt a bit intimidated, anyway.

We did a showcase gig for both labels on November 25 at a local venue in Walsall called The George Hotel along with some other acts that were also on Alan's books. The George Hotel had a large ballroom inside with two stages. Robert Plant was in the audience, and like Sabbath, Led Zeppelin had started to make a name for themselves as a hard blues rock band. But Zep was a bigger entity, much bigger. By the end of 1969, Planty had toured the States an unbelievable three times with Led Zeppelin and had even headlined the prestigious Carnegie Hall in New York. They supported bands like Vanilla Fudge and MC5 and went down a storm. I was really envious of Planty but he was a top man and a real influence on me. Before his Led Zeppelin days, I used to see him quite often when he lived just around the corner from where I worked at Prestage, which was a small Vauxhall/Bedford garage on Birmingham Road. We would sometimes bump into each other at the Lewisham Hotel where we both had a beer or two. I remember him buying his first second hand car from my old mechanic mate Kenny Chipchase who also worked at Prestage. We went to his house with another old pal of mine named John England and listened to him sing and play on his old Fender Telecaster. How little did we know that in the next couple of years we would both form two giant names of rock: Led Zeppelin and Judas Priest.

On the night of the gig John Ward introduced me to Planty; we shook hands and exchanged pleasantries. I hadn't seen him for over a year and I asked how he was keeping. He was always a larger than life figure but Ernie thought he was a bighead. I always had time for him. Ernie liked him less in 1980 when he was playing guitar for The Ricky Cool Band and Robert decided to use them for his new project The Honeydrippers; they fired Ernie so they could bring in Robert's own lead guitarist Robbie Blunt.

I noticed Planty had got married to his girlfriend Maureen Wilson on November 9. Headlines in local newspaper said things like: 'King Of The Hippies Gets Wed.' I'd only met her a couple of times so I didn't really get to know her but I got on well with her two brothers: Glen and Bruce. Glen played guitar and at one time I teamed up with him for a duo and we had a jam at my friend John England's house on acoustic guitars. Bruce fancied himself as a drummer.

Anyway, at The George Hotel, we played a good set but we got carried away; we finished set with us going over the top smashing a few things up on stage, hoping it would leave an impression with the record company guys.

I went wild; I smashed Ernie's guitar across the neck so hard with the mic stand it cut the strings right into the fret board and nearly broke the neck clean off. He wasn't very happy because it was a lovely cream coloured Fender Strat that he had borrowed from Roy Wood just to try it out. Ernie fell off stage, which everybody thought was a bit of a joke. We got banned from playing there again when the management caught me pissing in the sink in the kitchens, which we were using as a changing room.

The guy from Harvest Records didn't like us at all and said we behaved like animals and sounded nothing like the demo we had sent him. I thought we had blown our chances of getting a deal but the other guy, who was simply named D'Abo, liked us and thought we were really exciting. He had been over to the States looking at various new bands to sign to the Immediate label and saw nothing that impressed him enough but was blown away by us. He wasn't very old probably late 20's/early 30's. I later found out that he was Mike

D'Abo's brother, the vocalist from The Manfred Mann Band. D'Abo gave us a handshake deal on the spot and in the following weeks we received and signed a four year record contract with Immediate Records.

"We've got a fucking record deal at last!" I shouted to the lads in the band.

Now we were on a label owned by the guy who discovered The Rolling Stones and had also been press agent for The Beatles at one time. Andrew was an eccentric guy who was like an English Phil Spector. He was one of the most important people in the music business during the sixties.

He created Immediate Records in 1965 so it was one of the country's first independent labels which covered all styles of music like rock, progressive, blues and psychedelic. When we got signed to Immediate they had on their books artists like John Mayalls Bluesbreakers, Chris Farlowe, The Small Faces, The Nice, Amen Corner, Humble Pie and Fleetwood Mac to name a few, so to say we were very pleased was an understatement.

Alan Eade threw a champagne party at his home at Cheslyn Hay and was really pleased because the other label Harvest Records (who were part of the Decca/EMI group) also signed another one of his acts called The Extreem, which featured a few of my old players from the past like Geoff Furnival (The Sugar Stack), Pete Boot (Blue Condition) and Barry Civil (The Jug Blues Band). I was also really pleased because The Extreem had got the deal playing a song I wrote with Barry some time back called "Out Of The Sky", which became the title of their album release.

We soon began to write some new songs, which would feature on our first album when Alan contacted us with the bad news that Immediate had folded and from now on would cease to exist. Our dreams had been smashed to pieces as easily as crystal. This was a bitter blow for us and it meant everything was back to the drawing board and back on the road to start all over again. I've never had much luck in this business; in fact, if I fell into a crate of nipples I would come out sucking my thumb.

So it was a case of onwards and upwards; we had to stay positive.

When we had our first series of live dates booked outside of England we felt like we were making progress. We were set to tour Scotland for three weeks in the winter of 1969/70. We kicked off in December and finished the following month, so we did lots of rehearsing and then we hit the road. To say everything went wrong preceding the tour would be an understatement. The first thing that happened was that our road manager Magnet broke his left arm but he said he would still try to drive us there if someone could change the gears for him as he steered the wheel with one hand. Then just as we had loaded up the van with all the equipment, the clutch broke so Bruno, Magnet and myself had to fit a new one; it was a good job Magnet was a bit of a mechanic, only we couldn't afford to take it to a garage. So now we were covered in oil and grease as we went to pick up Ernie and John before setting off on our long journey up North. Things would only get worse ...

When we got to Ernie's matchbox sized terraced house at about nine o'clock that night, he decided he didn't want to go because of the weather. Like bloody hell, he wasn't going to go!

"You're coming with us whether you like it or not, so go and get fucking ready", I shouted.

"Okay, okay ..." he said with no enthusiasm whatsoever.

I dragged him along with no further arguments.

When we arrived at John's house he came to the door in his pyjamas saying he had come down with flu and wouldn't be coming with us. By now I was really pissed off and told Magnet just to drive, and I would sing and play the fucking drums as well if I had to. I would have called this tour 'The Winter Of My Discontent Tour,' which is named after a horrible period in British history when in 1978/79 there were trade union strikes all over country and Britain was brought to a halt.

"I hate this bloody tour already and we've not even started driving up to Scotland yet!" I balled.

So off we went at about ten o'clock: Magnet drove us with his good arm and I sat along side him changing the gears for him all the way to Scotland, but our bad luck didn't just end there because as the night drew near we took on the notorious Shap Fell in Cumbria just as snow began to fall. Luckily, those old Thames vans had timber floorboards so the van was strong enough for the trip.

Half way up the mountain it became much worse and the flakes were as big as half crowns, the old English coin. Then we finally came to a standstill behind a traffic jam of cars and lorries that were all snowed under. The nearside door window of the van had jammed open earlier so we had to hang up an old grey army blanket to keep out the freezing conditions (it didn't!) I swear, I have never been so cold in my life. During the middle of the night we all looked like Scott of the Antarctic with icicles hanging off our beards. I thought we would all die of hypothermia when some guy banged on the van door saying if we walked down the hill with him he would show us an all night café, so we all jumped out and started walking in the snow, which by now was at least a foot deep.

As we walked down the hill we saw some lights in the distance somewhere on the old A-road and at first I thought I was having hallucinations because it said The Jungle Café. I mean, who thought of a name like that on top of a bloody freezing mountain? But it was our saviour on that cold winter's night. We sat there eating beans on toast and drinking plenty of hot drinks until the next morning when a snowplough came to dig us all out.

We missed the first gig of the tour but our luck finally changed and everything else went really well, including me playing the drums and singing but those bloody blisters on my hands were sore for days.

We stayed at a small bed and breakfast house in a town called Elgin and according to the guest book, which we were asked to sign, nearly all the stars had stayed there at sometime or other while touring Scotland. Just some of the signatures I remember were The Beatles, Cilla Black, Status Quo and Slade to mention a few; in fact, I wish I had nicked it now because it would be worth a fortune on ebay.

The first gig we played was at Dingwall Town Hall and we were told to arrive at eight o'clock, which seemed quite late, and when we arrived there wasn't a soul about apart from this old chap with the keys to open it up. I asked him where the audience was and he replied: "Up the pub getting drunk. When it closes they all come in here to finish off their night's entertainment."

Sure enough at about 10:30, the place started filling up. We kicked off our setlist and all was going well but then all of a sudden Ernie disappeared off the front of the stage, the next minute he was thrown back on again by a six-foot Jock with long grey hair and a beard to match, apparently he grabbed Ernie by his legs, dragged him off stage into the audience, requested the song "Summer Time Blues" and threw him back on stage again. Of course, we willingly jammed it out for him, after all there were no bouncers and our only roadie Magnet was hiding behind the stage curtains. (I didn't blame him).

The rest of the night went down really well but we were hoping we didn't encounter any more drunken Jocks dragging us off stage on the rest of the tour; having said that, I don't think anyone would be going by 20 stone Bruno.

Other venues we performed at included, The Beach Ballroom in Aberdeen, The Caledonian Hotel in Inverness, Fort William and even two nights at the Naval Base in Lossiemouth. There were a few others but I can't remember those.

One song in particular that the audience kept requesting us to play was the old classic "Born To Be Wild" by German/American group Steppenwolf; in fact, I recall that on one night we had to play it three times! It was the first time I had heard the words Heavy Metal used in the lyric. Steppenwolf sang "heavy metal thunder", which I understood they borrowed from a book by William S. Burroughs called »Naked Lunch«. Burroughs used it to describe a motorcycle. They were words I never forgot.

Halfway through the tour we had a two day break and took in a bit of sightseeing. One place we visited was an old monastery tucked away in the forests on a mountain side and you should have seen the look on the monks faces when we pulled up outside the place; with our beards and long hair and a van that had JUDAS PRIEST painted on the side in big psychedelic lettering, we looked a sight ... they must have thought we'd come from another planet.

"I think we're the odd ones out here", I said to the lads with a smirk on my face.

On the night we went down the local pub to taste a few beers, as this was one of Bruno's favourite pastimes. The only problem with this was that Ernie had a weird allergy to certain food and drink and it would bring him out in an awful rash if he wasn't careful. Anyway, Ernie, being just 17 years old, had never tried ale before but once he had a sip he liked the taste of it and for once forgot about his allergy; in fact, after about four or five pints of some strong Scottish brew he forgot his own name and came out in big red blotches. His face started to puff out and he looked like the TV comedy character Mr. Blobby on a bad day; although we laughed at him we were all a little bit concerned. Fortunately, after a good night's sleep he was back to normal the next day.

At one of the Lacarno Ballroom gigs that we played, Bruno broke one of his bass strings and walked off stage to change it at the end of the song. Rather than stop the music while he did this, Ernie put his guitar down and began to sing and play harmonica as he broke into an old Sonny Terry and Brownie McGee blues number; I picked up his guitar and accompanied him during the impromptu bit and when Bruno finally replaced his string he too joined in on the jam, which went down really well with the crowd, so much so we had to play it every night on the rest of the tour at the request of some audience members who used to turn up at every gig we played. Clearly, we made some sort of impact! Actually, at that time – late sixties/early seventies – most groups had to adlib and jam to get them out of trouble. I remember Robert Plant making the headlines of the local newspaper once because he sang a solo set at The Queen Mary Ballroom venue; for some reason or another his band's technical gear just randomly turned off on stage so he had to improvise. Rather than walking off stage with the rest of his band he sang and played his harmonica without a mic or P.A. system to a very quiet crowd for about half an hour before they all went wild with great applause.

Thank Christ it's over, I said to myself as we headed back to West Brom.
However, it wasn't all bad because I had been writing lyrics during our stay in Scotland; I scribbled down some lines for a new song to remind me of this tour which I aptly called "Winter".

"Winter"
(Atkins 1970)

Got no silver in my pockets
Got no pillow for my bed
And the winter it gets stronger
Got to ease my aching head
In the morning when I wake up
Get this feeling deep inside
And I wonder if I'll die young
Or just go out of my mind
I still get this awful feeling
When the snow falls to the ground
And it sends my senses reeling
Going winter underground

At some point in early 1970 with the Scottish tour nothing but an unwanted memory, we were asked to go to a Marshall Amplification Exhibition at a venue near Yardley's music shop in town. The band that was playing was Deep Purple and I was blown away by them and the guitar wizardry of Ritchie Blackmore; my ears were ringing for two days afterwards. Like a lot of bands Purple had a complicated start (well, a very complicated history come to think of it) but they released their first album »Shades Of Deep Purple« in 1968. It wasn't until the tremendous »In Rock« album in 1970 that they really hit the big time as one of the country's top hard rock outfits. The album featured the most successful line up (and they've had many) in their history: Ritchie Blackmore, Ian Gillan, Roger Glover, Jon Lord and Ian Paice. Blackmore's a bit of an oddball but then most geniuses are. They followed »In Rock« with more great albums such as »Fireball«, »Machine Head« and »Who Do We Think We Are?«. I also liked the stuff Deep Purple made when they recruited David Coverdale, especially the album »Burn«. Coverdale is another one of my favourite singers and I think in many respects he's underrated; he certainly doesn't deserve the criticism he's received over the years. I know Robert Plant's not been to kind to him, calling him 'Cover-Plant' and things like that.

Free was another great hard rock band of that era. »Fire And Water« was their biggest selling album and oddly, it doesn't have any blues songs on it even though they made their name singing the blues. Who could forget first hearing "All Right Now"? What a bloody brilliant song! Paul Rodgers quickly became one of my idols; his voice is very powerful and even now as he sings with Queen he still has a strong set of lungs. For a while, I wanted to be Paul Rodgers. He's been in the business for 40 years and still looks and sounds bloody amazing.

Anyway, we carried on gigging in the coming weeks playing places like Masonic Hall in Walsall, Community Centre in Wednesbury, The George in Walsall, Club Westbourne in

Edgbaston, Rugby Club in Shrewsbury, Old Swinford Hospital School in Stourbridge, Moor Farm Inn in Nottingham and the Hereford Town Hall in Hereford.

In the early days when I was in the band, Judas Priest attracted crowds that listened to heavy American bands like Blue Cheer, Iron Butterfly and Vanilla Fudge. Black Sabbath had charted in the UK with their first album »Black Sabbath« and this gave us a big boost of encouragement – Judas Priest could do the same! So from January through to March we worked our arses off on the road; it was good training for us. But we ran into problems when the band started to drift apart musically.

Personally, I wanted to explore the heavier side of rock and roll as played by bands like Black Sabbath, Deep Purple and Led Zeppelin; those great bands eventually broke away from the bluesy hard rock style of playing that they had started with but that didn't stop me from being a big fan. As a band, we couldn't agree on the issue of Judas Priest's sound and image: Ernie leaned towards a blues rock sound but I wanted us to get heavier and explore a bigger rock landscape. We decided to split midway through the year and go our separate musical ways. It wasn't a bitter spilt; we were actually quite mature about it. Our last gig was on April 20 at the Youth Centre in Cannock. That was the end of Judas Priest Mark I.

Bruno teamed up with a soul band called The Roy Gee Explosion and went off to tour Denmark for a couple of months; I wished him all the best even though I was slightly jealous that he got to travel abroad. Ernie moved to London to work with some friends on a blues project and John, the drummer, also drifted away from West Bromwich to join another group. He moved out of town to live in Lye; I haven't seen him since.

Magnet, our faithful roadie, teamed up with Robert Plant for a while before working with Jeff Beck. He then got a job with Deep Purple as Ian Paice's drum technician for several years before ending his career with Whitesnake. I believe that he also worked for AC/DC.

As for myself: I decided to take a short break for a while and then I got a job as a gardener for West Bromwich local council and even married my girlfriend Linda Cowley and moved in with her and her mum Anne; her father was killed in an industrial accident when she was a child. I met Linda in 1969 and fell in love with her straight away; she was young, had lovely long blonde hair and was also from Stone Cross. I was 23.

Let me tell you, times were tough in 1970. Tory leader Ted Heath moved into 10 Downing Street in 1970. Things didn't get better, the seventies was an awful period in this country's history, ridden with unemployment, strikes and bad politics.

But all that meant very little to me and to my own little world in West Brom. It wasn't long before I began to think about my next musical adventure ...

I received another message from guitarist Adrian Ingram; this time he asked me to join him in forming a new band. Adrian was the guitarist in The Bakerloo Blues Line in which guitar wizard Clem Clemson had made famous before he left to join Colosseum. The band reformed with Jim Simpson as manager.

He asked me to take over on vocals and at first I didn't fancy going back to a blues rock style of music, which was one of the reasons why I disbanded Judas Priest, but Adrian convinced me that this group were going places. He said Jim Simpson had gotten them a record deal lined up, along with a tour of Europe and that was enough to convince me to join.

They were a six-piece group with George Northall on saxophone; they were all very competent musicians with a lot of potential and a bright future. We rented out an old disused shop in Old Hill by Dudley Town and we lived there over the next month just rehearsing and living on peanut butter sandwiches, because that's all I could afford on my dole money (I swear I will never eat that stuff again). As rehearsals progressed it became obvious that this version was more of a jazz band than the previous incarnation, so it was really something of a departure for me. I honestly can't remember many of the songs we performed; there was a song by Donovan which they made jazzier and there were some original Bakerloo songs.

One day Jim Simpson dropped by to see how things were shaping up and told us he had secured a record deal for us and was sorting out the tour just as promised, and then out of the blue he introduced the band to their new vocalist who was some black dude named Kirk St. James who had just finished a stint in Paris with the musical »Hair«.

I was totally gobsmacked because not only had I made good friends with everyone, I thought they could go all the way to the top. And I also felt that I did a good enough job with them ... and so did the band!

It was the first time I had been fired from any sort of job and Adrian apologised to me on behalf of the rest of the band but said it was out of their hands. It seemed Jim Simpson was pulling all the strings and they were just performing for him; George Northall has stayed a lifelong friend.

If they had made it to the top naturally I would have been slightly envious. Jim Simpson finally whittled them down to a four-piece when Bill Hunt, the keyboard player, joined Roy Wood's Wizzard. Then Simpson changed the band's name to Hannibal when they got singed to Chrysalis Records. Hannibal had one flop album and after a year, they split up. Adrian Ingram went on to have a brilliant career as one of Britain's top jazz guitarists.

After my dismissal from The Bakerloo Blues Line, my confidence was knocked, badly. I decided against doing any more auditions and to form my own group, yet again. This time I would be in charge! I would write the songs for the band and play the kind of heavy rock and roll that bands like Black Sabbath played. I wanted to form this kind of band for the past year but wasn't given the chance and so it was at this point that I decided it's about time I gave it another shot ...

1970 was nearly over and what a disappointing year it had been, but I was looking forward to what 1971 had around the corner. I tried to be positive, to think about the future rather than the past.

I was about to advertise for musicians when I thought about some old rehearsal rooms, which, on most nights, were always full of groups practising their songs. I had been using one particular hall since the 1960s. It was an old disused school by the side of a church called St James in Wednesbury, just a few miles outside of West Bromwich, but us locals called it Holy Joe's. It was run by a peculiar vicar named Father Husband who was once a naval padre.

"Fares please", he would shout out at the top of his voice, as he held out his hand for the five shilling fee he charged for renting out his rooms.

He was a stout old chap and always wore spectacles and a dog collar; and after collecting all the money from the groups he would walk up to the pub, which was called The Butlers, on the corner of the street and spend it on beer. He was a hefty drinker. He even let people practise in his house if the money was right.

All the old classrooms, of which there were about ten to 15, were turned into rehearsal rooms for local bands. Slade, Robert Plant and Trapeze used Holy Joe's. One story was that

Robert got banned when Holy Joe caught him smoking dope but apparently it was just a Camel cigarette.

Anyway, I dropped by Holy Joe's one cold night in October, 1970, to see if there were any upcoming local rock bands that I might like the sound of.

In October, 1970, I stood outside each room listening to the echoing sound the old-school made and there was one particular group that sounded like they'd be right up my street; it was my type of music. So I put my head around the door to see which band was playing. In the room stood three young longhaired guys, head banging away with their amps turned up to maximum volume, giving it all.

"Great", I muttered quietly, "just what I was looking for ... a hard rock and roll band."

I later discovered that the lad sitting in the corner of the room was their roadie, Trevor Lunn. One guy I recognized straight away was Kenny Downing who I had auditioned a year earlier and I must say his guitar playing had improved a lot in just twelve months, even though he still loved his wah wah pedal a bit too much. The other two players were Ian "Skull" Hill on bass guitar and John Ellis on drums.

I walked into the room, shook hands with them and introduced myself. I told them I liked the sound of their band and asked if they were looking for a vocalist. Lord and behold, Kenny said they were considering adding a singer to their line-up and I asked them if they would consider teaming up with me. They told me that their band was called Freight, which I didn't like the sound of very much. I suggested using my old band name Judas Priest, which had already gained a bit of a reputation on the local live music circuit. I told them about our deal with Immediate and the many gigs we played. They all agreed. Judas Priest was resurrected and the Mark II version was born. In a way it was quite sad for me because it was the first band in several years which I had formed without my good mate Bruno.

Over the next couple of weeks we discussed which direction we were going to take and what type of music we all preferred to play. We agreed on heavy rock, the louder the better.

Ian, Kenny and John were all about 18 years of age and were old school friends who had been seduced by rock music at an early age while attending Churchfields School at All Saints. They grew up together on the Yew Tree council estate, which borders Walsall and West Bromwich.

My initial suggestions were to rehearse at my mother-in-law's council house at Stone Cross; she had a vacant spare bedroom that we could use. As I've already said she was a widower named Anne, a lovely woman who never moaned about the noise we made or the smell of the funny cigarettes we smoked or the frequently loud belches from our binge drinking. We would practice there on most nights and then go to Holy Joe's at the weekend and try out all the songs we had learned with the amps turned up full.

I did, occasionally, get into her bad books: one night at bedtime I fell asleep while smoking a joint and it set the bed on fire along with my wife. They were both running round the bedroom screaming their heads off but I just sat up in bed laughing at them through the smoke, luckily they put out the fire, but, boy, did I get a telling off them the next day. My wife wasn't injured but her night dress was!

At first we were all working in day jobs apart from Kenny. Ian worked at a small firm called Regent Spring that sold motorcar springs and accessories; John worked at a well-known paper mill called K & J's and I carried on working as a gardener/handyman for the West

Bromwich Council but over the next six months Ian and myself gave up our jobs to concentrate on the music. John decided to try and do both, which he found very stressful.

We all seemed to get on well together and had a mutual friend called Beverley Stone who was dating a lad named Keith Evans. But if there was one thing that we all had in common then it was our love of Jimi Hendrix; he died in September, 1970, after an accidental drugs overdose. His genius has never been bettered. I remember the look on Kenny's face when he found about about Hendrix's death; it was one of complete shock.

John had a musical background; he started playing drums at an early age. He was a Mod during his teenage years and used to ride a scooter around West Brom with Ian who also owned a flashy scooter. I know they'd drifted apart from Kenny at one point but through music their paths crossed again and so they formed Freight.

On several occasions, I had to tell John about him bringing his girlfriend along to rehearsals; I needed them all to focus on the music and take it seriously if we were going to make it big time and so I had to stop girls from coming to the rehearsals.

I used to stress to him: "You don't take your woman to work with you! You leave her at home!" Apart from that, we all got along okay.

As for Kenny, well, I would often say that Kenny was only allergic to one thing and that was work but I've heard since that after leaving school he was a trainee chef for a while at the Littleton Arms in Worcester. He was a lazy sod who left school at 15.

Kenny was much more outgoing than Ian and John and I used to see him prior to joining the group, hanging around West Bromwich town centre, especially the local Billiard Hall and the local hang out café the Cassa Bamboo where all the teenagers would drink their Espresso Coffee, listen to music and smoke a joint or two. Every now and then the police would raid it and make us stand outside with our arms above our heads while they searched us for drugs (happy times).

I think he had a troubled history; he suffered from asthma and lived alone in lodgings at the appropriately named Lodge Road. He left school at 15 and had been on his own for some time after falling out with his parents over his long blonde hair ... so I was told, anyway. He had a girlfriend called Carol Hales who also had long blonde hair and I always thought they would stay together forever as a couple. I sensed she didn't like me too much but I liked her and thought she was good for him. Kenny loved fishing and snooker and could also be found doing either. He was easy enough to get on with but he would not work for love or money.

Ian was a quiet and unassuming lad who I had never seen or met before Judas Priest Mark II formed. Ian got his nickname "Skull" because he was really thin and gaunt like a skeleton. He was a very good, natural bass guitarist for his age; he bought his first bass with the insurance money after he crashed his car.

Ian's dad had died a few years before when Ian was just 15 and he too was a bass player in a jazz band so maybe that is were Ian got his talent from. His mum later married a carpenter and he used to help Ian make his bass cabinets. They moved to Chester but Ian didn't want to leave his Black Country roots and all his friends behind, so he stayed locally and moved in with Trevor Lunn and his dad. Not much later he moved in with his Nan at her council flat in the Bermuda Mansions part of Yew Tree Estate. As it goes, Ian is one of the nicest and most generous people I have ever met which is a rare thing in this business.

The Yew Tree Estate was part of the housing projects built after World War II; with the influx of immigrants and the poor housing conditions caused by the war the government invested in new schemes to rebuild houses all over Britain. Yew Tree was like a self-contained world with its own shops, community centre, public toilets, clubs and even a doctors and dentists surgery. There were also bus routes into Birmingham and nearby towns. I got the impression that Ian and John liked living there because there were loads of families in the area in similar situations to them. The Yew Tree kids had places to play football, rugby and other sports like cricket. They had places to hide from their families if they wanted to get up to mischief and the area was generally well maintained with hot and cold water and free from litter.

None of them were into hard drugs but sometimes the three of them would experiment with LSD on a weekend at Kenny's lodgings. They also told me about one occasion when they took a "trip" down the valley, which is the local greenbelt surrounding Sandwell, on one Saturday night; they stripped off and ran through the trees naked!

One weekend John had a bad trip at Kenny's and they had to tie him to the bed when he hallucinated about rats that were crawling all over him. I think this put Kenny and Ian off using LSD but John continued to dabble with the hallucination drug. We certainly didn't take anything like cocaine or heroin, mostly weed, uppers and sleepers.

Times were hard and Kenny and myself signed on the dole in Paradise Street, West Bromwich on Thursdays and as soon as we picked up our weekly bit of cash to live on we would eat breakfast at the Country Girl café. Kenny told me how much he loved his music more than anything else and wanted to make it successful so badly that he couldn't see himself doing anything else in life. I used to wish him all the luck in the world because no matter how good a musician you are, you will need a lot of luck in this business because it's so tough to break into, but above all else, you should enjoy the ride no matter what the outcome may be.

As I said, it was a difficult period, and I remember once when Kenny's jeans became so ragged from wear and tear that his arse practically fell out the back of them, so my very slim wife found him a pair of hers to give to him because he couldn't afford a new pair, and they actually fitted him because his waist was so narrow. Kenny couldn't afford to eat a lot which explains his physique way back then.

Once, after one of our rehearsals, I took Ian and Kenny to a party I had been invited to; it was some relative's wedding anniversary at the Friar Park Community Centre and we filled our faces with food and drink but I couldn't believe Kenny when I saw him stuffing sausage rolls and sandwiches inside his jacket for the next day. Kenny had a good set of mates and I don't think he could have survived otherwise. He was lucky, that way.

When I first rehearsed with Kenny and Ian, we jammed out the obvious blues songs like BB King's classic "Rock Me Baby" and the other blues song I can remember us playing was a Savoy Brown Blues Band track called "Wake Up My Mind", which didn't stay in the set very long. Anyway, after some tight rehearsals in which we practiced modern songs by Cream and Hendrix, Judas Priest Mark II was almost ready to hit the road at the tail end of 1970; we decided we would need at least another roadie to help Trevor Lunn so we took on board Keith "Evo" Evans. He was a shady character, anything you wanted he could get you and a lot cheaper but he was a great guy and we got on really well with each other. He came off the Yew Tree Estate like the rest of the lads.

1964. The Medallians. Yuck, what a stupid fucking name (yes that smart young lad is me on drums.)
This band later became The Bitta Sweet.

In the graveyard taken with some old war veteran who could tell a few stories. "You lot get your hair cut." Ian Hill, Chris "Congo" Campbell, the war vet, Kenny Downing and Me. Judas Priest Mark IV.

In Barmouth, Wales circa 1970-71.

Sitting down relaxing in Stonehenge, Wiltshire.

Kenny posing (I like the shirt, mate!)

Judas Priest Mark II (me, Kenny Downing, Ian Hill and John Ellis) circa 1970-71.

Keith Evans and Trevor Lunn with John Ellis and Kenny.

John Ellis and Keith Evans share a joint ... I mean share a joke.

Nicky Bowbanks, friend of the band and one time partner of Rob Halford. (He was killed in a car crash in 1992.) Nicky was the uncle of The Holy Rage guitarist Chris Johnson.

Kenny with his new amp thinking will this be loud enough for Madison Square Garden?

Taken from rare poster of a tour of Scotland. (1971)

Early posters, 1973. The band poster shows Judas Priest Mark IV. My final tour with the band was the Heavy Thoughts jaunt, 1973. Chris "Congo" Campbell, Kenny Downing, Me & Ian Hill.

Cuttings from my old scrapbook.

JUDAS PRIEST
HEAVY THOUGHTS

Judas Priest's first two albums featuring my songs.

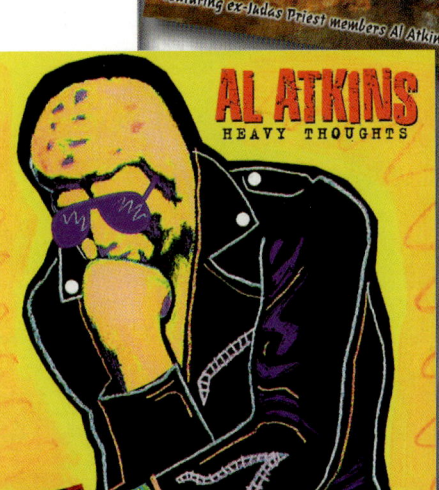

Some of my solo albums.

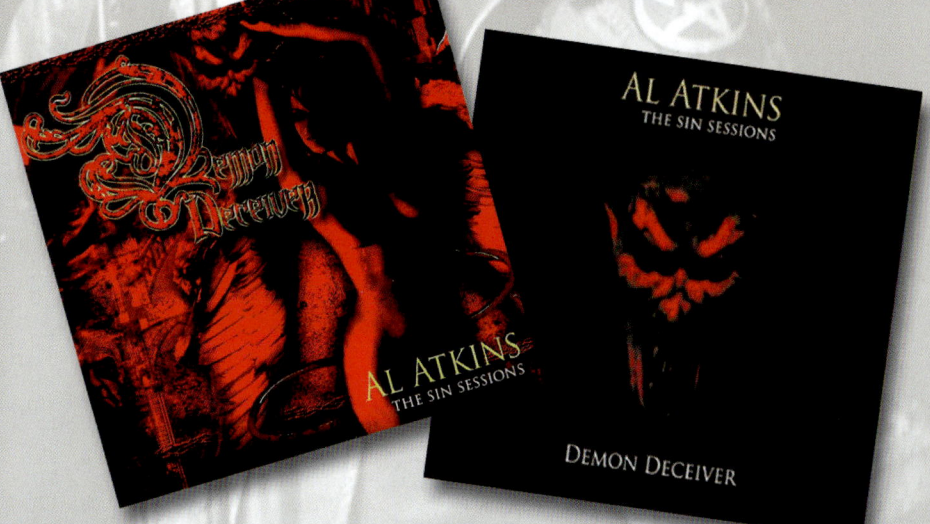

Paul May and myself at Outlaw Studios in Birmingham, 1989.

Pete Emms, me and Paul with roadie (l) Archie Cole (r) Eric Bloodaxe.

Having a beer at our local brewhouse, The Wheatsheaf.

Meeting up with Paul May again in 2007.

Me posing.

Pete Emms, me, Dave Holland and Paul May in 1998.

Some cool pics of us live at JB's nightclub in Dudley, 2006.

Nice solo shot of Chris with his Moser BVI Custom Guitar.

More JB's live shots with our one time drummer Alex Reynolds giving his skins some stick.

More mug shots of me on stage at JB's.

My band rehearsing at The Madhouse in Birmingham.

Poster from Hollywood gig with the great Graham Bonnet, formally of Rainbow.

Promotional shot of me posing for the fantastic guitar company from California 'Moser Custom Guitars.' Chris Johnson, me and Mike De Jager.

Holy Rage supporting Diamond Head in August 2008.

Ex-Judas Priest manager Dave Corke (left). Dave Corke with Simon Austen from Light and Sound Design (right).

Also, another friend of theirs named Dave Corke fancied himself as a rock and roll manager so we hired him in an instant. He was a West Bromwich lad and very eccentric; he was of average height, wore big specs and had black curly hair. He was a friend of Ian's and wasn't musically talented but he was good at talking to people to get what he wanted.

I kid you not: Dave Corke used to have a phone box as an office. It was one of those phone boxes like the one Doctor Who has in the TV series. I think he used the phone box because his parents wouldn't let him use the house phone; they were probably afraid of getting expensive phones bills and I don't blame them.

After a week stuck in a phone box, Dave Corke finally came up with some gigs for us to play. Dave played a significant role for us over the next few years and just like the road crew, he became the fifth member of the group. Motörhead's main man Mr. Lemmy Kilmister – who briefly roadied for Jimi Hendrix – wrote "We Are The Road Crew" as a tribute to his road team; some people don't realise how important roadies actually are. Without them, bands would not be able to make it to gigs.

Each of us would work really hard and pull it together over the years to come; we all ate, slept and wept together. He would use pseudonyms like Eric Smith to get us more gigs; he was brilliant at the administration side of the music business.

Our sound was raw, fresh and loud and what we lacked in experience we certainly made up for in enthusiasm. Kenny played a Gibson S G; as a big Jimi Hendrix fan he longed to own a Flying V. Ian played an Epiphone E.B.O and later bought a black Ned Callan bass. They played their instruments through Laney 100 watt stacks.

We had the name, the transport, the roadies and some gigs lined up and so it was at this time that the JUDAS PRIEST machine began to roll ... again.

We played our first gig on March 16 at St. Johns Hall, a working man's club in Essington. We got paid a grand fee of £6 to cover our petrol expenses – it was rubbish money but it was better than nothing! There were only about 60 or 70 people in the crowd. I remember Kenny being a bit nervous about walking out on stage for the first time, after all this would be Kenny, Ian and John's debut live performance, but when he saw all the girls in the audience dancing in their hot pants we couldn't hold him back. Kenny was definitely a ladies man, always has been and always will be, and what better job to have to attract the ladies than a rock star.

I don't think our style of music was quite what the audience wanted and some even tried dancing to it but we didn't go down too bad considering how loud we were. We had to start somewhere and this type of low-key gig was just what we needed to iron out the mistakes that we made.

Trevor would like to add a few words; we hadn't spoken in years before I decided to write this book so his thoughts are more than welcome.

Trevor Lunn (road manager 1970-72): "I first made friends with Ian Hill in early '67 while riding our Vespa and Lambretta scooters during the Mod movement. The music we were listening to at this moment in time was stuff by the The Small Faces and Amen Corner, etc., but we soon realised Cream, Jimi Hendrix and Pink Floyd were the bands everyone was talking about and as soon as we heard them, it changed our lives and musical tastes forever.

So with a group of friends we started to explore the underground and progressive rock and blues scene, and collecting albums by bands such as Colloseum, Jethro Tull, Fleetwood Mac, John Mayall, Cream and Jimi Hendrix.

In the summer of '68 we were going to music festivals and meeting up with a crowd of friends we had all known from school, one of them was Kenny Downing, another was John Ellis. After watching numerous bands across the country during that summer it seemed everyone wanted one thing and that was to play in a band, myself included.

Ian chose to play bass; maybe because of his father's influence because he played double bass in a jazz band. John chose drums because he once had lessons in the boy's brigade. Kenny chose lead guitar because of his hero Jimi Hendrix.

One of my first memories of Kenny playing guitar was when Ian and myself went to watch him rehearse at the Yew Tree School, West Bromwich with his cousin Brian Badhams on bass. Not long after this he bought himself a brand new Gibson SG Junior and when I asked him how he was going to pay for it (he was unemployed at the time) he turned to me and said: 'The guitar will pay for itself,' and told me he was going to make a living playing the instrument. I must say that single-mindedness got him where he is today. Hats off to you Kenny!

Some time later he auditioned for a job in a local band who were making a name for themselves called Judas Priest but he didn't pass the audition, the vocalist in this band was Al Atkins.

Not long after Kenny teamed up with Al's wife's cousin named Robert 'Skip' Spencer to gain more experience. Skip was another good local guitarist and he gave Kenny a job in his band called Stagecoach; he also gave him some guitar lessons to improve his playing and this definitely made a difference over the next six months. I heard Kenny played a few local gigs with this band but I don't recall what the venues were.

After leaving Skip he went back to the music he liked best and teamed up with Ian, John and myself. I had always wanted to play guitar in a rock band but I couldn't keep up with the progress Ian and Kenny were making so in the end I opted to be their road manager instead, that way I could remain friends with them and still play a part in the music business so I sold my guitar and bought an old Commer van for us to travel around in. So Ian, Kenny and John finally came up with a name to call themselves, which was Freight and they started to rehearse at Holy Joe's in Wednesbury town centre.

One evening at rehearsals, Al Atkins entered the room, stood and watched for a while then asked the band if he could have a word. They all went outside for about 20 minutes then John, Ian and Kenny came back in and said to me that Al wanted to form a band with them

Me, Ian Hill and Chris "Congo" Campbell. The other two guys are the old roadies Trevor Lunn and Keith Evans. It was supposed to be a Judas Priest reunion night at 'The Rock' pub run by Keith to auction off different things for charity, Glenn turned up earlier and gave one of his guitars but Kenny never turned up, can't think of the year but Halford had left them and they were looking for a new vocalist.

and they all agreed it would be a good idea and from now on they would be known as Judas Priest.

The first thing I noticed at rehearsals was how professional Al was and how he organised everything, he knew exactly what he wanted from the band and I admired him and still do today.

Their first gig was at Essington near Cannock and needing a second roadie, we recruited Keith 'Evo' Evans. My old Commer van broke down and needing another more reliable one Evo and myself put our money together and bought a second hand Ford Transit from a local farmer for £150.00. And that was because the van had been a farm vehicle, so it smelt like pig shit and it took nearly a week of disinfecting and hosing it out to get rid of the smell.

Over the two years that I spent with the band I had some great times and memories of them playing alongside Black Sabbath, Status Quo, Thin Lizzy, Slade and The Pink Fairies, to name just a few.

I have remained Ian's friend to this day and we meet up now and then and also go to West Bromwich Albion football matches together when he's not on tour or recording his next album with now the world's famous heavy metal band Judas Priest …"

From April until the end of summer we gigged tirelessly playing at venues such as Burntwood Baths, Three Mile Oak in West Bromwich, Youth Centre in Cannock, Dudley Tech in Dudley, Technical College in Walsall, The Plaza in Old Hill, Henry's Blues House in Birmingham and Coppertops in Worcester. We supported Black Sabbath at the Masonic Hall in Walsall. When Priest played with Sabbath a few years ago at the US Ozzfest; they were asked if it was the first time they had appeared on stage together. Apparently, Rob Halford said yes but then Kenny corrected him and mentioned the gig Judas Priest Mark II played supporting Sabbath on April 21, 1971. Trevor Lunn, our roadie, remembers this gig too but I just can't recall the events of that night – I probably smoked too much pot! Honestly, I don't remember a thing! You'd think I would considering that Black Sabbath headlined the evening's shindigs.

Coppertops was a big pub with a large dance room at the rear. Everything went well until the end of the night at closing time when a large group of skinheads started fighting with another group of people and all hell broke loose. We ran back into the changing room and locked ourselves in and attempted to climb out of a small window, first pushing Ian out but he started shouting something about the drop and it was then when we realised we were about 20 feet above a flight of steps. Luckily for him, Trevor and Evo didn't push too hard and it wasn't long before the police came and broke up the fight.

After playing gigs at Three Mile Oak in West Bromwich and The Plaza in Old Hill, we supported the Chicago Blues Band at Lafayette Club in Wolverhampton on June 30. Kenny's guitar strap broke just before we were due to go on stage so he went into their changing room and asked if he could borrow one but their guitarist Peter Haycock said to him: "Fuck off! What do you think this is, a music shop?!"

"I can't believe that bloke", Kenny said to me.

We could never understand people like that, big headed bastard. Luckily, the roadies patched it up just enough to get us through the show.

We stormed through places like Three Mile Oak in West Bromwich, Central Hall in Birmingham and another show at Dudley Tech College. We supported a young band called Status Quo at Quaintways in Chester; they'd already had hit singles with "Pictures Of Matchstick Men" and "In The Sun" although their first two albums, »Picturesque Matchstickable Messages« and »Spare Parts« flopped despite good reviews. I became an instant fan as soon as they dropped their psychedelic image and moved toward a blues rock sound, which they are brilliant at. Their denim jeans and white shirts image was a damn sight better than that pompous Carnaby Street clothing they used to wear. After supporting Quo, the gigs rolled on, playing in Derby, Coventry and Liverpool.

Another one of our earlier gigs was in London at a place called The Gunn Inn; you'd think that playing in the capital city would be a big step forward for a young band, well, it's not. When we arrived at this venue it was just a large shed behind a pub and there were not very many people in the audience that night.

"I'll strangle Corky when we get back", I said to the lads. "I can't believe he put us in this fucking dump."

"All right calm down, Al."

Just for laughs some cockney band that opened up for us let all four of our tyres down on the van. The bastards. Dave was now working at a tyre company, which was very useful because he had access to the office and a free phone line to book us into gigs. Similarly to the first line-up of Priest we played some Hendrix stuff, Spirit and I even threw one or two of my own songs into the setlist. Anyway, as the year progressed we began to get better with every gig we played; I also started to write more songs too, bigger venues came our way (via Dave who worked tirelessly) and we started to feature alongside some big name bands such as Supertramp.

It was at this time in July 1971, that we decided to go into a recording studio and record a couple of my songs so Dave booked us a quick session at Zella Studios in Broad Street, Birmingham. It was the best studio in the Midlands at the time; Zella was run by Johnny Haines and most top bands used to record there, including Black Sabbath. When the BBC radio moved out, Zella moved to bigger premises at Walker Hall in Ampton Road but now ceases to exist under that name. A rather good local group called Magnum took it over years later; the studio is now called Mad Hat and is based in Wolverhampton where it is run by Mark Stuart

We recorded two of my songs at Zella titled "Mind Conception" and "Holy Is The Man".

"Mind Conception"
(Atkins 1971)

Big black room is closing
Closing on my mind
Walked around it time and time
See what I could find
Doors they open for me
Winds blow from behind
Hold me back and warn me
Look out for a sign

But I don't hear a thing, except a distant ring
Tolling bells are a calling me
And I will go to them, when the nightmare ends
And the waker sets me free

Confused confrontations
How long will this last
Dark hallucinations
Hide behind their masks
Shadows in the hallway
Turn their true form shape
Warning that a darker day
Waits when I awake

Falling, falling deeper and deeper
How the night holds on to me
Falling, falling weaker and weaker
Page the keeper bring the key
Calling, calling over and over
In this endless night of nights
Burning, burning running for cover
Until another dawn and light

"Holy Is The Man"
(Atkins 1970)

Don't have no fear
And live a lot on the wild side
Got so many files
Every day is a hard life
Like my noise real loud
Spirits strong and neat
Take on any young pretenders
And all that's so on the street

And holy is the man
Who can turn this sinner out of me

Never hid from danger
Never got much loving
Learned to look out for myself
And find I hard forgiving
Got a real mean nature
Never one for giving
Had to fight out to survive
Just to keep on living

Never ran from trouble
Always stood my ground
Got this reputation
Got to live it down

Built-in destruction
Hard to the core
Just hold contemption
When it comes to the law

But there was a problem: when I asked Johnny to tape them live I wouldn't listen to his advice so we found ourselves with loads of overspill and no overdubs, in other words it sounded awful. I had a cold at the time and being stoned out of my head didn't help either. Ah well, we put it down to experience; it was a learning curve at best. The rest of the band was a bit annoyed with me but at least we actually made a demo.

But there you have it, the first ever recordings by Judas Priest and I still have the master, a 45rpm record. I believe I have the only copy. (Wanna buy it?)

One day after our demo session, Dave called us all to a meeting and asked us if the Judas Priest name had ever been registered; the entire band turned and looked at me, and I said: "No, why? What's the problem?"

"The problem is", he replied, "there are two groups out there using this name, one in the USA and one in Scotland who I think must have stolen it from the tour you did there once. Leave it to me ..."

I heard later from him that he threatened to sue both of them if they played or recorded under the Judas Priest name again, saying we had already registered it (although we hadn't) but clearly they both hadn't because they stopped using it after that.

We realised what a great group name we had got in Judas Priest and wanted to hold on to it.

In September, we supported Gary Moore at the Town Hall in West Bromwich; the band Skid Row had released »34 Hours«. And then we blitzed places like: Plough and Harrow, British Legion Club and Moor Farm Inn in Nottingham, Kinetic Circus in Birmingham, The Babalou Club in Liverpool, The Fighting Cocks in Mosely and County Cricket Club in Northampton as support to a long-forgotten progressive rock band called Curved Air. They formed in 1969 and a year later released their terrific debut album »Airconditioning«.

We kicked off October with yet more gigs; Angel Underground in Nottingham, Kings Head in Stafford and the Kinetic Circus in Birmingham. A gig I recall with particular vividness was at the Borough Hall in Stafford on October 4, 1971. We supported a local band called Strife and the awesome Thin Lizzy; they'd formed in 1969 in Dublin and were still a struggling band when we supported them. They had a big hit a couple of years later with the powerful single "Whiskey In The Jar" and after that "Jailbreak" and "The Boys Are Back In Town" from the album »Fighting«. Listen to »Live And Dangerous«, you'll understand just how great they were on stage.

Unlike Peter Haycock from the Chicago Blues Band whom we had supported weeks before, Phil Lynott would do anything to help you if you needed it. I remember he offered me a joint in the dressing room before the show started, which made me feel great but I felt really blitzed on stage; I couldn't remember what my performance was like on that night but the roadies assured me it was okay, so I took their word for it. I don't know how Phil got through his gigs; Christ, you couldn't even tell he was stoned at all and was always a true pro. Kenny and Ian were against me doing any drugs but to me it was all part of rock and roll.

Some of these local gigs were great because it meant we could go home to our own beds for a good night's sleep but the gigs that were not so close to home were awkward; we would travel anywhere just to play, so we had to find bed and breakfast or sleep in the old van with the equipment. In the winter it was bloody freezing and when the roadies started farting it was not very pleasant at all. Some bands have certain roles for the tour van but we didn't have any because it was a rusted piece of metal on wheels. We didn't have the money to care about rules; we just acted our usual selves even if it meant annoying the hell out of each other. I know in the eighties when rock bands sued really expensive tour buses they made certain rules like no shitting in the toilet. Again, it's all part of the rock and roll experience.

During October we would see a change in the line-up of Judas Priest Mark II. More and more gigs came our way and our drummer John just couldn't handle the frantic pace. He was the only one of us left in the band who stayed in employment; he worked at Kenrick & Jefferson printers in West Bromwich. Kenny, Ian and myself had by now given up everything for the cause, we were on a mission and nothing was going to stand in our way until we had made it to the big time.

We could tell that the pressure of work and the band was taking its toll on him; he was under pressure from his bosses at work because he was taking too much time off, so he decided his destiny lay with the security of his full time day job and not us. His dad has recently died so he was trying to cope with the grief which must have been tough on him.

I could tell he was having some sort of breakdown because of his unusual behaviour; someone told me he was having flashbacks because he was tripping out on too much LSD. I've told you, we gave up but John carried on taking hallucinogens. He would vomit before a gig, sweat profusely and get really nervous about performing.

On the night he left the band he sat crying in the tour van and we all felt sorry for him, some weeks later he was admitted to a mental home. His girlfriend, who became his wife, was with him that night, trying in vain to calm him down.

John's last gig was at The Yeoman in Derby on October 6, 1971, and for the first and only time we topped the bill over Slade but only because they had another gig after this one so by default we headlined. I remember that there was a lot of shouting between Dave Hill and the promoter about it. Also, we had to reorganise our equipment so they could go on first. It was some sort of end of term bash so the place was packed with college kids.

John Ellis later moved down to Northampton and we enjoy our reminisces whenever we have the chance to speak to one another.

John Ellis: "Allan did most of the writing. He was a Jack of all trades. I mean, he could play a bit of guitar, a bit of drums, a bit of bass and he could sing. He actually came up with the material, we were just glad to follow really. He'd been playing a bit longer than we had."

Due to our constant gigging, hard work and sheer determination to play no matter where, for whatever fee and to how many people, it was beginning to pay off in the long run and our name and fan club were getting bigger all the time.

But we were brought back down to earth that night because I had never heard Slade play so well; they truly rocked The Yeoman that night. They performed an absolutely stunning set with their new wall of sound and got applause after applause. I think they played

A flyer of Judas Priest circa 1972: There's me and Alan Moore on the top and Kenny Downing and Ian Hill on the bottom.

two encores as well. There was no way we have followed them or played better but we did our set and went down really well.

About this time Slade were just about to break through into the big time in the UK; they were a great bunch of blokes and you just knew that they were going to be a star rock band of the future. In the early seventies they had a batch of massive hit singles: "Cum On Feel the Noize", "Skweeze Me Pleeze Me", "Coz I Luv You", "Mama Weer All Crazee Now" and "Merry Xmas Everybody". I think they used to drive English teachers crazy because they'd deliberately misspell words in the songs titles. Slade would influence the likes of Kiss, Mötley Crüe and Whitesnake. Even Oasis are Slade fans!

Years later, Slade were featured in the centre pages of the New Musical Express in an article about St. James rehearsal rooms: the article had some pictures of them with Father Husband and when asked about the groups that rehearsed there he reeled off all sorts of memories but asked about Judas Priest he never batted an eyelid.

After John left, it was time for Judas Priest Mark III …

Over the next couple of weeks we auditioned new drummers to take the place of John and we finally found one who was quite an experienced professional player named Alan "Skip" Moore. I met Alan after looking through some musicians adverts in a music shop window in town. The ad read something like: 'DRUMMER LOOKING FOR BAND, LOTS OF EXPERIENCE, KIT ... BLACK LUDWIG etc ...' There was a telephone number so I rang him and arranged an audition at Holy Joe's and he came along and passed, it was really that simple. Alan had already done the rounds with bands like Glad Stallion from Birmingham so he was a valuable member to the fold. Alan had loads of energy and enthusiasm.

There was also a big change in my personal life in October: my wife gave birth to a beautiful baby girl who we named Sharon, this was fantastic news but with another mouth to feed it put pressure on me to make more money. We only took a few nights off and worked our socks off playing gig after gig. The winter of '71 was really hard and although we had many gigs in the schedule they were spread over the country; Mark III played gigs in Wales, Bristol, London, Birmingham, Manchester and Liverpool.

Those days were a world far apart from the likes of »The X Factor« and »American Idol« and similar dross like pub karaokes and tribute bands. It was just hard graft and we got very little money, but it was not in vain, bands like us hoped to land a record deal just to get you on to the next level. So many musicians fell on the way to the Promised Land and should have made it there; others battled on against all odds and eventually got their spoils.

By now Black Sabbath were getting bigger with three albums under their belt, but I still hadn't met them until one day in Birmingham. As with a lot of bands it's much easier to recognise their music then their faces.

There used to be a little music shop in Hurst Street called Wasp which was run by a really nice guy and brilliant guitarist named Peter Oliver. I remember going in one day to trade in some Impact P.A. columns and told Peter that they had 4x 50-watt speakers in each one. But this guy sitting on a Marshall 4x12 in the dark in the corner of the shop piped: "No, they haven't ... they are only 25 watt speakers mate."

I told him to mind his own business but he kept arguing the fact until I nearly chinned him.

Peter said that the only thing to do was to open up the back of one of the cabs and in doing so we found that I was right. This guy then walked out of the shop in a huff.

"Prat", I shouted.

Peter then said: "Do you know who that was?"

"No, why?"

"Because it's Ozzy Osbourne!"

Sadly, Peter Oliver passed away in April 2006.

By the end of '71, we still hadn't got the elusive record deal; we seemed forever doomed to be a warm up for other contracted artists but it was still a good experience for us to play to large crowds and to mix with the top named bands.

Everything was going great with us in the group but there's always some idiot who throws a stick in your wheel when you're rolling along nicely, and for us it was Birmingham band called Sundance who had offered our drummer Alan a record contract and an easier life playing country/rock music, so off he went and left us. As with previous incarnations of the band, Judas Priest Mark III came to an abrupt end. Alan later left Sundance and joined another group called Pendulum and toured North Africa, little did he know he would join Judas Priest again to record their second album with them, the powerful »Sad Wings Of Destiny«.

Before Alan buggered off to another band, he recommended a Brummie drummer named Chris "Congo" Campbell as his replacement. Chris happened to live right opposite Aston Villa football ground. We took him on but I always remember it being a pain in the

Judas Priest Mark IV: Ian Hill, Kenny Downing, Congo Campbell and me.

arse when we used to pick him up for a Saturday gig when Villa were playing at home, we were always stuck in traffic jams for about half an hour or more so consequently we were always late for our gig.

Chris came along with us to Alan's farewell booking at The Catacombs in Wolverhampton and as the name suggests, it was built to look like a cave with underground galleries; the small stage ceiling was very low.

I tried to impress him with my stage presence during the show and swung the mic stand around my head but the base of it went straight through the mock cave above us and the legs got stuck. Red faced, I tried to pull it out and half the bloody ceiling came down too, there we stood covered in dust and polystyrene to the amusement of the audience.

"This can't be happening", I muttered to myself.

It's not that Chris noticed anyway because he was in the toilet being sick from too much booze, it was another gig and another ban from a club and I don't think Kenny and Ian were very impressed at all, especially when they were told that he had ripped off the toilet seat and smashed the bog up as well, but I liked Chris because his wild character reminded me a little bit of myself in my younger years. He was always laughing and joking; most bands have this sort of character.

Chris was more photogenic than our other drummers; he was a young, strong-looking Jamaican black lad with a big Afro, which was obviously a complete contrast to Kenny's long blonde mane. A local photographer noticed this too and asked us to be featured in a photo exhibition about people living in the Black Country.

The photographer took some shots of us – Judas Priest Mark IV – at Ocker Hill; the old cooling towers (which have now been demolished) in the background were very promi-

Judas Priest Mark IV: me, Kenny Downing, Ian Hill and Congo Campbell.

nent in the pictures. The pictures were shown in an advertisement about his exhibition on A.T.V television alongside other shots he had taken. I was well chuffed seeing my face on TV for the first time even though I was next to a pigeon fancier from Tipton.

1972 brought some more changes. The year kick started with gigs all over the place: Hucknall MWC (Miners Club) in Nottingham, Gold Diamond in Nottingham, Youth Wing in Penarth and Bristol Legion in Cwmbach, Wales and then up to Scotland to play at the Youth Centre in Kincardine and then down to Cheltenham to perform at the Pavilion.

We even played a set at Henry's Blues House (with Trapeze as the support act) on February 17th, 1972. It was the first time I met Dave Holland and I bet he would never have imagined that he would one day be playing drums in Judas Priest. I remember briefly talking to Glenn Hughes backstage after the gig; he seemed like a really nice, friendly guy. And what a voice! He's called 'the voice of rock' for a reason, you know. Trapeze was a local band that had everything going for them and I really thought they would be massive one day. Sadly, they have remained nothing but a cult band. As a side note to this little anecdote about Trapeze: Dave Holland (after a few vodkas) once told me the story behind their break up but made me swear never to tell the story to anyone else. I think Glenn Hughes would be pissed if I spilled the beans on that one …

JUDAS PRIEST

Judas Priest are a hard-working Birmingham band, boasting perhaps the largest following of any up-and-coming 'Brummies' at the current time. The interest is aroused by their loud, adventurous music and visual stage presence, almost harking back to the freaky, progressive days of a few years ago. A very exciting live band.

The Band consists of :-

           KEN DOWNING (lead guitar)
           IAN HILL (bass guitar)
           CHRIS CAMPBELL (drums)
           ALAN ATKINS (vocal)

We were playing all over the country by now from Southern England to Scotland and we even played a gig at Douglas, on the Isle of Man at a venue called the Palace Lido. This was in April and we felt like superstars at this show because we had a rough journey on the ferry across the Irish Sea with a few of us being sick overboard, a taxi waited for us in the harbour, which took us to the five star Casino Hotel where we stayed for the night. Talk about luxury. But I let the side down when I ordered a packet of Number Six, which were really cheap cigarettes and came in packets of ten, but that's all I could afford at the time and I was dying for a fag. A lovely waitress bought them to our room on a silver tray and even she looked embarrassed when I paid for them.

    The Palace Lido was a big venue, which held about a 5,000 capacity crowd and lots of top bands played there over the years like The Rolling Stones, Pink Floyd and Led Zeppelin.
    "We're in good company then", I said to Kenny.
    It was a good gig and the next morning we had a smashing free breakfast ordered from the menu. I can tell you we ate as much as we could, after all we probably wouldn't eat again for a day or two because we had to travel back across the sea to Liverpool, hoping it would be a calmer crossing (which it was) and then on to the next gig. See what I mean … gigging is tough! It takes a lot out of you.
    I was over the moon when we were booked to appear with the American progressive rock band Spirit in April. They were a group I had always been a big fan of but when we got to the venue which was the Wellington Hall in Shropshire, we found out that they had got lost and ended up at the Wellington by Taunton in Somerset. Corkey somehow ma-

naged to get them to the proper venue in time, less their equipment so they had to borrow ours that night. I think they bought us a few pints at some point during the evening as a thank you gesture.

Another good gig was at our own Town Hall in West Bromwich, which was a first for the town; it was organised by Dave Corke. In fact, Corkey put together about three or four Saturday night rock shows that included Eric Clapton's Derek and The Domino's and Wishbone Ash who were the first group I had heard playing rock music with twin harmony guitars, a style that Judas Priest would adopt in the next few years.

We played there in September with Gary Moore who was, and still is, one of my favourite guitar players of all time; he makes one slow note sound better than some guitarists play a hundred fast ones. Back stage in the changing rooms Kenny and myself were chatting to him while he practiced with his small amp and Gibson guitar, which he let me have a play with; it was a green Les Paul which he said was given to him by Peter Green when he retired from Fleetwood Mac. Apparently, he said that Gary was the only guitarist worthy of playing it – I'll second that! It was another night to remember and another good gig for us but I wished that someone had carried a camera with them to some of these gigs because they would have captured some great moments in time.

We basically zigzagged all over the country but not all of them were what I had hoped for and I hated the travelling. We had some memorable times in '72 at places like The Marquee in Wardour Street, London. The Marquee was the place to play if you wanted to be noticed by record companies and The Temple just up the road was another famous venue. The Greyhound pub in Fulham Palace was another gig we played but it didn't start too well when some Scottish guy asked: "Who's the nigger at the bar?"

Congo and myself took a drink before we hit the stage and our roadie Mickey Botfield had to intervene before it got nasty. Mickey was a little hard case and a close friend of Kenny's and would come along with us if Trev couldn't make it and I'm glad he came that night. Another good gig was at The Speakeasy which was always full of celebrities. On the night we played there, I recall seeing Mark Bolan of T-Rex, Maggie Bell and Mott The Hoople, to name a few. Mott The Hoople was a great band; their bassist Pete "Overend" Watts was born in Birmingham. In 1973, a young band called Queen supported them on tour.

We also played more gigs at The Cavern in Liverpool, which was a place The Beatles made famous in the early sixties. The original Cavern was a damp and dingy little place that was not as glamorous as the press made out.

In fact, I have two memories of playing there: the first was not a good one because some twat in the audience spat on me during a gig we played there back in August 1971. I didn't see who did it because if I had I would have jumped on him and beat the crap out of him. Spitting is something I hate and I walked off the stage in disgust and refused to go back on. The band said I was making a big thing out of nothing and I replied: "I don't mind being booed if someone doesn't like me and I certainly don't mind being applauded if they do, but nobody gobs on me."

"C'mon Al, you're overreacting."

I replied: "If I was walking down the street and someone did that to me I would rip their fucking head off their shoulders."

Anyway, the next time we played a year later it was a really good gig and in fact the owner of a club just up the road called The Pyramid asked us to cover for a band that had failed to turn up for him, so we did and got double money that night. We didn't tell the agency though because they would have asked for another ten per cent. We went back to play the Cavern again a few days later on October 21st.

When I've been asked during various interviews "What was the worst gig Judas Priest ever played in the early days?", there is one gig that immediately jumps to mind. It was a gig in South Wales after travelling down from the Palace Lido.

We arrived early, about four o' clock in the afternoon and sat in the car park of the club waiting for them to open at six. The manager of the building drove past in his car and spotted us and decided to open up the club earlier than usual leaving us to unload and set up our equipment.

Once inside, I noticed he had left the bar door open from the night before. So Congo, Ian and myself helped ourselves to the 'top shelf' mixing half a pint of whiskey, gin, brandy and vodka cocktails each! Taking a load of bottles of beer backstage and hiding them in the dressing room for consumption later.

By the time we hit the stage we were totally legless and couldn't even stand up, let alone play a gig. It sounded absolutely awful! The audience booed us off the stage (rightly so)! A sober Kenny was fucking fuming ...

"That's the most stupid, unprofessional thing we've ever done. Absolute bollocks."

I will never forget that gig we played on one especially scary night in the West Country during the 1972 workers strikes as Britain battled through blackouts and food shortages. It was horrendous – the gig and the aftermath of the workers strike. As we played our set, the electricity in the whole of the building went off and although someone managed to get the lights back on, powered by a generator, it was still very dim and so it was not powerful enough for us to continue. Instead, we took a break until the power resumed. I went backstage to our dressing room to get a cigarette from my jacket pocket and standing either side of the door stood two really cagey characters dressed in black clothes in the dark, but I could see enough to notice that one of them had got a knife in his hand. I swiftly turned around and ran back down the stairs to the stage area with these two guys running down behind me and just as I burst through the doors to the side of the stage all the lights came back on to a very loud cheer from the waiting audience, I turned around and they had both disappeared.

We went back on stage and finished the show and I later told the band about my experience but they just laughed in my face.

"What drugs are you on now, Al?!"

"Very funny, lads."

But after we had got changed and returned to the tour bus one of our roadies – the ever faithful Evo – told us some psycho had tried to stab him as he was loading up the equipment and ran away. He had a small puncture of the skin in his back and was very lucky that the blade didn't go right in him. We had nowhere to sleep that night but a couple of friendly hippies from the audience said two of us could stay at their nearby country cottage, Kenny and myself won the toss of the coin but I was still a bit scared of the night's adventure and wondered if it would have been safer sleeping in the bus with the rest of the band. I hardly slept at all that night thinking about what could have been …

One memorable gig I remember playing was when we had to cover for Vinegar Joe at a last minute call out by Corkey and the audience were told the band had to cancel the show only seconds before the curtains opened. I thought this was really bad for the paying crowd that had been waiting patiently to see them and should have been offered a refund or been told earlier that Judas Priest was replacing them. It was bad for us as well because we got booed off the stage by the upset crowd (what was left of them) because most of them walked out. I mean, I'm not that bad a vocalist but I'm no Elkie Brookes.

In December, 1972, we played support to The Sensational Alex Harvey Band at the Boat Club in Nottingham. Alex was smashed and I didn't feel much better because I was suffering from an alcohol induced headache; I threw up in the river Trent outside the club. God only knows what the audience thought about the two groups that night! They'd only formed earlier in the year and were already making an impression. They were part of the glam rock movement that was sweeping the country.

Alex taunted and insulted the crowd and in the end got his band booed off stage but we didn't go down too bad with the audience and I'm glad no one took any photographs of me that night with all the vomit still stuck to my beard.

Anyway, back to the touring schedule at hand: one group that we started gigging a great deal with in '72 was the great Welsh band Budgie. They reminded me a lot of ourselves, in that they were a hard working down to earth act and played heavy rock music but had some bizarre titles to their songs like "Nude Disintegrating Parachutist Woman", "Hot As A Docker's Armpit" and "In The Grip Of A Tyre Fitter's Hand".

The first time we appeared with them was on their own soil in Wales and they blew us off stage playing a very loud and tight set, but over the next few gigs we played together there was nothing between us except that they had a record deal and we hadn't, so we had to back them every time. But we were also making a name for ourselves now and headlining over some good bands like the up and coming melodic rock band Magnum.

For years I'd have a close relationship with Budgie; they formed in 1967 and over the years built up a hell of a cult reputation as a classic hard rock band. Even Metallica are Budgie fans; they covered the songs "Breadfan" and "Crash Course In Brain Surgery". Before Sabbath, Priest and Wishbone Ash, Budgie were rockin' hard and riding free. They've never achieved the success and reverence they deserve which is an absolute crying shame but at least they're still going strong after all these years.

Another group we played alongside with in 1972 was Status Quo; we supported them about a year ago at Quaintways in Chester but this time we gigged with them at place called Quarthouse, which coincidentally was also in Chester.

I still maintain to this day that they were a great bunch of guys and gave us a good game of 301 at darts; we used the dartboard our roadies used to carry around with them.

The venue was packed to the roof with people. I recall the stage manager going mad and shouting at us to get on stage because the audience were going crazy, and I remember saying: "I've just got to get this last double", as I threw a dart.

"Hurry up, the fans are waiting!"

When we finally thrashed them at darts we walked out on stage to a mighty cheer, the crowd were only here for one group but we had to try to win them over. We kicked off with a song everyone knew which was our version of "Spanish Castle Magic" by Jimi Hendrix and it went down a storm; we then continued with the rest of the set with our own songs for the next hour and received two encores. We nearly always finished our gigs with an epic song called "Caviar And Meths" which I wrote and the band re-recorded and re-wrote for their debut album »Rocka Rolla« on Gull Records. I can't recall why I wrote it but it is about two people: one rich and one poor. The poor man questions himself about why he was born poor and the other man rich. I guess I was trying to be philosophical.

"Caviar And Meths"
(Atkins)

I've got no home … I just pretend
Building a world of trouble 'til the end
Out all alone … facing the cold
Nothing comes easy not like you, all turns to gold

Situations never change … it was meant this way
Never to own … always to strive
Just want a little piece of something in this life

Always the dreamer … never to rise
Nothing comes easy, not like you always the prize

Out on the road ... devil may care
That's the way it was meant to be ... always to bear

Shooting deals, chasing wheels, running from the wild dogs
Downtowns pretty if you know how to keep everything on a lock
Greasing wheels, shining steel, taking on the odd jobs
Gotta survive, just to keep alive in this hot cross gun shop
Breaking laws, kicking down doors, gotta find a way through
Out of this place that lives off hate I was born into
City smoke seems to hurt and choke gotta find some room to breath
Want to be like you, want to see the views, want to taste the life of ease

Anyway, after getting changed out of our stage gear Kenny and myself moved over and stood at the side wings of the club amongst the audience to see what the audience thought about Status Quo. They walked on stage to a great roar from their waiting fans and showed us just how to please an audience not with guitar wizardry but superb, good time entertainment. They'd improved massively since the last time we supported them. Quo have always worked bloody hard on the road; even to this day they must tour at least six months a year. And at their age, that must be commended.

They also played much louder than any other group we had performed with, and went down a headbanging storm with the crowd. Overall, it was a great night and we also saved a few pounds by staying at Ian's mum's who lived near Chester. The only trouble was there was only one double bed and there were six of us so we had to toss a coin to see who got the bed and who got the floor, but we were always grateful and she gave us a good (greasy) breakfast the next morning before we set off back to Brum.

Listening to the volume Status Quo played at made us realise that if we were going to compete with any of these top bands who played much larger venues than us, we would need a bigger P.A. system with monitors, so some months later we hired extra road crew and rented out a new sound system from a company called Green Goblin. The first time we used it was at the Hippodrome Theatre in Birmingham on April 15, 1973, when we opened up for Family, which featured one of my all time favourite vocalists Roger Chapman. Other singers I rated were Paul Rogers from Free and of course Robert Plant; both of these guys got better as they got older.

Evo took over the mixing desk and cranked it all up full volume and when we started playing the set some of the audience went running for the exit doors it was so loud, but after a couple of songs he got the mix right and it was great to hear myself through some good monitor speakers for a change.

Other groups I recall supporting in 1972 were Curved Air featuring Sonja Christina and future Police drummer Stewart Copeland who wore a top hat and tails, and The Flying Hat Band featuring Mr. Glenn Tipton. The Flying Hat Band deserved more success; they were a cracking blues based rock trio. Like The Sensational Alex Harvey Band, they only got together months before we supported them so they were moving fast, already making a name for themselves.

We also supported Dr. Ross who was a one man band blues player from the Mississippi; he carried all his harmonicas in an old doctor's bag hence his nickname. We played with him over two nights at The Ceda club in Birmingham. Atomic Rooster was another band

Judas Priest Mark IV circa 1973.
This line-up featured me, Ian Hill, Kenny Downing and Chris "Congo" Campbell.
At this point the band was signed to Tramp Entertainments/I.M.A.
(co-owned by Tony Iommi) in Birmingham.
These are promotional shots, which were professionally done.

Flying Hat Band, featuring soon to be Priest guitarist Glenn Tipton (looking like a real HM star).

we supported; the band featured the late keyboardist Vincent Crane and Chris Farlowe. Both bands got banned for smoking grass and playing cricket dressed in full cricket attire stolen from the dressing rooms used by the Northampton Cricket Club. We also supported Supertramp, Rory Gallagher, Wild Angels, Trapeze and Hookfoot, which featured Caleb Quaye who rolled a lovely joint ... and he wasn't a bad guitarist either.

At the end of '72, Dave Corke got a job working for Norman Hood at a company called Tramp Management in Lichfield, Staffordshire, before Tramp joined forces with Pactmoor Agency, which was owned by Black Sabbath guitarist Tony Iommi. This business coalition was eventually trademarked as International Management Agency; they relocated their offices to Hurst Street in Birmingham on December 12, 1972.

Norman had professional associations with Jim Simpson; they'd promote UK tours headlined by American blues players which became known as the American Blues Legends. After Simpson split with Sabbath, Norman still retained his friendship with Tony and the pair joined forces by creating an Agency which, initially, was set up to promote one of Tony's favourite bands – Necromandus – who hailed from Cumbria. Ric Lee, the drummer in Ten Years After, became the third partner of IMA.

While Dave was working there, we were one of the first groups to be signed to IMA and they promised us lots of work with the intention of getting us a record deal. Dave worked hard to plug us at Tramp and we actually got signed on January 19th, 1973, before the company officially changed its name to IMA on February 26. We used to take the piss with Norman and say it was called Iommi Management Agency which would really wind him up. Tony was the famous partner but Norman worked just as hard, if not harder, because Tony was business with Sabbath.

I don't think Norman was a big fan of us at first but we tried bloody hard to please him, especially considering he gave us a twelve month contract. So now Judas Priest Mark IV – myself, Kenny, Ian and Congo – were finally heading somewhere.

IMA was great because it gave great opportunities to all upcoming rock bands, offering gigs and promotion. There were other groups IMA signed to their books, among them: The Steve Gibbons Band, who later had a hit single with "Tulane". And there was Bullion, which featured my old bass mate Bruno and The Flying Hat Band with Glenn Tipton, bass player Mars Crowling and drummer Steve Palmer who is Carl Palmer's brother from ELO.

> Now seems like a good time to have some recollections from Norman. His website has some vintage photos of Judas Priest Mark IV: www.normanhood.co.uk.
>
> Norman Hood: "Tony Iommi was my best buddy for years and he had roots and connections in Cumbria and wanted me to push a band he had found up there called Hot Spring Water (honest). He eventually persuaded me to leave the Jim Simpson camp and set up Tramp Entertainments in Lichfield. His favourite band was later named Taurus before finally becoming Necromandus.
>
> I became aware of Judas Priest around this time as David Corke (we just knew him as 'Corky') worked for me for a while, and I already knew John Hinch who would later play drums for Judas Priest from the days when I managed Jeremy Spencer prior to the formation of Fleetwood Mac.
>
> We started booking gigs for our bands but Priest became more and more Corky's pet project. We also took on artists from my blues days such as Champion Jack Dupree, and worked extensively with the likes of Wild Turkey, Thin Lizzy and so on.

> When we moved to central Birmingham from Litchfield, Corky was still more or less with us and still had responsibility for Judas Priest, which we managed to get some big support gigs for, like with Sabbath, of course, and Family at the Hippodrome in Birmingham.
> The company began to get stretched when Black Sabbath went massive Stateside with Tony spending more and more time in America and could not devote much attention to the agency anymore and Ric managed to lose money in the property boom and so wanted out as well.
> It was then we formed IMA, the initials for International Management Agency, no false modesty in those days. This ran for a couple of years and then I received an offer to go back to work with Jim Simpson on the Birmingham Jazz Festival with King Pleasure so that was that.
> Probably the last thing I had to do with Priest was driving Glenn Tipton from The Flying Hat Band who was another one of our acts down to a session at Track Studios. I remember Keith Moon, drummer of The Who, buying me a drink and Glenn talking about joining up with Judas Priest permanently …"

After signing to IMA we suddenly had a lot more gigs coming our way. We launched the »Heavy Thoughts« tour, which would be our last road jaunt together, in February 1973, beginning with a three week tour of Scotland. This time the weather up North was not nearly as horrendous as it was when I toured with the first line-up of Priest. It went quite smoothly actually; we played much tighter and heavier.

Dave Corke came up with the title for the tour and he had posters plastered on every bare wall he could find in and around Birmingham.

We continued to play the usual setlist, which featured quite a bit of our own material. I fucked around a lot with lyrics. There was one song I wrote called "Joey" which had a big bloody riff but was a much slower song that we were used to playing. It wasn't a very clever song but the first two lines went: "Joey had a crime mind waiting for his time to come/Joey walked a fine line always ever on the run." Another one I penned was called "Voodoo Rag" which had totally mind boggling lyrics that meant nothing to anyone … including me! Sometimes if I didn't know what to write about I'd turn to the great lyricist Felix Pappalardi for inspiration. He was the bassist in the great American band Mountain and produced Cream's masterpiece »Disraeli Gears«. He wrote some great but weird psychedelic blues rock for Cream and Jack Bruce, like "Rope Ladder To The Moon" and "Tickets To The Waterfalls".

Don't ask me about the lyrics to "Voodoo Rag" but the song was an outright rocker. I just wished we had recorded some of those early tracks and kept the lyrics. Norman Hood once taped us live at the Hippodrome in Brum but lost the tape. Shame.

Also, one of our favourite cover versions was "Black Sheep Of The Family" by Quatermass which coincidentally got Ronnie James Dio and Ritchie Blackmore together to make the mighty hard rock band Rainbow. Our setlist looked like this:

Judas Priest Setlist

"Spanish Castle Magic" (Hendrix)
"Winter" (Atkins)
"Voodoo Rag" (Atkins)

"Never Satisfied" (Atkins/Downing)
"Joey" (Atkins)
"Whiskey Woman" (Atkins)
"Mind Conception" (Atkins)
"Black Sheep Of The Family" (Quatermass)
"Holy Is The Man" (Atkins)
"Caviar And Meths" (Atkins)

Kenny had started to write his own songs now and during this tour he was half way through one set of lyrics that was to become "Run Of The Mill" which featured on their first album »Rocka Rolla«. It was the first song he'd ever written. I'd written a song with Kenny called "Never Satisfied" which we played live; the song also featured on »Rocka Rolla«.

"Never Satisfied"
(Atkins/Downing)

Where do we go from here
There must be something near
Changing you, changing me
Forever

Places change, faces change
Life is so very strange
Changing minds, changing times together

We are never satisfied

There's nowhere, left to go
This could be our last show
Changing dreams, changing schemes forever

Love has gone, so has fun
Now we're reaching for the gun
Changing class, changing fast
No more tether

We are never satisfied ...

The only problem within the group now was my problems with drink and drugs, which became my downfall. I was having terrible nightmares, perpetual headaches and nasty mood swings. I was once too scared to sleep; I kept taking uppers and managed to stay awake for three nights before collapsing from exhaustion. I then went into a deep sleep like a coma and what happened next is what people call an out of body experience which frightened the shit out of me. There I was stuck to the ceiling of my bedroom one night looking down on my wife and myself in bed with our baby daughter Sharon who was sleeping blissfully in her cot. I was screaming at them but the words came out in slow motion before I bellowed: "Somebody help me …"

My wife said she suddenly woke up and looked over at me. She said I looked like death itself and I was really cold to touch; she began to shake me and shout my name and it was then that I returned back to my body.

I grabbed hold of her and wouldn't let go and was crying with fright; I noticed patches of my hair had fallen out with shock. I kid you not; I never want to go through that again.

I never really confided with the group about my personal problems but they must have noticed something was wrong with me being sick all the time and my erratic mood swings. To the band I must have been intolerable; my poor behaviour was definitely getting on everybody's nerves.

I had some wicked headaches and to this day I will never know how I sang with them live on stage. I just wanted to sit in a corner of a dark noiseless room with a blanket over my head, the last thing I needed was to stand in front of Judas Priest with their amps on full volume but somehow I did. I'd always finish the gigs feeling like shit but somewhere deep inside me, I knew that this is what I wanted to do in life regardless of how I felt or how hard the journey might be. It turned out that the journey itself was a lot harder than I ever anticipated. I wasn't sure if I could continue with the way I was feeling.

One particular tablet which I took frequently was called Mandrax. Basically, in the sixties and seventies, these tablets were thought to be non-dependant sleeping tablets. But they became very addictive and had side effects when taken with alcohol; symptoms such as serious headaches, nausea and depression. I look back know and think how lucky I was that I didn't have much money because I know which road I could have easily taken. Rich and famous rock stars often have a void in their lives and so it's usually the case that they take to drugs on a bigger scale than the average Joe.

The last straw was when Norman Hood stopped me from being the spokesman for the band because of my bad attitude and told Kenny to take charge.

"You're not up to the task anymore, Al", he said.

I was no longer heading the band I had formed; my addictions had got the better of me.

My problem was down to my own arrogance because for the last few years we had played everywhere we had been asked to play, no matter what the size of the venue or how little money we were getting paid. With IMA we were only getting £10 per gig and even in those days it was simply not enough. I was getting really pissed off and wanted us to play the big gigs in the top venues alongside the famous bands or headlining ourselves. We seemed to be going backwards, playing in the small local clubs and making hardly any money. In fact, when IMA did book us into the small gigs, we would turn up on time but I would write in bold black pen on the advertising posters: 'NO CHANCE.' Then we'd all return back home in a huff. You might think I was being a bit petty but I wanted us to have standards.

It always felt great playing the bigger stages with name stars like Black Sabbath and it gave me that much needed adrenalin rush and it felt like this is exactly where I belong but without a record deal we were forced to play the usual rounds of civic centres and clubs.

I always hated playing the smaller clubs. I remember one night up North in Southport during the »Heavy Thoughts« tour in March, we turned up early at this joint we were supposed to be performing at but there was no one there, so we all went for a quick beer to kill the time while we waited for it to open. When we returned, this geezer wearing a black

An old picture of me belting out a song.

suit and dickey bow who was on a power trip was shouting at us about turning up late, he happened to be the club owner and I nearly told him where to stick his club.

"Let's just play and get out of here", said Kenny. "We've come a long distance and need the cash."

"Yeah, alright then", I replied.

As we were changing the club manager put his head round the door and said we had to play three 45-minute spots. By this point I started to get really annoyed with him, saying we only do a one spot performance especially for the money he was paying us. He said it was in the contract that the agency had signed and Kenny who was now spokesman had forgotten our copy so we had no choice but to do it. I wouldn't have minded but in the first spot we played there, were only about six people in the club.

At the end of the night Kenny went to collect our fee and was told by the manager that he was paying us by cheque and deducting some money for being late. I stormed into his office and demanded to see the contract which I snatched out of his hand. It read: 'One hour playing time and to be paid cash on the night.' So now I had him round the throat screaming at him for messing us around like this but then a burly bouncer turned up and grabbed hold off me trying to get me off the manager.

I wasn't finished with this guy yet or his sodding bouncer and precious night club; we needed some cash to get us fuel to get back home so I went outside to the tour bus and fetched Trev and Evo to come back inside with me. I told them what had happened and that they should expect a big fight. We walked back in and the first thing I did was pick up an empty pint glass by the handle and threaten to smash the manager's pretty mirrors behind the bar and then smash his head in if he didn't cough up the money he owed us. I must have been having one of my mood swings! He soon paid up in full but IMA wasn't very happy with me; when we finally returned home the next day, Norman said the manager had cancelled all future acts from his club. I think I did them all a favour; Kenny was told to take full control of the band and that was that.

Another small club we gigged at was a local one in Birmingham. We were booked to play there by a black DJ and small time promoter; let's just say I don't have any kind words to say about him.

After we played the gig for him he did a runner, so we never got paid. I tried contacting him but he always put the phone down on me but I found out where he lived and went round to see him one Sunday morning. He lived above a small shop in town but wouldn't answer the door so I threw some stones at his window.

I shouted: "The next stone will go through your window if you don't bloody speak to me!"

He eventually looked out and said: "Meet me at the club tonight and I will pay you."

He never turned up and I swore I would catch up with him one day and wondered how many other bands he had ripped off.

The funny side to this story is some years later when Judas Priest got signed to CBS; they walked into the company's London offices and there sat behind the big desk was the guy who had ripped me off.

His first words were: "Where's Al and Kenny?"

They told him I had left the band in '73 and had been replaced by Rob Halford.

"Thank god for that!" he said.

I don't think the band could believe he had got such a high position job with a company like CBS after being such a shit of a man.

Kenny and Ian were now living in a penthouse suite in Birmingham, which was usually full of scantily dressed young ladies but I was still living at my mother-in-law's council house with my wife and daughter who was now two years old. Kenny used to joke that he mastered the art of silent sex because their flat was always packed with friends. I was finding it hard keeping my family together while playing away all the time with the band and for very little money although to be honest Norman at the agency was good to me and would give me a cheque or two to help pay my bills and keep the wolf from the door. I hope he doesn't read this, only I still owe him about £300 ...

So we're stuck in '73 and by now we were offered two or three record contracts but they were all by independent labels and they were too small to consider; I could never have signed to a tiny label for the next four years just to keep struggling on. I never told the group about them but just told Norman that the band had turned them down, knowing Kenny, he would have taken one, after all we had waited this long we might as well wait a bit longer and hope that a major deal might come our way.

One Saturday night before a gig we were scheduled to play, Congo hadn't turned up to meet us in town to be picked up so we could go to the venue together; we received a phone call from Dave Corke telling us to carry on without him and that he would bring Congo to the gig later on. Apparently, he had been arrested for stealing alcohol the night before so Dave had to bail him out of jail so he could play. Nice one Congo, I thought.

Personally, I was getting really pissed off with everything and everyone so I had decided to leave the band for a couple of reasons. After all the hard work we had put into the group over the years I honestly thought we had missed the boat and would never make it big or get signed to a major label for reasons I couldn't understand; I doubted the band's ability and doubted mine sometimes but I knew we could be really good if we had something to push our confidence. My enthusiasm had waned. I tried for over a decade to make a career for myself in the music business but to no avail.

Most of the groups we had played alongside over the years like Slade, Black Sabbath and Thin Lizzy had become household names and were continually charting with their hit singles and albums. Deep down, I knew we were good enough to make it and we had got a good fan base but never had the luck to go with it. It was a depressing period.

The second reason was down to my finances or rather lack of. I couldn't stay with them, because the bigger we got, the more overheads we got, so we always ended up with little or no money left to live on and I had my family to consider.

One of the last gigs we played on the »Heavy Thoughts« tour was at St. George's Hall in Liverpool in March, again with our old mates Budgie. They had just left College Entertainments who had kept them in good gigs for some time but they had now signed to MCA Records and were looking forward to bigger and better things ... at last. We were really envious of them and as usual went on stage first as the warm up act; we played a storming set and got three encores. Budgie weren't too pleased though when all our fans came crashing into the dressing room that we shared with them, chasing after us for our autographs just as they were getting changed to go on stage; Burke Shelly got trampled on as he lay on the floor doing his usual meditation sessions.

If only every night could have been like that; we could have got a record deal to make more money. I know we would have survived but I just felt we had come as far as we could and we still had as many lows as highs even after all this time.

After the gig, Budgie's old agent from College Entertainments spoke to Kenny and myself about leaving IMA and signing up with them, taking Budgie's place on the College circuit. Kenny agreed but I didn't see the point and didn't agree with him, but looking back now I wished we had gone with them. Who knows what's around the corner, after all it didn't do Budgie any harm. This led to yet another argument between Kenny and myself and finally drove a bit of a wedge between us. Actually, we played on the same bill as Budgie at the College of Art and Food in Birmingham although it wasn't quite as exciting as the Liverpool show. I later found out that a certain Robert Halford and John Hinch were in the audience that night.

The »Heavy Thoughts« tour drew to an abrupt close in May after dates in Scotland, Manchester, Liverpool, Southport, Birmingham, Wolverhampton and Shropshire. We'd also supported Family at the Hippodrome in Brum on April 15th; it was another step up the ladder for us performing at a bigger venue, which Tony Iommi had booked for us to play. As I've said, Norman Hood taped the show but we never got to hear it and it got lost like a lot of things do. As far as the show went, I think it was good because I can't think of any accidents that happened that night, like breaking strings, valves popping or anything at all.

Family were a good band and what's more annoying is that they'd only formed in '67 but had way more success than us before splitting in '73. Their debut album »Music In A Doll's House« was brilliant and part of the reason for that is because it was produced by Dave Mason from Traffic, a favourite band of mine. Mason is a Midlands man and has a cracking CV that included names like Eric Clapton, The Beatles, Hendrix and the Stones; if we had somebody like that involved, we could have made a great album.

To be honest, I couldn't even be bothered to play the last gig with the lads and we had travelled all the way up the coast to Morecambe to do. I can't even remember the name of the club but it was so small that it reminded me of a fish and chip shop and I instantly refused to play there and stormed off, feeling really angry.

"I can't believe it. This must be a fucking wind-up", I said out loud, "We're better than this."

They found me about half an hour later propped up in a bar in some back street pub drowning my sorrows. I was absolutely sick of playing these little two bit gigs that the agency would throw at us now and then; I knew we deserved better than this after all these years of hard work and it was so frustrating at times.

Kenny looked me in the eye and shouted: "That's it! I've had enough of you and your bad attitude, I'm leaving the band!"

"I can't be arsed with this anyway", I said, and walked off.

I couldn't really blame Kenny but Ian and Congo understood my frustration and said they would stick by me no matter what happens. No one spoke a word in the tour bus all the way back to Brum and you could have cut the atmosphere with a knife.

The next day, Ian, Congo and myself dropped by IMA to tell Norman not to book us into these types of small gigs again; if he did, I said, we would leave the agency. He wasn't very happy with me and was less happy when I told him Kenny had left us. I also told him that we wanted to bring in a new guitarist and asked him to finance us while we resolved the situation.

Then Tony Iommi walked into the office and said he wanted us to come off the road for about three months to sort out our problems, take a rest and concentrate on writing more songs to get us that deal we were after. I said that I couldn't survive that long unless they funded me and my family but they said that they wouldn't do that, and Congo and myself sensed a bit of conspiracy going on behind the scenes to get me out of the band because they knew I couldn't live on fresh air alone. I know now that I shouldn't have done some of the things I did but everything I did was done for the good of the band and my family. Basically, they wanted a 'yes man' and saw me as a troublemaker so I basically told them to FUCK OFF.

After about an hour of heated arguments, in which time we had not come to any sort of agreement on anything whatsoever, I decided to call it a day for Judas Priest because without any income coming in, I knew for a fact that my family wouldn't be able to survive on pennies. So that was it, the end of the story for me, the roadies dropped me off at Anne's (I was still living at the in-law's) along with my equipment and I said my last farewells to them all.

After properly disbanding Judas Priest some weeks later I got myself a normal nine to five job at a cost office in Sutton Coldfield; my role was to price up vehicle repairs at a garage. I had a nice haircut to go with my new job. I started to sort my life out without music; I was already missing the tours up and down the motorways and got told off a few times by my manager for daydreaming. I couldn't hack the day job, even after a week I got bored.

Congo called me one day in '73 and asked me if I was interested in reforming Judas Priest with him, his brother – who played guitar – and another black dude on bass; now that would have been a novelty act in the seventies … a white singer with three coloured musicians playing heavy rock! I told him that I would think about it, which I did, but declined the offer, but thanked him very much for thinking about me.

Congo's brother, John Campbell, formed a band some years ago now called Are You Experienced who are a very talented Jimi Hendrix tribute band that Kenny Downing would have been proud of. John has appeared in Guitar Magazine and was featured on the BBC arts programme »Arena« in 2007.

Judas Priest would not die …

One weekend Kenny and Ian dropped in to see me at Anne's house and asked if I was going to form another group, and if so, was I going to use the Judas Priest name. They also laughed at my new haircut. Deep down I knew I wanted to reform Judas Priest again but I wasn't prepared to put more work into a band that produced pennies and played small clubs. Kenny and Ian said they had found another vocalist named Robert Halford who came from Walsall; Ian was dating Rob's sister. The story goes that Ian mentioned to Rob that they were looking for a singer and one day Kenny and Ian were at Rob's house in Walsall waiting to go on a night out with Ian's girlfriend; they heard Rob singing along to a Doris Day song on the radio or the TV. They liked his voice and asked him to audition. I mean … Doris Day! Of all the singers … bloody hell!

Judas Priest Mark V circa 1973-1974: Drummer John Hinch with Kenny Downing, Rob Halford and Ian Hill upfront. I believe it was taken at Holy Joe's in Wednesbury using a fish eye lens.

Along with Rob, they had found a drummer named John Hinch and they said they wanted to form another heavy rock group. Rob and John's old band was called Hiroshima which they had folded to join Judas Priest; after all, it was already established and Priest had a Ford Transit van, a better P.A. system and a tour arranged with Budgie. I told Kenny and Ian about Congo's idea.

I said: "No, I don't want to use it, go ahead … if you want it, you can have the name. I'm fed up with Judas Priest now."

They also asked me for the lyrics to the songs because they wanted to keep the same setlist that we used to play, and again I agreed that they could take the songs and the name. They deserved that, at least for all the hard work they had put into the band over the last few years.

When they left, my wife went crazy at me saying I had just threw away four years of my life and I would never come up with a great name like Judas Priest again.

"I can't believe you've been so stupid and naïve", she cried.

"I've had enough anyway. I need to move on with my career", I replied. I've never been one to get depressed. I had other ideas to work with.

I never heard from the band, which was now Judas Priest Mark V, for a few months; then a friend of mine told me he had seen an advertisement that said Judas Priest was scheduled to play at a local venue so we went along to watch them. I wasn't very impressed with Rob's vocal range; to be honest, I felt his voice wasn't meaty enough for some of the songs. I always preferred a singer like Paul Rodgers, Robert Plant or Terry Reid. It seemed

Rob "The Queen" Halford.

a little strange to hear someone else singing more or less the old set that I used to sing. It was a bit uncomfortable too. After the gig I would see Rob quite a few times in the seventies but not so much after that, maybe just to say hello at after-gig parties or something.

They were about to start a three or four week tour with Budgie and I started to feel a little regretful now about leaving them and was missing my music more and more, so I decided to start up again but this time to try and hold down a job as well, so I would be financially more stable.

Chapter 4
Life After Priest & The Story Of Lion
(1974-1978)

1974 was a fucking good year for rock music. Led Zeppelin was probably the biggest band in the world after having released two mesmerising albums: »Led Zeppelin IV« and »Houses Of The Holy«. They followed up those albums with the magnificent double record »Physical Graffiti«. Paul Rodgers had formed Bad Company a year before with his Free pal Simon Kirke, Mick Ralphs from Mott The Hoople and Boz Burrell from King Crimson. What a band! I love them to this day.

British rock had dominated the European and American charts for most of the sixties but by this point American rock bands had started to emerge and all hell broke loose. Even to this day, America would dominate the mainstream rock and metal scene. The ultimate shock rocker Alice Cooper was a huge star in the seventies; he had hits with albums like »Killer« and »School's Out« and songs such as "Under My Wheels". He still has an incredible knack of creating classic rock and heavy metal songs although he made a name for himself with the punk sound which was inspired by his home state of Detroit, a working class place like Birmingham or Manchester. It's a great thing that Cooper is still touring and making top quality music; he's definitely somebody I admire.

Iggy Pop comes from Detroit and he too would influence the dominant sound of the late seventies, which I'll get to later. Alice Cooper influenced a crazy band from New York called Kiss. And another band from New York called Blue Öyster Cult were having some success with an album called »Secret Treaties« but I've always felt that they have never had the full respect which they deserve.

In Britain, glam rock was enormous; it was like a fantasy. You'd see singers on the TV dressed like strange colourful characters from another world. The optimism of the swinging sixties had disappeared and the country was in despair; glam rock provided a welcome antidote. You'd never see me dressed like somebody from The Sweet or Marc Bolan but I loved the music. I was happy in jeans and a shirt. The guys in Slade dressed in silly clothes but their music was heavier and more working class than the other glam rock bands.

In years to come, one of my favourite bands of the glam era was Queen; they were emerging as a force to be reckoned with after having released the stunning »Queen II« opus but it was in '74 when they released »Sheer Heart Attack« that they got the breakthrough they deserved.

Bowie had proved that he was one of the country's greatest song writers and musical geniuses with the creation of Ziggy Stardust. Like many of his peers Bowie reached his creative peak in the seventies. To a lot of rock fans David Bowie is a deity; he's an intelligent, eccentric character and like most rock stars egomaniacal. It's those kinds of traits that make a rock star so bloody interesting. There have been many phases in his career from psychedelia to glam rock to R&B to pop and even electronica. He's never always gotten it right and most people believe his seventies work is his best. Bowie had a close working relationship with Iggy Pop and even produced Lou Reed's superb »Transformer« album with

Mick Ronson. People like Bowie and Elton John and Freddie Mercury are one-offs. There have been younger singers like Justin Hawkins from The Darkness who have tried to emulate their heroes but have fallen flat on their arses either because they're too annoying, lack charisma or any other number of reasons. I think to stay popular you should have a sense of irony and self-parody. It's like the crazy bat eating Ozzy on stage is not the crazy bat eating Ozzy off stage.

I watched it all happen but in my own little world, things were not quite as exciting although the pace would pick up in due course.

After leaving Judas Priest well and truly behind me I continued to work at a cost office in Sutton Coldfield, which believe you me was truly soul destroying, especially after having spent most of my adult life up to that point rockin' and rollin' around the country. What did I do next? Huh, well, I went back to what I do best – play in bands. I just couldn't cope with the tediousness of working in an office anymore, I had to get out. And the eight hour days nearly killed me, not through exhaustion but sheer mind-inducing boredom. I kept dreaming about band life and how much I missed being on the road with my mates; drinking all hours, having a laugh and playing music to an audience. You just don't get any job satisfaction in a minimum wage day job.

Around the end of '73, I decided to team up with whom else but my old buddy and bass man Bruno Stapenhill. Bruno had come back to West Brom after having played in the soul

The New Cavern club in Liverpool. It's the Wall of Fame, featuring all bands that played at the original club back in the sixties and seventies. The band Oasis (who are situated next to Judas Priest) was a progressive seventies outfit and not the Manchester Gallagher Brothers band we all know today.

band The Roy Gee Explosion. He did about twelve months with them before the band went stale and he got bored. He told me he enjoyed the three months they spent touring Denmark but sometimes the shows could be a massive letdown. I think Bruno always preferred playing songs by The Shadows than Chicago and Blood, Sweat & Tears. Rock and roll was in his heart and it was in mine too so it was fate that we'd once again team up together. I'd lost touch with the rest of the guys from Priest's past, except for Ian who is a great bloke and still a good friend.

Bruno's bass playing had become really sharp and heavy. The rock band Bullion with Pete Boot was a good band and I was pleased to see that Bruno followed his true path after quitting The Roy Gee Explosion. He was happy with what he was doing in Bullion. It was a different style of material and that was another band that I think would have made it had they continued but at the time they were broke. It was a good mix of material that they were doing; stuff with stage lights, flares – it was a proper show. Apparently, Bullion was the last band to play at The Cavern in Liverpool before it was pulled down. They played there on the Friday night and then had a big party on the Saturday with some local bands and then the bulldozers went in on the Monday and knocked it down. The Cavern has been rebuilt on another spot.

It was going down really well for the band but I think it was when Pete joined Budgie that the band collapsed. Of course, both Priest and Bullion were signed to IMA before fate dealt us a different set of cards. So Bruno and myself looked around for other musicians to join us in yet another quest to make our dreams happen. We were quite lucky because we'd had so much experience playing in bands around the Black Country that we built up a good list of contacts, which would help us find the right guitarist and drummer.

We hired one of the best guitarists to come out of the Black Country; his name was Harry Tonks and he'd recently played in a band called Stallion. Harry was a great guitarist and played with some really good local bands and made a name for himself as being one of the best guitarists in the business. Harry got his first band together when he is 13 years old even though he never had a single guitar lesson in his life; he taught himself just by playing for hours at a time, copying his guitar heroes as he played records or listened to the radio. Some of the bands he played in during the 1960s included the Cadenza, The Renegades and Johnny Love and The Spectres with drummer Alan Clements and bassist Barry Fidler. In 1965, Johnny Love and The Spectres played gigs in Germany which is what The Beatles did and what Black Sabbath did later in the sixties. Harry joined The Jug Blues Band after John Perry's death and after I quit the band to join Evolution. Harry was something of a local legend so to have him on board was flattering.

Jim Perry, the brother of the late John Perry from The Jug Blues Band, completed the rest of the band's line-up by taking the job as our drummer. I decided to call the band Lion after the famous British lion. I thought Lion was a really good name for a heavy metal band and the lads agreed. We began rehearsing at Holy Joe's almost immediately.

We went into a small studio in Birmingham as soon as myself and Harry had written the first few songs for the band. We recorded a 15 minute track called "Reminiscence" part one and two; it was two songs which were put together similarly to what Priest did with "Victim Of Changes". We sent it away to several record companies to try to get us a deal and start us off on the right foot but alas we got turned down by all of them. Maybe we weren't fashionable enough? Maybe our music was outdated? I don't know. The music business changes its mind about what music/bands it likes on a regular basis so who knows what the hell they're thinking?

My first post-Judas Priest band Lion: Jim Perry, me, Bruno and Harry.

Refusing to be put off by this, we continued to write more songs and started gigging in and around Brum; we gigged as often as possible. It was not easy to book a touring schedule without somebody as dedicated and knowledgeable as Dave Corke to help us. We initially played an instrumental mixture of jazz and rock. As well as being the vocalist, I played two tall black Natal Congo drums, tambourines and cowbells. And I suppose we tried to be a little bit too clever and we were really a sort of musician's band more than anything else.

After several gigs in the Black Country, we managed to get an evening's stint at the famous Castaways Club in Birmingham. Our roadie, John England, introduced me to two brothers who were fans of Lion. They said to me that if I or any of the band members were ever in trouble we should let them know and they would sort it for us. I thought that was cool but a bit random. Anyway, about a month later one of the brothers walked into an Irish night club in town with a girlfriend on his arm and was told he couldn't enter. Apparently, the big bouncer on the door thought they were with the couple standing in front of them in the queue. Well, that other guy was barred. A big argument started and the brother was eventually booted out. He went home and got his brother, who lived above a butcher's shop in town, and then went back to the club in black hoods armed with a twelve-bore shotgun. They kicked open the door and blew the bouncers head off. I don't think the police ever caught the brothers, even though their faces were shown on TV and in national newspapers. I remember telling my wife Linda that I'd met them not long ago at a club in Brum. I was told the brothers left the country on the night of the killing and were never caught. I kid you not, it's a true story.

One of our earlier gigs was at Birmingham Town Hall supporting The Heavy Metal Kids featuring the late Gary Holton (later of the TV comedy »Auf Wiedersehen Pet«), Keith Boyce, Ronny Thomas, Danny Peyronel (later of the fantastic hard blues rockers UFO) and Micky Waller. They'd only formed in '73, so they hadn't been around much longer than us yet they had already acquired a strong reputation on the live circuit. It was a sad thing that happened to Gary Holton: he died in 1985 because of his heroin addiction. Heroin is a terrible, destructive drug ... I wouldn't go anywhere near it.

To be truthful, we didn't go down too well with the audience that night. We had a different style of music than The Heavy Metal Kids so the crowd just didn't take to us. I was pissed off! It was our big chance to prove we were worth noticing. We eventually threw in the towel when Jim the drummer walked out on us. It was one of those occasions where we didn't gel and nothing good seemed to come out of the band.

This wasn't the start I had wanted; we appeared to reach the end before we'd even powered on full steam. But then came a lifeline when another one of our old mates, drummer Pete Boot, called me up to say he had just quit playing drums for Budgie through indifferences with the band and asked if he could join up with us. It was actually Dave Corke who told Pete about the vacant slot in Lion (Dave hooked Pete up with the Budgie gig) so all of us met up for a beer to discuss tactics and the first thing we agreed on was to change our style of music from a weird style of experimental jazz back to heavy rock, which we did and from then on things started to turn around for us. Pete was a great addition to the band; he was a better drummer than Jim Perry and had more experience in the kind of music I wanted to play. Like me, Pete is a rocker!

> I still keep in touch with Pete Boot, he's a top bloke. He has a website which you should check out: www.fillyourheadwithrockinternational.com. I have many fond memories of playing with Pete and I'm glad to share them with you.
>
> Pete Boot: "We were all young and had a whole life ahead of us ... Al Atkins must be one of the most dedicated musicians I have worked with; he helped me change my style from pop to rock. I have always had respect for Allan ... he has never given in and his songs are proof of his determination. Regrettably, he never found the recognition he so rightly deserves. Allan has stood in many doorways of the rock world, but for some reason never entered the room and shut the door behind him."

We mixed all of our influences into one sound – the sound of Lion – and we were pleased with the results. We'd also flirt around with the music each of us had played in our previous outfits so imagine early progressive Judas Priest and Budgie with a bit of Cream thrown in for good measure.

Lion almost got a major deal just after Pete Boot joined the band in late '73; Dave Corke, who I had remained in contact with, got us to audition at The Cooksferry Inn in Edmonton, North London for EMI Records. Dave wasn't managing us, he just did us a big favour even though he was busy doing business for Priest. I could not believe our luck. This is it, I thought. If we don't get this, I may never have another shot at the big time.

At the time EMI were looking for a new British rock group, they liked our music but not our stage presence. The one that beat us to the deal was a talented and clever young college band called Queen. (Say no more).

For one particular band 1974 arrived like a hurricane. After touring for about twelve months, Judas Priest – with the line-up of Rob Halford, Kenny Downing, Ian Hill and John Hinch – were about to at last sign a record deal; the tenacious Dave Corke got the band to sign on the dotted line of a four year contract with the independent label Gull Records which was based in London.

David Howells who ran Gull knew a thing or two about rock music, and he also had a lot of contacts in the music world but personally, I didn't think it was a big enough label for Judas Priest; it was the type of deal I had turned down some years earlier. But one thing is for sure: what David Howells did do for them was add a second guitarist which would change the band's sound and image dramatically. I think doing such a thing was a stroke of genius and if such a decision had not been made, Judas Priest may not have been the band they turned out to be.

David Howells has been in the music business for a long time so it's a compliment that he should add some of his thoughts to my book. David can tell you the whole story about Judas Priest's first album for Gull Records and it's definitely worth knowing.

David Howells (Gull Records): "In 1974, soon after I left MCA with my partner Derek Everett to start Gull Records, their manager Dave Corke introduced me to the music of Judas Priest.

Dave was an interesting character, who depending on the situation used a variety of pseudonyms. He ended up sharing an office with me for a while and it was disconcerting sometimes to hear him introduce himself over the phone to promoters and agents as Eric Smith, Eric Corke or one memorable occasion as Halibut. I often wondered how this affected his personal life; mind you I have been told that prior to joining us his previous office had been a telephone kiosk.

One of his less endearing habits was to constantly pace up and down the office when on the phone, and has he lived on the phone, this was all the time he was in the room. The complication was that we'd just moved offices at Morgan studios in Willesden, and our temporary home was about ten foot by ten foot, and in that space were four desks and four people, well five, if you count Eric's split personality, a tight fit at best, so his pacing was something to behold.

I first saw Judas Priest live at The Greyhound in Fulham, London, in 1974 and thought they were terrific. Unlike most new bands they had a strong set of songs that complimented their sound. I didn't realize at that moment watching them that the band in various combinations of personnel, Kenny Downing, John Hinch, Ian Hill and Rob Halford had been together for quite a while, and had built up a good song repertoire through the hard slog of pubs and clubs over several years.

So by those wonderful convoluted highways and byways, that bands go through to find the form that afterwards seem like the most natural, if not entirely organic entity, Al Atkins formed the band, then left in '73 ... Judas Priest [began again] when Kenny Downing and Ian Hill were joined by Rob Halford and John Hinch.

As John Hinch tells it, one of the reasons he and Rob joined up was because of a support slot the band had on a forthcoming tour their manager David Corke had set up. There is something of a 'six degrees of separation' vibe here.

Priest worked 20 days a month, extraordinary for an unknown act; mind you the itinerary was varied to say the least, covering the whole of the UK, not necessary in any logical order. The

REGISTRATION OF BUSINESS NAMES ACT, 1916

as amended by the Companies Act, 1947

Application for registration by an individual

Registration cannot be effected in advance of the date of the commencement of the business, particulars of which should be furnished within 14 days after

I, the undersigned, hereby apply for registration pursuant to the provisions of the Registration of Business Names Act, 1916, as amended, and for that purpose furnish the following statement of particulars:—

(1) The business name. (Note A)	JUDAS PRIEST
(2) The general nature of the business	ENTERTAINMENT (POP) GROUP
(3) The principal place of the business. (Full address)	D CORKE 56, SOUTH MOLTON STREET LONDON W1
(4) The present Christian name (or names) and surname of the individual. (Note C)	CORKE
(5) Any former Christian name (or names) or surname of the individual. If none say "None" (Note D)	~~None~~ DAVID
(6) The nationality of the individual.	ENGLISH
(7) The usual residence of the individual. (Full address)	56, SOUTH MOLTON STREET LONDON W1
(8) The other business occupation (if any) of the individual. If none say "None"	AGENCY MANAGER FOR RECORDING COMPANY
(9) The date of the commencement of the business by the present proprietor under the name given in space (1)	5/4/74
(10) Any other business name or names under which the business is carried on. If none say "None".	NONE

Signature ....D. Corke.................... (Note B)

Date ....4/4/74....................

Form RBN/1
(Registration fee £1)
(not stamps)

V231   Please see notes overleaf

benefit, of course, was the closeness of the band, the honing of their skills and the tightness of their set.

What marked them out from their competitors and peers at the time was the remarkable balance in their songs and set.

After the gig, I offered them a recording contract with Gull Records and also one piece of advice. The only thing I felt could improve their act would be the addition of a second lead guitar.

At MCA, I'd worked with Wishbone Ash and it seemed to me that the adoption of their twin-guitar signature to Judas Priest's heavier, fatter sound would beautifully underpin the extraordinary voice of Rob Halford.

I've always admired Kenny Downing for the fact that he not only embraced the idea of a second lead guitar, but he went out and found an arguably stronger guitarist partner in Glenn Tipton who was in fellow Birmingham group The Flying Hat Band.

For Judas Priest's first album I brought in Rodger Bain who had produced [for] Black Sabbath and who I'd worked with in my MCA days when he also produced Budgie's albums for me.

The song selection was easy; it was the basic set they performed live. One of the reasons so many first albums are so good is simply that, a repertoire developed over a long period of time and the lack of expectation.

The reason for second album is often due to shortness of time to develop new songs and a high expectation by media and public leading to a whole new set of pressures on the band. As history shows this was not a problem for Priest when they came to record their second album, as there were a lot of songs from the original set not used on their debut album.

But back to the first sessions for what was to become »Rocka Rolla«. The first demos I'd heard I seemed to remember were 'Run Of The Mill' and 'Caviar And Meths.' To this they added amongst other tracks 'Never Satisfied,' 'One For The Road,' 'Dying To Meet You' and 'Cheater.'

The original Al Atkins compositions 'Never Satisfied,' 'Caviar And Meths' and 'Winter' remained, in some cases, evolved. The newcomers put their mark on the songs and developed new ideas.

Another Atkins song, 'Whiskey Woman,' was one of the first song demos I ever heard by Priest and grew into the classic 'Victim Of Changes' once Glenn and Rob were on board.

As well as a record label and publishing company, Gull also had a design division called Gull Graphics. My partner was John Pasche, who designed the memorable Rolling Stones 'Lips and Tongue' logo. Other clients included The Average White Band, The Bay City Rollers, Isotope, The Rocky Horror Show Movie and The Who.

One of John's designs rejected by The Rolling Stones around the time of the »Goats Head Soup« album, was an air brushed image of a bottle top with 'Rocka Rolla' written on it. This struck me as being in keeping with Priest and a great title for their debut album. So I showed it to them and suggested that they write a song around it and they came up with one of the strongest tracks on the album.

The album was recorded over three weeks at Island, Trident and Olympic studios in London. During which time, I seem to remember, they met The Rolling Stones and Supertramp amongst others, all in their first visit to a recording studio. Heady times.

Their big breakthrough was their support appearance at the Reading Festival, which won them a rapturous reception from a hostile crowd. Not a forgone conclusion prior to their entrance, as the previous act had been bottled off the stage."

Glenn Tipton in action.

    Glenn Tipton quickly became the dominant figure of the band. He's a brilliant guitarist but it's surprising to learn that he'd only started playing guitar at 18. Prior to learning the guitar he played piano because his mum owned one while he brother played guitar and it was his brother that inspired him to pick up a guitar. He quickly gained a lot of experience through playing in bands such as The Flying Hat Band and two earlier bands; Merlin and Shave And Dry. Glenn had had some pretty tough factory jobs so it's no surprise that like the rest of us he wanted to make some HEAVY music.

With Glenn's inclusion, Judas Priest had now entered the Mark VI phase of their career. I just couldn't believe what had happened to the band. It had been five years since Judas Priest had been formed and now the band featured none of its original members but that's the way it goes, I suppose.

Anyway, »Rocka Rolla« had been released to little patters of applause and so it largely went unnoticed. The band have always blamed Gull for its lack of success and the strange album cover. Personally, the only thing that I didn't like about the »Rocka Rolla« album was its production which sounded very tame, and with John Hinch's laidback style of drumming, it lacked power and drive in the songs. Hinch comes from a jazz and blues background which is not necessarily the best for a hard rock band so it's not a surprise that he didn't last long in Priest. They needed someone like Led Zep's John Bonham to really bring out the best qualities of the band and give it some backbone. Most of the songs sounded pretty weak too despite some good melodies and guitars.

»Rocka Rolla« (Gull Records – 1974)

"One For The Road" (Downing/Halford)
"Rocka Rolla" (Downing/Halford/Tipton)
"Winter" (Downing/Hill/Atkins)
"Deep Freeze" (Downing)
"Winter Retreat" (Downing/Halford)
"Cheater" (Downing/Halford)
"Never Satisfied" (Downing/Atkins)
"Run Of The Mill" (Downing/Halford/Tipton)
"Dying To Meet You" (Downing/Halford)
"Caviar And Meths" (Atkins)

There are quite a few songs relating to cold weather/winter on the album. My song "Winter" was written after the horrendous tour of Scotland I had back with the first line-up of the band and the rest (not written by me) are about similar experiences Mark V had whilst during Europe in January-February 1974. Priest hit Europe for the first time, playing shows in a very cold Scandinavia. Kenny has told stories about brushing his teeth in snow and struggling to drive through a blizzard and one of the band members (I don't know who!) even took a dump in an envelope at the back of the tour van because it was too cold to go outside and there wasn't a toilet in sight. They do say artists suffer for their art …

Bands have it easy these days in terms of promoting albums because you have things like MySpace and YouTube but back then you had to tour the length and breadth of the country to promote a record. It doesn't matter what the weather's like or how much (or rather how little) money you have because you had to go out there and bloody play for peanuts. I'm sure most British bands of the sixties and seventies have some great stories about life on the road but I can tell you from my own personal experiences that it wasn't all fun and games. Sure, the gigs were great but touring was really hard work, it was more like a necessary evil.

Even now, I play gigs in the Midlands and abroad and it's tough work. I love seeing the audiences sing to my songs, it is very gratifying, but driving up and down the motorway or fly-

Judas Priest Mark VII circa 1975-76: Ian, Kenny, Rob, Glenn and Alan Moore.

ing out somewhere is very tiring and stressful. If you're in a big band, you've got all sorts of people to help you – a whole entourage – but if you haven't, then it can be very hard arranging a tour schedule and sticking to it without making some kind of cock up along the way.

»Rocka Rolla« never really took off but at least they had an album out. They continued to play live which helped push the sales of it for another year or so. They were well ahead of me in the game. My band Lion was still gigging around Birmingham and the Black Country, and I was still struggling to earn a living from making music.

In '74, Priest made their first live television appearance playing on the famous BBC music TV show the »Old Grey Whistle Test« introduced by the legendary presenter "whispering" Bob Harris; they played three songs which they used in their regular setlist: "Rocka Rolla", "Deceiver" and "Dreamer Deceiver". They looked like a crazy psychedelic band; Rob Halford had long hair! Kenny was wearing a Panama hat! (You'll never see them doing anything like that again). It was their early image and I guess they were perfecting their sound rather than spending time concerning themselves about the way they looked. Obviously, they had an image change later on but the sound of the band was more important to them. I remember hearing keen music fans in West Brom talking about seeing Judas Priest, saying they were really impressed that a local band had made it on to the TV not realising that there was still a lot more hard work involved. People think that if you have an album released and appear on TV you become automatically rich, it couldn't be further from the truth. Sure, Priest were certainly on the right path to glory but I don't think they understood that it would be so hard.

The Black Country is a small place. It may look like a big area on a map but word of mouth gets around quickly. I lived here most of my life and because of all the bands I've played in I've made a lot of friends and acquired some good contacts.

1975 saw me going through a low point in my life. Judas Priest were busy preparing for their second album for Gull Records and they'd seen most of Europe, playing gigs just about everywhere. I was back in the Black Country thinking about the next move for Lion; I felt more confident about the band since Pete came onboard but things were still moving too slowly for my liking.

I think I reached an introspective phase in my career; I was looking at my life and thinking about what I had achieved. Like most aspiring professional artists I wanted to be remembered. I wanted people to recognise me and my music. Going way back in time to when I was in The Medallians I had been in a handful of bands since then and really gotten nowhere; sometimes, as with Judas Priest, I had come really close to making an album, something I had always wanted to do but nothing panned out. Okay, I had gained tons of experience but it seemed to be to no avail. But I was and still am headstrong and continued to follow my dream despite all the setbacks. It's a tough business and if you are weak, lack confidence and believe in yourself you will not survive. You have to be tenacious and headstrong.

At the end of '75, Judas Priest recorded their second album at Rockfield Studios in South Wales and this time it was produced by Jeffery Calvert and Max West. The album was christened »Sad Wings Of Destiny«. It was apt that they recorded their first masterpiece at Rockfield. Maybe the aura of the place gave them enthusiasm and extra boost of energy and passion. After all, Queen and Black Sabbath had recorded there and over the years Rockfield has become Britain's most famous rock recording studio. They mixed the album at Morgan Studios in London the following January.

After splitting with John Hinch, who really wasn't the right drummer for the band, they called in my old drummer Alan Moore to pound the skins. Why did they re-hire Alan? I would have thought it was a similar situation like with Lion and Pete Boot: they knew him well enough to put him back in the band. Why they didn't keep him in is another story entirely?! So with Alan Moore on the drum stool Judas Priest was in its seventh line-up since 1969!

To me this album was a completely different animal to »Rocka Rolla« and featured some classic songs like "The Ripper", "Dreamer Deceiver", "Tyrant", "Genocide" and, of course, the ultimate heavy metal screamer "Victim Of Changes". It was a heavier and more mature album, and it still remains one of their most accomplished pieces of work. It's an angry album which probably reflected the way they were feeling at the time.

"Victim Of Changes" was concocted from two songs: one being my old song "Whiskey Woman" that I used to sing live with the band; and the other was one of Rob's numbers called "Red Light Lady" which was much slower. They put them back-to-back, added more guitars and re-titled the whole composition "Victim Of Changes". When I first wrote "Whiskey Woman" I had the idea of making it like Led Zeppelin's song "Black Dog" from their best album »Led Zeppelin IV«. You can hear Robert Plant singing a passage on his own and a riff coming in straight after; it worked really well and I wanted to try something like that on one of my songs. "Victim Of Changes" was to feature on many albums over the years and has become a classic song and covered by many bands too. I read in some magazine that Jimmy Page said they in turn had adapted "Black Dog" from listening to Fleetwood Mac's song "Oh Well". It's funny how songs evolve …

K.K Downing – Question: Favourite Judas Priest song?
Answer: "Victim Of Changes".

Rob Halford – Question: Favourite Judas Priest song?
Answer: "Victim Of Changes" – that's essentially what Priest is all about.

(Taken from the 'Facts File' section in »Heavy Duty: The official Biography« by Steve Gett. Published by Cherry Lane Books, 1984).

"'Victim Of Changes' set the template for all progressive metal that followed ..."
(Classic Rock Magazine)

"Victim Of Changes" has one of the greatest riffs ever composed; it's tremendous. Of course, when I wrote the song I never imagined in my wildest dreams that one day another singer/songwriter would add more lyrics and turn it into one of heavy metal's greatest songs. By now, heavy metal was an acknowledged term and bands like UFO and Judas Priest were flying the flag for the genre.

"Victim Of Changes"
(Atkins/Halford/Tipton/Downing)

Whiskey woman don't you know that you are driving me insane
The drink you give stems your well to live and it gets right to your brain
You're trying to find your way through life
You're trying to find some new direction

Another woman's got her man
And she can't find a new connection
Takes another drink or two
Things look better when she's through

Take another look around
You ain't going anywhere
You've realized you're getting old
And no one seems to care
You're trying to find your way again
You're trying to find something new
Another woman's got her man
And everything just seems bad news
Takes another drink or two
Things look better when she's through

You been fooling ... with some hot guy
I want to know why is it why
Get up get out you know you really blew it

I've had enough ... good god you shook me
Once she was wonderful, once she was fine
Once she was beautiful, once she was mine
Now a change has come over her body
She doesn't see me any more
A change has come over her body
She doesn't see me any more
Changes. Changes. Changes. Victim of Changes

»Sad Wings Of Destiny« was released in March 1976 and in my opinion it was (still is!) a brilliant album and set the standard for heavy metal in years to come, and I wasn't surprised that later on they came to the attention of a much bigger label than Gull. I noticed that Glenn Tipton was putting his own contributions to the songwriting side of their new songs and this showed; they had not only found a brilliant guitarist but a talented songwriter too. In 1989, Kerrang! magazine placed the album in the '100 Greatest Heavy Metal Albums Of All Time.' They got that right!

»Sad Wings Of Destiny« (Gull Records – 1976)

"Victim Of Changes"
(Atkins/Halford/Downing/Tipton)
"The Ripper" (Tipton)
"Dreamer Deceiver" (Atkins/Halford/Downing/Tipton)
"Deceiver" (Downing/Halford/Tipton)
"Prelude" (Tipton)
"Tyrant" (Tipton/Halford)
"Genocide" (Tipton/Halford/Downing)
"Epitaph" (Tipton)
"Island Of Domination" (Tipton/Halford/Downing)

Not only did they use "Whiskey Woman" but they also used another one of my songs called "Dreamer Deceiver". Basically, I came up with the riff for that one so I got credit on the album. I guess they had been playing it live and liked the song enough too add some lyrics and record it for their album. It's a good song and I play it live all the time – the fans love it. In fact the late Michael Llilljhammer, a fan of mine from Sweden and the guy who designed and compiled all the material on my website, had requested to have my version of the song played at his funeral.

"Dreamer Deceiver"
(Halford/Downing/Tipton/Atkins)

Standing by my window breathing summer breeze
Saw a figure floating 'neath the willow trees
Asked us if we were happy we said we didn't know
Took us by the hands and up we go.

We followed the dreamer through the purple hazy clouds
He could control our sense of time
We thought we were lost but no matter how we tried
Everyone was in peace of mind
We felt the sensations drift inside our frames
Finding complete contentment there
And all the tensions that hurt us in the past
Just seem to vanish in thin air

He said in the cosmos is a single sonic sound
That is vibrating constantly
And if we could grip and hold on to the note
We would see our minds were free
We are lost above floating way up high
And if you think that you can find a way
You must surely try

And at this point with the release of »Sad Wings Of Destiny«, which included my songwriting contributions, it's where my connection with Judas Priest ends.

I still receive royalty cheques from the band (thank you!) but after the release of »Sad Wings Of Destiny« in '76 I tried to move on and leave Judas Priest behind. I wanted to get away from the name and the music but somehow I just couldn't ... the name 'Judas Priest' and its history was always at the back of my mind. I followed their career and to this day, I will continue to buy their albums but as a fan not for any sort of yearning to remember the past.

Dave Corke prefers to live the quiet life, so it's really a privilege for me that I get to include this lengthy interview with him which I conducted. He's a really nice guy and worked his arse off for Judas Priest; it's just a shame the band didn't appreciate him as much as they should have done. I am pleased that he played a part in my life. Cheers Dave!

Dave Corke (Manager of Judas Priest from 1970 to 1976): "The first time I saw Al was at our Churchfields School leaving party in the mid-sixties. It was held in the large hall of the school and on stage playing live that night was Al's blues/rock band called The Jug Blues Band; the band consisted of John Perry (guitar), Bruno Stapenhill (bass), Barry Civil (guitar) and Jim Perry (drums).

Another year would pass until I saw him playing live again when Kenny Downing and myself went to see his new band called Judas Priest whom Kenny had earlier failed an audition for. They were playing at a local Community Centre in Friar Park, Wednesbury and there were only about 20 people in the audience but they still played a storming set and Kenny was well impressed by their performance and loved their version of 'Woman' by Free as he was a big fan of them and really admired Paul Kossoff on guitar.

The new band was Al (vocals), Bruno (bass), John Partridge (drums) and Ernie Chataway (guitar). I later told him that this was the standard and the benchmark to set his new band that he was starting up.

Judas Priest were a hard working band playing anywhere and everywhere all over the UK and already had A&R scouts watching their every move.

During 1970 Kenny and his band called Freight – a three piece rock outfit – that featured Ian 'Skull' Hill (bass), John Ellis (drums) and Kenny himself on lead guitar, practiced and worked hard at becoming a tight unit and getting all geared up to hit the road. Then one night at Holy Joe's rehearsal rooms, who would walk in but Al Atkins. He asked them if they needed a good vocalist. He told them that his old band had split up after twelve months of hard work, but with more than their share of bad luck and the other members just didn't want to continue and had lost heart. But he was determined to carry on and explore new avenues of rock music and find a new line-up of musicians. He said he liked what he heard of Kenny's band but they needed a voice to go with it and recommended that with the reputation Al's Judas Priest had already acquired, they should also use his old band's name and they all agreed, so that was that and the new Judas Priest was born.

Kenny, Ian, John, Trevor Lunn, their roadie, and myself all grew up on the Yew Tree Estate and attended the same school together. We were all good friends and all liked the same music, which was seventies style blues/hard rock. Kenny was always out of work when we left High School so it was me who bought him his first guitar, which was a red Gibson junior from Wasp Music in Birmingham. (By the way, if he ever reads this book, he still hasn't paid me back for it yet!)

It was a real coup for them to get Al on board with all his playing experience; he could play guitar, harmonica, and drums and also write his own songs.

I would have loved to have been a musician but, unfortunately, couldn't play a damn thing. That's why I offered my services by way of getting their gigs as I fancied myself as some sort of agent or even going into management, this way at least, I would be a part of the music business and would also stay close to my buddies. They all agreed to my offer and we all started to pull together to get Judas Priest back on the road.

The first gigs I got them were all local and very low key and also for very little money but the most important thing was getting some playing experience behind them. If I remember correctly, they played a very mixed bag of songs at first that ranged from Quatermass, Savoy Brown Blues Band and some of Al's own compositions called 'Winter' and 'Never Satisfied.' With Trev and Keith 'Evo' Evans their friends and roadies supplying the transport they were soon pounding up and down the motorways of England. (Delivering the Goods).

By now, I hardly saw them performing live as I had to stay back home phoning round for more gigs for them to play and also trying to hold down my day job at a tyre company in West Bromwich. The only time I did see them is when they played locally and they got more confident and more aggressive with every performance bettering the last.

After a while I felt the time was right that they should go into the studio and record some of Al's new material that he had just written so I booked them into Zella Studios in town, which was one of the better studios around and often used by Black Sabbath. They recorded two songs titled 'Mind Conception' and 'Holy Is The Man,' the songs showed Al's writing ability but the quality of the recordings sounded pretty poor so I decided to shelve them until we recorded something that really captured the band's energy.

In 1971, John Ellis, the drummer, decided to quit the band and was replaced immediately by Alan Moore and by now we were playing bigger clubs and colleges across the UK. Alan Moore lasted into 1972 and then Chris Campbell, otherwise known as 'Congo', replaced him.

It was about this time through general enquiries I met Norman Hood via the Jim Simpson Agency by booking various bands into the Three Mile Oak through him. Norman later split up with Jim and set up his own company in Lichfield called Tramp Entertainments and asked me to work with him, by this time I had given up my day job to concentrate on Judas Priest and the agency.

While working alongside Norman, I got to know that Black Sabbath guitarist Tony Iommi was financing us. Basically, I was booking bands like Necromandus, Judas Priest and The Flying Hat Band, which were their three main bands, but also at this time I started booking another little known band called Hiroshima (featuring Rob Halford) who were also based in Lichfield.

This continued for a while until we moved the company to Hurst Street in Birmingham [in December 1972]. I was constantly trying to promote Judas Priest because I didn't really think Norman believed in them that much and he was always pushing Necromandus who were Tony's big pet project.

Just to contradict a lot of rumours that Tony Iommi managed Judas Priest, these are not true; their main manager was always myself from 1970 to 1976. Sometimes I couldn't make up my mind whether I was their manager, promoter or their agent because, basically, I did all of these jobs just to keep them going.

I was bitterly disappointed when Al left them, along with Congo, and they came to a full stop in May of '73. At this point in time, I had built up a lot of experience although being only 22 years of age and I had been staying a lot in London and made a lot of new contacts. After their departure from the band I thought this might be the end of them but Ian's girlfriend Sue told Ian that her brother Rob was a good vocalist with a band called Hiroshima and they should check him out.

The first time I saw Rob perform was at the Three Mile Oak, which I had booked his band to play. My first thoughts about him was that he had no stage presence or image and sounded very much in the style of another local singer made good called Robert Plant. But what did stand out was his very high range of vocals and what a very interesting voice he had.

Later, after meeting him off stage I found him to be a bit of a drama queen and a little over the top, but a friendly guy with a very sincere attitude to his music.

It was no surprise to me when he teamed up with Kenny and Ian and he also brought in his drummer John Hinch; John was a very experienced drummer and had played in The Bakerloo Blues Line with Clem Clempson and I think they learnt the whole set of songs, which they used to play with Al within weeks of rehearsing and were ready to go back on the road.

I was quite exited at this point in time with them re-emerging with the new line-up and soon took over the reins again as their manager and made up my mind to push them on again, but even more determined this time to make them a success.

I later met a contact in London who turned out to be Budgie's manager named Graham Maloney and we became really good friends and I have fond memories of us speeding around in his open top Ford Mustang. Budgie was now signed to MCA and their A&R man was no other than David Howells. They were still playing the clubs around the UK and were coming to their second album »Squawk« and my aim was at this time was how to make Judas Priest look bigger than they were. I knew it would take more than the large posters that I stuck up everywhere (oh, that's another job I forgot about that I did for them), so I persuaded Graham to book Budgie into bigger halls and actually put together a proper tour even side stepping their agent.

Knowing at the time I could put Priest on with Budgie, I knew this could be the perfect fit and at the same time we could capture Budgie's audience on a big scale. This tour at the end of '73 was a great success in many ways and a platform to build them on.

During the tour I met David Howells via Maloney and thought he was another good contact for the possible future. As it was to be, David left MCA and founded Gull Records through Decca Records.

Around this time I needed the band to record a really good demo as we were like a gun but without any bullets to fire. It was now that I was also approached by David Howells to work for him in South Molten Street, W1, London. Again, I saw this as a great move for Priest and myself. I proceeded to do next to nothing for Gull but concentrate all my energies on Priest courtesy of David's phones.

The first thing I did was put up a massive poster of them on David's office wall which I think confused him, but one thing was for sure, he realised my belief in them.

I basically spent the next year sleeping on people's floors and blagging hotels and also at this time changed my name to Eric Smith due to the massive debts I had built up all over the country with the band.

I eventually told Howells my real name in the back of a taxi going to Morgan Studios in Willesden and he looked at me gob smacked but saw the funny side of it.

During this period I was also concentrating about approaching major record labels in London that included Island, Vertigo, Harvest and several more, speaking to them at length and trying to get them to see the band perform live.

"[In 1974] it was now time to record those demos so we recorded two songs back at Lee Sounds in Pelsall, Walsall in the Black Country. One was a song Al wrote called 'Whiskey Woman' and the other was one of Kenny's called 'Run Of The Mill.' Once finished I took them to the record companies and making sure their image was right I set up a showcase gig at the well known Greyhound Pub in London. The reaction was that everyone loved Rob's voice and with his new charismatic stage presence he had worked on but the overriding opinion was Kenny couldn't cut it and so they all passed on them. To this day I never told them that all these A&R men's eyes were upon them, but knowing I had an even larger tour coming up again with Budgie I still had some aces up my sleeve.

I was a massive fan of Kenny from day one and he oozed stage star quality and looked one hell of a sexy guy for the female side of the fans. Basically, I was the one who came up with all the ideas for them, image/style, etc. Does any one remember that sheepskin Panama hat that Kenny wore on the '74 tour and on the »Old Grey Whistle Test« on TV? I bought that for him from a shop in Bond Street, London, and it was very expensive too, but everyone loved it ... Result.

Also, Kenny's stage name 'K.K.' was an idea of mine and didn't come from some groupie in Denmark as quoted in some circles. I was always coming up with names for them and looking at him I knew the name Ken just didn't fit the bill and 'K.K.' was pure international. One name that I gave Rob didn't go down too well though which was Queen, and he went ballistic when I showed him some press photos I had done and so we had to have them all scrapped because at the time he didn't want anyone to know he was gay. But since he has come out and announced it to the world I gave Al one of the old photos which I kept behind all these years to show in his book.

Anyway, after playing the demo to David Howells he said: 'I think they should add another guitarist and make it a heavier twin guitar sound.' [This was] similar to one of his other signings Wishbone Ash.

This got me thinking and I had always admired Glenn Tipton from Birmingham and his Flying Hat Band and phoned him and suggested he should join Priest. At first, he thought they were not good enough for him but I kept on to him and said he would be a major player in them and then I got more of a response from him and knew I was getting closer to my goal.

One day I was in a music shop on the Bristol Road in town and bumped into him and again asked him to join them and a few days later he came over to our flat that we lived in at Handsworth Wood.

Basically, I left him to chat away to Kenny to see what he could come up with and luckily they hit it off and so now we had the five star line-up and this time I knew we would turn more heads. It was also time to register the 'Judas Priest' name just in case anyone else tried to use it, so on the fifth of April 1974 I registered it in my name.

Glenn teamed up with the band just in time for the '74 Budgie tour and during this tour I found that I had converted David Howells to do the record deal.

At this point in time, I had decided not to approach any more record labels and stick with Gull. I have to admit that looking back, it may not have been the right move for us, also the restraints on this deal were poor in respect of a very small advance of just £2,000 which also included the group's publishing on which Howells insisted on, or he would not have moved forward.

I thought the basics of this arrangement weren't right but I had no choice (the scale of advances given to groups between '74-'76 became astronomical) but the deal was done and they went into the studio to record their first album with Rodger Bain at the helm who had previously produced Black Sabbath at Basing Street Studios, West London. I felt at this time I still had the group's ear and creative control but this was all blown out of the window when they approved of the cover to their debut album »Rocka Rolla« which was a concept of a 'Coca Cola' bottle cap, hence the title. It did the group more harm than good in my opinion; I tested the water back home to Al, the original vocalist, by playing it to him on a cassette player in my car and asked for his opinion on the sound quality, his reaction: a poor production with no bollocks.

I had lost that much interest at this stage, they even spelt Glenn's name wrong on the back of the album cover using only one 'n' and we had a massive argument.

Against a back drop of mistakes, I tried again in 1975 to launch a couple of fairly high profile tours through Sherry/Copeland; basically, I worked on the proviso that they needed a major record deal and also major money because at this time we were starting to headline large venues such as Newcastle Mayfair, Wigan Casino, Roundhouse London, and Liverpool Stadium, etc. I also realised their stage presence had to be more defined so I incorporated extra lighting and pyrotechnics via Terry Lee who later went on to be boss of one of the biggest stage lighting companies in the world called Light & Sound Designs, and along with his partner Simon Austen they later worked with artists like AC/DC and Prince, to name a few.

I threw everything on their stage shows, including smoke machines and massive wind machines. I believed that when the kids who came to our shows saw that the music was important but they would be also blown away by the stunning stage set.

I, David Corke, do hereby dissolve any management interests, connections, debts etc with the Group Judas Priest and as such do officially resign my status as a Third Management Partner. I am, therefore, no longer involved with Judas Priest in any way.

Signed DAVID CORKE

Witness

Dated this 6th day of August 1976.

Alcazar Productions.
York House, Leamington Spa, Warwickshire. Telephone John Tully on: 021-643 3137 or 021-523 9623.
Partners: John Tully, Neil French, David Cork

At this point in time [autumn 1975] I just knew they were going to be massive and they had already [started] recording their second album »Sad Wings Of Destiny« which was better than the first but again I felt it was poorly recorded but my live strategy was paying off with the amount of kids who now knew of Judas Priest and we finished the year off at a sold out concert at The Roundhouse in London [on December 28.]

The most important event of '75 had to be the Reading Pop Festival which we got through devious means via a bit of cock sucking in Jack Barry's office after a show at The Marquee. The deal was that we opened up the festival literally in the daylight but we still blew everyone else away ... which included UFO.

1976 was the point in time that the band decided they didn't require my services anymore. This was in my opinion all the fault of Glenn Tipton who turned into the real Judas when he decided to get some of his own contacts involved which included the late David Hemmings and Mike Dolan, this move would prove costly for them later on but I had other plans up my sleeve anyway and moved into the new punk scene working with The Clash and The Sex Pistols after forming new relationships with Malcolm MaClaren and Bernard Rhodes.

Priest went on to get their major deal with CBS, Hemmings and Dolan coming to an arrangement with Gull Records and David Howells citing that the Gull contract was invalid and unfair due to the group being stitched up with the publishing deal and they persuaded David to release them from the contracts but to keep the rights to their first two albums.

Sitting in my office in Birmingham one afternoon during the late seventies, I received a postcard from Glenn in the USA saying they were on tour and missing my presence so much they offered me a job with them selling T-shirts. How ironic that they saw me as a small time operator! To me this was a total insult and for all my years of hard work I never received a penny from them!"

Al Atkins: "David was a great character and went on to be very successful, managing bands such as Dexy's Midnight Runners who had a Number One single with 'Geno' and a Number One album called »Searching For The Young Soul Rebels«. He also managed Uli Jon Roth formerly of the great German band Scorpions and the group Fashion; he was also involved with Duran Duran during the eighties.

In the nineties, he successfully managed bands like Babylon Zoo, The Sandkings, and Laxton Superb who were signed to Sony and also political rockers 25th Of May who he signed to the Arista label."

1976 was the year which saw Judas Priest shred some uncomfortable ties with their old manager and friend Dave Corke and tear up the four year contract they had signed with Gull Records after being spotted by an agent working for CBS over here in the UK. This agent got them to sign a major deal with the big American label, a deal which would eventually see them move from England and set up camp in America. A very good move and about time they had a change of luck. Their new manager David Hemmings of Arnakata Management would help propel the band to global success. Little did they know just how bloody popular they would become in the States the following decade.

A classic shot of my seventies band Lion.

By now, Lion had been struggling for about two years; it's not a long time but we had some good stories to tell. I remember when we battled through the IRA explosions in November 1974. 21 people had been killed in those devastating attacks. The IRA blew up The Tavern In The Town and the Mulberry Bush, which made us really scared to play anywhere in Birmingham just in case some other club or pub we might be appearing in was on their hit list. The public outcry for justice was enormous. People were scared to go to any public building in case of more bombings. Ten people were arrested for the Birmingham bombings and the bombings in Guildford earlier in the year. Shockingly, the people who were arrested were found innocent; the Birmingham Six were released in 1989 and the Guildford Four were released in 1991. The trial and imprisonment of those men has become one of the most famous miscarriages of justice in British criminal history.

We also had to battle through the punk explosion of '76 with the emergence of UK punk bands like The Damned, The Clash and, of course, The Sex Pistols who we played with at Birmingham's Barbarella's club a year before the release of their controversial record »Never Mind The Bollocks«. Even now, some 30 years later, a lot of people still ask me what it was like to play alongside the Pistols but I honestly can't remember much about the gig at all; I think we finished our set and went for a curry in town. I can tell you that the Pistols were a rough looking crew: Johnny Rotten, Steve Jones, Paul Cook and Glen Matlock.

Since we started in '74, Lion always pulled in a big crowd at Barbarella's, which was like a residency gig to us and lots of local musicians would also come along to check us out and have a good time, including Kenny and Rob from Priest. In fact, Kenny and Rob went to Barbarella's a lot but the one time I remember well was when they had just signed with Gull Records and I sat at a table with them after our show drinking beer with them; it had to be 1974. It was good that they came along and supported me and my new venture. Priest had made a name for themselves so as far as they were concerned there was no snobbery: Lion and Priest were two upstarting Midlands bands.

The Stranglers also supported us once. They were only a three piece then but a very good one actually. We played with them above a large pub in the centre of Birmingham. I remember JJ Burnel played some mean bass lines. They even brought some of their own audience up from London. They were mostly considered to be a punk band but crossed over into other fan bases such as the Goths and the New Wave rock bands of the 1980s, like Joy Division. Perhaps their broad appeal had something to do with singer/guitarist Hugh Cornwell who was actually trained as a blues player. They had some big hits in the eighties and I respect them more than the Pistols and a lot of other punk bands because they could actually play. They had a huge single with "Golden Brown" and another hit with "Strange Little Girl".

I think supporting bands like the Pistols and The Stranglers really helped us attract a decent sized audience in the Midlands although we were careful not to be labelled a punk band.

I hated most of the punk groups; to me they just made a racket and relied mainly on shock tactics like swearing and spitting at each other and the audience. I didn't like the music and I didn't like the image either, skinheads and ripped jeans. Nope, not my thing!

A band like the Sex Pistols weren't very talented. They could barely string a note together. The Pistols were not unlike a lot of modern pop bands; they put together and marketed by their manager Malcolm McLaren. The reason why they proved to be so popular was because of their attitude and the ideas they stood for. The press made a big deal about Johnny Rotten's attitude on Granada TV; he cursed at the presenter Bill Grundy who was slightly pissed anyway. The next day, Johnny Rotten was all over the papers and it made Grundy look like a complete dick. I think he lost his TV job after that little incident.

Punk was more than a musical movement; it was a subculture that changed everything – clothes, music and even the movies. You couldn't get away from it at the time, punk was everywhere and old rockers like me and even the likes of Led Zeppelin looked like out of fashion relics of the past. In fact, a lot of bands made several digs at Robert Plant and Led Zeppelin; after all their stage shows had gotten bigger, Plant had long hair and they were mega rich rock stars. Zeppelin recently reformed to play a gig at the O_2 Arena in London and millions of people applied for tickets. Johnny Rotten is that desperate for money he even appeared on ITV's »I'm A Celebrity Get Me Out Of Here!« Who's laughing now?!

A lot of bands who had success in the late sixties and early seventies struggled to be taken seriously in the wake of punk music but the one band who seemed to avoid it all was Queen. They were having the biggest hits of their career. I really admired the way they tackled America. Instead of going straight over there with just an album they waited until they had a strong reputation over here in the UK, and after the success of »A Night At The Opera« they hit the States big time. Freddie Mercury even moved to New York for several years. »News Of The World« is a fantastic rock album with a great cover. Singles like "Bohemian Rhapsody" and "We Will Rock You" are classics known the world over. I think it was because they were so inventive and brilliant that they really didn't care about any other style of music; they just did their own thing fusing jazz, blues, and rock, classical and pop. Their productions were huge and extremely professional but they knew how to have a laugh especially with songs like "Fat Bottom Girls". In this business, you need to have a sense of humour. Brian May's riffs were incredibly imaginative, Freddie Mercury's voice and songwriting talents were unparalled and the rhythm section of Roger Taylor and John Deacon was unique. Put simply, the chemistry between the four of them just seemed to work so bloody well. Queen were a one-off.

Punk was the complete opposite of glam; they couldn't have been further apart. In my view, I suppose the good that came out of punk was the political aspect; punk was anti-establishment and anti-authoritarian. I didn't like the social rebellion with skinheads terrorising the streets but at least politicians took notice of what punk rockers had to say. I loathe politicians; they're manipulative and selfish. Look what they did to this country in the seventies. Look at what Margaret Thatcher did to the working classes in the 1980s. At least punk rockers had the balls to stand up and say something.

When I was a kid my parents and people their age were shocked at the sight of Elvis gyrating on stage; imagine the shock on their faces at them hearing Johnny Rotten spew a torrent of verbal abuse on the TV. The sixties had affected people's senses; artistic types were no longer going to be chained down by censorship or irritable public figures and right-wing politicians.

The Sex Pistols became the most famous band on the planet for a brief period but they weren't the best punk band. The Clash laid down some incredible melodies as did the Ramones in NYC. Other UK bands of the era included The Stranglers, The Damned and the Buzzcocks but punk was mostly localised to London and in America, the Big Apple. Truthfully, I think I preferred the bands that preceded punk like Alice Cooper, Iggy Pop and Patti Smith because I could relate to them.

Punk was relatively short-lived although since the late seventies there has been a ridiculous amount of sub genres, and today bands like Green Day and even Good Charlotte are labelled punk. It just goes to show how music can transform itself. Take my genre, heavy metal, just look at the amount of styles there are: thrash, death, hardcore, industrial and extreme. It's crazy. I prefer good old-fashioned metal with bands like the Scorpions, Iron Maiden and Black Sabbath. UFO was another favourite band of mine; they formed in 1969, the same year Priest began. As soon as I heard their cover of Eddie Cochran's "C'mon Everybody", I was hooked. Basically, if it rocked and it was loud, I loved it.

A lot of the older metal heads like me didn't take to punk all that much. But there was a small selection of bands in the mid-seventies that crossed both fan bases. Take Motörhead, for example. What a bloody good band! They appealed to both the punks and the metal fans and even now in 2009 they are still the top underdogs, still going strong. Lemmy will keep coming at you. He's a legend; there's nobody like him in the business. He's unique.

Anyway, punk rock was a bit of a shock for me and people of my type. With a name like Lion, I don't think we did too badly when it came to selling tickets to punters in the Midlands. I mean, we weren't pretentious and we basically dressed in denim jeans and shirts although we did have long hair. We were at the beginning of our career but when we stripped the sound down and played basic rock Lion had more success and good feedback from people. But we still had some music fans calling us old farts.

Lion was by far the loudest and most talented band I had fronted and also the craziest group of nutters you could ever come across. Even the road crew, Moose, Big M, Cowboy, Ken, Johnny England and Mick "Zoom" Hughes, were hell bent on competing with Pete Boot in his mad challenges on the road. Mick was an electrician and throughout the years with us he became a really good friend of the band. When we split up, he formed a sound and lighting company in Birmingham and toured with bands like New Model Army until he eventually joining up with Metallica as their sound engineer and has been with them ever since. He has also worked with Motörhead and Slipknot.

Looking back at the short career of Lion, I really think we should have secured a record deal and it wasn't for the lack of trying. Again, I think that for those luckier enough to get a deal it

Mick Hughes behind Midas XL8

is down to the right time, right place and a hell of a lot of good luck. I was not that lucky, hence all the bands I had formed. Deep down we were too proud to cash in on our past relationships with certain bands (i.e. Budgie/Priest) who were doing really well by the end of the decade.

We had now signed up with John Tully and Eddie Fewtrell of Fewtrell-Tully Associates at 41 Cumberland Street, Birmingham. They owned some nightclubs in town, including the famous Barbarella's by Broad Street. It was a good thing for us because it gave us some much needed confidence when we were at a low ebb. They got us some gigs which was the main thing.

I remember one night at Barbarella's when we opened up for The Kevin Coyne Band; they were amazed at our crazy antics. Mick and Big M stripped off to have a go at sumo wrestling in the changing room. You have to understand that Big M was 17 stone and Mick was about three stone heavier; Kevin and his band just fell about laughing at them.

"What the hell are you doing?" I shouted to them when I walked into the changing rooms, and saw them stripped down to their underpants.

"We're going to have a sumo wrestle!" shouted Mick. "Wanna have a go?"

"No chance!" I balled. I was not gonna make myself look like a prat.

Later on when we were performing on stage, Kevin stood behind Bruno's double Marshall Stack whilst Bruno was playing a solo and I said: "If I were you, I would move from there."

Bruno used to hold down a feedback note with one hand as he was downing a pint of beer with the other. When Bruno was finished, he would throw the empty glass over the back of his Marshall Stack. As soon as I warned him Kevin soon moved away, and just in time as the pint class shattered on the floor behind him.

Kevin shouted: "You lot are completely fucking mad!"

"You haven't seen anything yet … Now you know what I have to put up with", I laughed.

That wasn't the end of our antics because Pete was about to do his drum solo and when he pounds his skins believe me, anything could happen. Pete was one crazy guy back in those days. When Pete was excited and the adrenalin was pumping he would play for ages. We stood behind the stacks as we watched Pete do his solo, every now and then he would double up on his bass drums then he'd stop playing so he could stand up and scream at the audience and they would in turn scream back.

In those days something like that – interaction between the drummer and the audience – wouldn't happen as often as it does now. You see drummers do that all the time now; it gives them a chance to show off their talents and actually get some acknowledgement from the audience whilst at the same time it gives the rest of the band a chance to have a break. I remember watching a Queen gig on TV; I was really impressed by Roger Taylor's drum solo. He can sing really well too, especially with the more rock stuff like "Tie Your Mother Down". He knows how to excite an audience even during a drum solo which is often the time when most of the audience goes for a piss or buys a hot dog.

Anyway, there was this one guy who stood right in the front of the stage and it was a packed house; he continually heckled and shouted at the band all night and Pete got really angry. He made a move towards this guy while he was beating the floor with his drumsticks, and then he'd hit the mic stand and he'd run up and down the stage hitting whatever he could until he stood right in front of the guy and then suddenly Pete kicked him in the head.

"Jesus Christ!" shouted the audience member.

"Served you right", Pete said before he went back to his drum stool and started playing.

"Bloody hell", I said to Pete after the gig. "That was brilliant mate … Did you see the look on that guy's face when you hit him. Classic."

"I can't say I felt sorry for him", Pete replied with a pint in his hand.

Anyway, the crowd cheered at Pete and we never heard from that guy again; he must have felt really embarrassed. We continued with the gig with huge smiles on our faces. We were proper working class guys who didn't take shit from anybody.

We included some original material in our setlist and even "Pride Of Man" by Quick Silver Messenger which was a Judas Priest Mark I song. We also covered the Cream classic "N.S.U." from their brilliant album »Fresh Cream«.

Lion Setlist

"On The Wheel" (Atkins/Tonks)
"Journey" (Atkins)
"Rain" (Atkins)
"N.S.U." (Jack Bruce)
"Reminiscence" part one (Tonks)
"Reminiscence" part two (Atkins)
"Life Goes On" (Atkins)
"Pride Of Man" (Quick Silver Messenger)
"Another Country" (Atkins)

A song we played which I liked was "Life Goes On". I don't have the lyrics to it anymore but I remember the chorus went: "Life goes on and on/Being weak, being strong/Based around the sun/Burning on ever long."

After the gig Kevin Coyne said apart from being crazy, we were one of the most exciting bands he had seen for a long time and would recommend us to someone he knew at Virgin Records – the label his band was signed to – so without any hesitation I gave him my telephone number.

"Bloody hell, Kev! That would be brilliant, mate." I said to him.

Kevin was really nice to us so I was saddened to hear of his death in 2004 but when we met him he liked his drink. I later found out that he, like most musicians, had a serious drink problem which led to a nervous breakdown. He moved to Germany in the mid-eighties and never lost his passion for music. He was a really good blues guitarist and singer and somebody I will never forget, even though I only met him once.

Rightly so, in a couple of days I received a phone call from an A&R guy and he asked us to arrange transport down to London so they could see us play live. I booked us into the famous Marquee Club at short notice for expenses only and we had to open up for Polydor recording band Dirty Tricks.

So two weeks passed between the phone call and the gig. When it was time for us to make our way down to London, I got really nervous. We arrived a little late and when we got there we saw Dirty Tricks on stage doing a soundcheck. When they had finished running through a song we asked them if we could get our gear set up; they didn't reply. They just smiled at each other and carried on messing around until it left us with only ten minutes before the club was due to open. By now, our patience started to get a little thin and Mick shouted at them to unplug their guitars and get off stage.

"You better bloody well hurry up or I'll do it for you!" Mick shouted.

Pete went off to fetch the promoter but it was too late, Ken grabbed their drummer and Mick unplugged all their guitars and then their roadies took offence to this and fists started flying.

"Here we go again", I said out loud to myself.

By this point the promoter came in with Pete and they broke it up.

We had to kick off without doing a soundcheck but soon got into our stride and we played a great set to a packed crowd and we even got three encores. Lemmy came backstage with his son to congratulate us on playing such a good show. Lionel Morton was also in the changing room but didn't speak to us so he must have been with the other band Dirty Tricks. Lionel was massive in the sixties singing; he played guitar with The Four Pennies, they had a huge hit with a song called "Juliet" in 1964 and he was at one time married to actress Julia Foster. And the resident DJ came up to us, raving about how much he liked the gig. The only trouble was the guy from Virgin Records didn't show up. Just our bloody luck …

Do you remember Dirty Tricks? They were a good band but they acted like a bunch of arrogant tossers to us. They played a mixture of Led Zeppelin and UFO so they played a style of gritty hard blues rock. They released their final album in 1977 and haven't been heard of since. It's a case where another bites the dust. I know that one of their ex-members is in a successful Led Zeppelin tribute band called Stairway To Zeppelin. I think we wiped the floor with them on the night; we definitely played better.

We had loads of great times; Lion didn't reach its full potential as a rock band but we knew how to have fun and that's part of the game. One night Pete got up to his own dirty tricks on the way home from the Black Rock club in Derby, which by the way had some lovely groupies; he told Ken the driver to stop the van, on doing so Pete started to take off all his clothes.

"What the bloody hell are you doin'?" I said to Pete. "Are you mad?!"

He folded them neatly and placed them on the passenger seat. He then told Ken to put his headlights on and he started jogging naked down the country lanes in front of our slow moving van. You should have seen the look on people's faces on the other side of the road.

I said to Ken: "Pete is an absolute nutcase but he is bloody funny."

We later teamed up with another new manager named Stewart Fraisse who really took a shine to us. He told us he was once a DJ and had worked in America. He proudly showed us photographs of himself with a host of different stars, including one of him and Jimi Hendrix, and he promised us loads of gigs up North where he was based. Stewart was a good guy – one of few in the business. I liked him. I'd worked with that many managers – some of them great, some of them not so great – that I didn't know who to trust any more. I'd had a lot of knockbacks but with Stewart he knew how to treat bands with respect and to boost their confidence.

One weekend he invited us up to Gentle Giants studios in Leeds to record two of my new songs: one was called "On The Wheel", which I co-wrote with Harry, and the other was called "Journey" which turned out quite well. Unfortunately, they never saw the light of day, and nor did we because we basically locked ourselves into the studio for the weekend. They had a 16-track mixer which for us was the height of glamour. "On The Wheel" can actually be heard on the Budgie fan album by Pete Boot's band The Hole In The Head Gang.

One funny road trip I remember is when we played The Penny Farthing club up North in the beautiful Lake District. Because it was a long way from Birmingham we used to make a weekend break of it and book ourselves into a nearby hotel. The Lake District is one of the most attractive areas of England so it was always a coup that we'd have a gig booked up there, it meant we could take a well-earned break.

The day after the gig we had a few beers by one of the lakes until we got bored and a little drunk; Bruno and Harry decided to play a round of golf at a small course nearby and the rest of us – Pete, Johnny England, Big M, Mick and myself – decided to hire a rowing boat. Pete took the oars (bad decision) and we headed out into the large lake. Half way across I said I needed a piss so I told Pete to drop me off on one of the small islands, in doing so I relieved myself but turning around I realised they had rowed away and left me in the middle of this fucking big lake.

"Where the hell are you goin' … you bastards!" I shouted to them.

For a while I panicked, but I heard laughter coming from the other side of the island and so I ran through the wild bushes and rhododendrons until I could see them. I waded out up to my waist hiding behind a big overhanging tree until they got closer and then I grabbed the side of the boat and pushed it up and down until it turned over and they all fell in the water.

"Oh, c'mon Al", Pete said. "We're only having a laugh."

"Not at my expense, you're not", I said.

When we got back to the hiring platform, the people waiting in the queue were in stitches, laughing at the sight of us. We looked like five drowned rats.

Over the next couple of years we became more motivated because we changed from being a part time weekend band to a monster full time hard rock band with a huge following all over the UK. I'm being serious when I say this: we had quite a lot of fans through our busy gig schedule and strong word of mouth. But like the first few line-ups of Judas Priest we just could not secure a record deal.

Also, things were getting crazier on the road because Mick, our sound engineer, used to play pranks which got a little scary: he'd plant small homemade bombs on stage and set them off when we least expected it (no bullshit). He tipped a large tin of talcum powder all over Pete one night while he performed his drum solo and then turned a strobe light on him and it looked fantastic but Pete didn't think so and threw his Gong beater at Mick; it missed him and smashed a light above his head and the glass shards fell down the back of his neck. There was blood everywhere.

Lion also played a charity gig for Possessed after Mick Reeves, whom I had played with in Sugar Stack, got killed in a motorway accident. It was held at the Coach and Horse, a rock pub in Hatley Heath, West Bromwich. We played on the Sunday lunchtime and it was a packed house, some other band played on the night but I can't remember which band it was. This would have been about November or December, 1976. Robert Plant played on the next night and landed in a helicopter on the Menzies High School playing fields next to the venue. The school was later made famous in the film »Clockwise« with the Monty Python legend John Cleese playing the headmaster.

As you know, we rode the storm of the punk era and soldiered on even when the spotty kids called us boring old farts and rock dinosaurs, but we still had the fight in us like the time we played at The Ford Green Hotel in Leeds, which Stewart had booked us into. The Sex Pistols had played there the week before us and there was very little trouble from them, but on the night that we gigged there, things turned very nasty indeed.

It all started when some drunken bearded Hell's Angel threw a large glass ashtray at Pete while he performed his drum solo, which fortunately just missed his head and smashed against the backdrop.

"What the fuck was that for?!" Pete yelled with the angriest look on his face.

The Hell's Angels guy ended up getting booted out of the club by one of the bouncers that worked there. So Pete, Mick, and myself decided to chase after the bastard and seek our revenge the only way we knew how. The bouncer bolted through the exit doors and left us on the car park alone to sort him out and he threatened to take all three of us on in a fight, it sounds very much one-sided but the huge Hell's Angel guy was built like a brick shit house and laid into us like a crazed bull running at a Matador.

"I'm not fucking scared of you lot", he said.

I was honestly quite scared for my life. Hell's Angels were terrifying. We all heard about the 1969 Rolling Stones gig in Altamont, San Francisco, when the Hell's Angels provided security. One fan was killed by a member of the gang and most commentators considered that to be the end of the Hippie era. Well, I was sacred this Hell's Angels guy would kill one of us.

"Fuck you!" one of the lads screamed.

Mick hit the guy with a right hook and put all of his 20 stone bulk behind it. The guy sank to the floor as Pete and myself dived in to give him the good pasting he deserved, but it didn't finish there because his gang of fellow Hell's Angels had started another fight inside the club which later spilled outside onto the car park. When they saw their buddy beaten up they went crazy and would have killed us if they could have caught us, but we locked ourselves in the changing room so they decided to take it out on our tour bus; they knifed the tyres, smashed the windscreen and basically smashed whatever else they could. The police came, eventually, and moved them on but we couldn't go anywhere so had to sleep on some cold hard benches in the clubs billiard room for the night.

The next morning we got the bus fixed up by the AA car service company which cost us all our gig money, and the police came back and told us to cancel the other two gigs we were booked to play in Leeds because they didn't want any more trouble, so we made our way back home down the motorway. (Just another crazy night of rock and roll!)

Sadly, Lion split up in late '78. It was an amicable end. Harry was the first to quit due to his day job; turning pro is always a problem when you have the security of a job to pay the mortgage where as being on the road away from your family and not looking beyond the next few gigs is a tough life. Lion had played together for a few years but still hadn't got the security of a record deal, which would have helped us especially when we had quite a big following and had the confidence of a major band.

We auditioned guitarists to take Harry's place but none of them seemed to fit in with our plans, or was as good as Harry. I had now started to write a lot of new songs but Bruno and Pete wanted to continue with our old setlist, which we had played for a long time so I quit to go back to doing studio work on my new material. Unfortunately, the band never got back together again. I always thought in hindsight that we should have tried this and we should have done that, but some things are meant to be, just look at The Beatles: they were turned down by every record company in the UK but eventually they proved them all wrong, a lot of bands have been in that position where you know how good you are but it's down to right time, right place sometimes.

Unfortunately, I never got to work with Harry Tonks again; in 1980 he had a major accident at his day job and wasn't able to pick up a guitar for the next ten years. He was a brilliant guitarist and what happened to him was a small tragedy but at least he recovered.

The annoying thing is: Zoom kept a boatload of stuff of the band, like pictures, live tapes from shows, ticket stubs and such. I've asked him for them a zillion times and he keeps saying they are in a suitcase under his old bed at his mother's and one day he will visit her and sort it out.

One of the saddest aspects about Lion's demise was that it was the last time I worked with Bruno in a full time band; we had become like brothers over the years.

Bruno eventually moved down to the South West where he plays in a tribute band called The Cadence. They're really good and have a website: www.thecadence.co.uk.

Bruno Stapenhill: "I don't really see Al. I speak to him on the phone quite regularly. He rings me or I ring him once a month or whatever. He did surprise me one summer. I remember I was sitting in the back garden and he came down South with his missus and the kids and he nipped in to see me. That was the first time he'd ever visited me here. I keep in touch with him on the phone. We're still good mates, I've got a lot of time for Allan – nice bloke. I mean, he's a little bit older than me and he's stuck at it. Normally people of our age, they've already made it back in the sixties and seventies and they're just carry on playing what they've already done but fool to retirement at his age for going for it the way he's going for it."

Chapter 5
Off The Road (1979-1983)

This period saw me coming off the road for the first time in 15 long years to concentrate on my songwriting. I decided I didn't want to be in bands ever again. I'd had enough of them; I'd jump in a band every couple of years and got nothing for it. A quick recap of my career proves that I'd been in more than enough: The Medallians, The Reaction, Blue Condition, Sugar Stack, The Jug Blues Band, Judas Priest and Lion. Any less persistent person would have quit years ago. Like the Lone Ranger, I decided to go solo, ride the horse on my own and see what the wilderness has to offer.

I started spending months at a time putting down demos of songs that I had written with producer/songwriter Phil Savage at the helm. I wrote probably hundreds of songs and laid down just as many demos. Not all of them were great, some of them were probably dreadful but you don't improve if you don't try. It was really good experience for me and helped me learn the craft of songwriting which I had never fully concentrated on before because I had too many band commitments. I used to write songs whenever I found a spare hour but this time around I promised myself that I'd spend days, weeks, even months, just scribbling down lyrics.

Phil owned Outlaw Studios in Birmingham and he was a great help to me and other local musicians. Phil was once the bass player in Sundance who, if you remember, were the

Phil Savage and myself in conversation at Outlaw Studios.

band that drummer Alan Moore had left Priest to join back in the early seventies. Outlaw Studios was very well known and used by most Birmingham bands, including Black Sabbath and Judas Priest.

The songs I had started writing were very varied in style because I tried to knock down the barriers of rock/metal music and explore more pop/rock and even acoustic ballads. So I recorded an acoustic set of songs on my own with titles like "Shadows", "Natural Destination", "Why", "Feelings" and "Nothing But A Heartache", to name just a few. And then, I recorded a heavy rock set with the help of lots of friends including some old faces like Jim Perry (drums), Harry Tonks (guitar) and Bruno. People like Kevin Knott (guitar), Kate Shanks (vocals) and Bob Slater (bass) from Alvin Stardust's band also gave me a helping hand, which was very kind of them. Pete Robinson turned up one day to put some drums down. Pete – or "Plug" as he was known – was one time drummer for Robert Plant.

Another group recording at the time was called The Killjoys and featured Kevin Rowland on vocals. Dave Corke dropped by one day to see me and liked the sound of Kevin's voice so much so he became their manager. After a line-up change and a name change to Dexy's Midnight Runners they were heading for the big time.

After I had finished recording all my songs, I asked Phil if I could settle up my recording fees and he said someone had already paid it for me but he wasn't allowed to tell me who. (Whoever it was – thanks!)

I remember one day I bumped into Kenny Downing as Judas Priest were just coming out of Outlaw Studios after recording a couple of demos; one of them was a cover song called "Race With The Devil", originally by Gun, and the other was Fleetwood Mac's "Green Manalishi (With The Two-Pronged Crown)". I asked Kenny if he would guest on one of my songs but he declined saying contractual problems stopped him doing so. (How times had changed)?

On a personal front, both Linda and myself got day jobs. I worked at a Ford Car Garage in charge of the goods inwards department. Linda worked in an office at an industrial components company. We bought our own private house and everything was good; we lived at Crockford Road on the border of West Bromwich and Wednesbury Town. Our lovely daughter was in primary school and things seemed to be going well. I was temporarily happy in the day job and very content in my home life.

However, after a couple of years idling around and missing the music scene (although I was still writing songs on my acoustic guitar) my weight plummeted to nearly 14 stone and I lazily let my hair grow back to shoulder length. My beard too was long and bushy and the overall state of my health started to fail, especially as I was smoking and drinking so much. Maybe my subconscious was telling me that this wasn't the life for me? Truthfully, I've never been a depressive type of person. I am always positive and always will be in everything I do. Frustrated, yes, at times, but I put my heart and soul into everything and know something good will happen.

But at this particular juncture, I was beginning to feel a little restrained. Of course, I was thankful for my wife and daughter but the big problem was I found it really difficult not to get bored in the trappings of a nine to five existence, so consequently I drank more and smoked more. I craved the excitement of the music scene, the noise of a crowd and the thrill of a gig. In the old days when I was on the road, I had something to occupy my mind; I was energetic on stage and didn't have time to think about eating and even though I was writing songs and making demos, it wasn't enough to stop me from piling on the pounds. I mean, sitting down playing the guitar is hardly a very active job. People started to notice that my waistline had extended. My mates would make a few jokes about it but I let them pass.

"Bloody hell, Al, I can tell you've not been gigging so much. You've put a bit of weight on, ain't ya?" one of them would say.

"Yeah, well I'm getting old. It happens to us all."

One night I collapsed with chest pains and thought this is it, my life is over. Fortunately when the emergency ambulance came, they said I only had a chest infection but my doctor gave me a warning that next time it could be my heart and so I needed to cut back on my habits and exercise more. It scared the hell out of me. I never put my health first; in fact, I never even thought about my health. I just ate and drank whatever I wanted to do, despite the amount of calories. There were no health guidelines on foods like there are today.

I decided to get myself sorted. I took the doctor's advice and at the behest of my wife I started jogging and gave up on the cigarettes. My weight dropped down to a healthy size, my breathing improved and I was happy again. I would run for miles at a time. Friends would notice me running in the local park and egg me on like I was Sylvester Stallone as Rocky Balboa or somebody like that. It was quite funny, actually.

One year later, I was down to my old weight of around ten to eleven stone and ran my first 26 mile marathon. My confidence had improved dramatically and I came out of that depression feeling renewed and re-energised. My head steaming with fresh ideas for songs and with bouts of enthusiasm I just had to have another musical outlet. Musicians are like children; we get excited about something and want to tell as many people as possible.

Even though I was out of the scene, as it were, I was still interested in how Judas Priest had progressed in the music scene. By the end of the decade, Priest were becoming more successful and more famous in the UK and especially in the USA.

Those first three albums for CBS blew me away; they are still powerful albums and very dark and moody. The first CBS album »Sin After Sin« laid down some really heavy songs: "Dissident Aggressor" and "Sinner" are absolute stone cold classics and it's clear where American bands of the eighties like Metallica and Anthrax took their ideas from. For that album, Priest used the delicate drumming skills of Simon Phillips who now plays drums in the AOR band Toto. Before being hired by Priest, Phillips had worked with many artists including the great Scottish band Nazareth. But Phillips didn't want to go on tour with the band and that's when a guy called Les Binks came into the picture. »Stained Class« was released in 1978 and like its predecessor it was a big Top 40 hit in the UK. »Stained Class« was the first album to feature Les Binks' drumming talent and I thought he sounded bloody good especially on the thrash metal anthem "Exciter", which has since become a classic song in the band's arsenal.

In 1979, they released their fifth album »Killing Machine«, their third release for CBS. In the States, they had to change the name of the album to »Hell Bent For Leather« because they thought it was too controversial and would damage potentially high sales. The same thing happened with Sabbath's second album; it was meant to be titled »War Pigs« but their US label felt that because of the Vietnam War such a title would be offensive to the American public so they changed it to »Paranoid« but it was too late to change the cover. »Killing Machine« features the blistering heavy metal monster "Delivering The Goods" and the brilliantly catchy "Hell Bent For Leather".

They had a hit single with the Queen-type anthem "Take On The World", which reached Number 14 in the UK charts and it was really funny to see them on »Top Of The Pops«. They were also breaking into the Japanese market in a big way. Not long after the release of »Killing Machine« they issued their first live release: the bloody awesome »Unleashed In The East« which captured their growing fanbase in East Asia, a part of the world that would give me some success as well in years to come. The album was a big chart hit, reaching Number Ten here in the UK, which is quite rare for a live album as most fans prefer studio recordings. Another really great live album which was a rare UK hit is Motörhead's classic »No Sleep Till Hammersmith«.

The audio quality of that album has always been debatable; some critics called it "Unleashed In The Studio" because it doesn't exactly sound like a live recording, it's a bit too polished. But it quickly became an instant classic and is rightly regarded as one of the all time great live metal albums. It was the first time they worked with producer Tom Allom who would stay with the band for the next decade producing a total of eight Priest albums, a couple of them are famous masterpieces.

Yet again another drummer leaves the band; the departure of Les Binks annoyed a lot of Priest fans because he was such a great talent on the drum stool. He pounded those bloody skins like nobody else. He left in July 1979, right before a US tour. The band had to find a quick replacement and they found one in none other than Dave Holland. I couldn't believe it when I found out that Priest had hired him as their sticksman. He was a good drummer, don't get me wrong, but he was more melodic than heavy. Some fans complained when the band took "Exciter" out of the setlist; the rumour was that Dave allegedly could not play double bass. It has been said that Binks was a bit too technical and clever for the kind of music Priest wanted to make on future recordings so Dave was right up their street, so to speak. He definitely had a more simplistic yet catchy drumming style than Binks'.

With everything that was happening in Priest's world – money, a big record deal, fame and success in the States, Japan and elsewhere, my own little world in West Brom was far from glamorous.

After losing weight and get myself-esteem back to where it should be, my enthusiasm had waned dramatically because there are too many people out there not willing to help you and putting you down when you're trying to make a name for yourself. I just wish I was as mentally strong and knowledgeable back then as I am now. I've learned to take everything with a pinch of salt and if somebody tries to put you down, just ignore them and move on. Look to the future, that's what I say.

I remember saying to my wife one night: "Jesus, I can't believe that after all these years nothing has happened and look at my old band."

"It's okay," she said, "something good will happen. You just have to stick at it." She always did try to make me feel good, even at the most frustrating periods.

And that's exactly what I did – stick at it. I've never given up, not completely, even at the most frustrating of times. I've just taken long breaks from bands and moved on to something else …

The rock scene was changing dramatically and before I move on to the details of my next escapade, I want to briefly take you through this transitional period in music …

Gothic rock music started to become really popular at the tail end of the 1970s. Those bands were definitely influenced by some of my favourite artists like David Bowie, Alice Cooper and Lou Reed. A lot of the Goth bands liked to dress up so in that respect they stole some ideas from the glam rock bands of my youth like T Rex and Slade.

Perhaps my biggest complaint about the Goth rock period of the late seventies and early eighties was that they were just a bit too miserable and drab. Sure, I liked a lot of the music but hard rock/heavy metal bands know how to have fun. Life is all about having fun! At least that's what I've been led to believe. And if you can make a living from being in a band whilst having the best time of your life, I'd say go for it and don't be so bloody moody. But then again, the Goth bands were very literary and they seemed a bit too middle class for my tastes.

A complete contrast to Goth music was UB40; they played their first gig on February 9th, 1979, at the Hare and Hounds pub in Kings Heath, Birmingham and became one of the most successful reggae pop bands of all time (selling over 55 million records!) It goes to show that the Midlands have always been producing good top selling bands and not just in rock and roll and heavy metal but bloody reggae too!

Now, I did become a big fan of the famed New Wave Of British Heavy Metal (NWOBHM) which commenced around '79 or as my old mate Dennis Stratton says 'Never Work On A Bank Holiday Monday.' I always found that quite amusing, Dennis has a strong sense of humour.

It wasn't a localised movement; bands started all over the country. NWOBHM legends like Samson, Girlschool, Blitzkrieg, Venom and local lads Diamond Head were just a handful of bands to make it big during the period 1979/80. But the big three – Iron Maiden, Def Leppard and Saxon – had long lasting success especially the former two who made it big abroad. There were lots of bands that didn't quite make it big after some initial periods of success: Tygers Of Pan Tang, Demon, Angel Witch, Vardis and Elixir. The list actually goes on and on …

A lot of those bands were quite amateurish but that's the appeal of the movement. Those guys just picked up an instrument and played. Isn't that how bands are supposed to start? From scratch.

Those bands represented the third phase of heavy metal. Phase one was bands like Black Sabbath, Led Zeppelin and fellow blues rock bands like Cream that played a much heavier style of music which nobody had ever heard before. I'm being simplistic here and I know those bands never refer to themselves as heavy metal bands but whether they like it or not, that's quite obviously where metal began. And phase two was Judas Priest, Scorpions and Motörhead and the rest.

If only Lion had stayed together a little longer – who knows? Maybe be we would have blazed through the NWOBHM. I think Lion would have fitted in perfectly with the New Wave bands like Saxon. We had a hard working class do-it-yourself sound which all of the New Waves bands had. What those bands were doing is what I had been doing for the past decade: getting a band together and working my arse off playing to as little and as many people as possible. Luckily for the NWOBHM bands, the punk scene was fading and I think a lot of rock fans wanted something different. It was the long-haired metal heads against the skinhead punks.

Between 1978 and 1981, Iron Maiden's singer was Paul Di'Anno – a tough hard drinking and hard smoking Essex bloke who would scare the shit out of your grandma just by raising an eyebrow. I have often compared my vocal style to that of Di'Anno, a gritty and harsh sounding voice. It's as if we've both drunk far too much whiskey and smoked too many cigarettes … which quite clearly we have! Paul has always been a volatile character and in the end Steve Harris, Maiden's main man, had to replace him. When ex-Samson singer Bruce Dickinson came into the picture, Maiden quickly became a top selling band; it was the same with Priest when Halford joined. Dickinson has since become one of the greatest frontmen in metal. His first album singing in Iron Maiden was »The Number Of Beast« which is rightly considered to be a heavy metal masterpiece; you can't deny the sheer strength and relentlessness of songs like "Run To The Hills", "The Prisoner" and "Children Of The Damned". Even now when I listen to that album it still inspires me after all these years. When Dickinson joined Maiden they moved away from being a kind of punk rock band to a fully fleshed out heavy metal band. The hits rolled on and just like Kiss the stage sets got bigger and more exciting.

As with Motörhead, Judas Priest have often been wrongly called a NWOBHM band. Motörhead's first record came out in the mid-seventies, not long after »Rocka Rolla« was released. I think Priest definitely inspired the heavier New Wave bands like Saxon but don't forget »Rocka Rolla«, their debut album, was issued back in '74 so that was a full five years before the NWOBHM began its short life. Even bands like Venom and Blitzkrieg are Priest fans. I think the fact that Priest had a profound influence on the NWOBHM showed how far they'd come in terms of their success and respectability even though their record sales were not that high at the time.

In 1980, Priest released their most famous album »British Steel« which spawned the hit singles "Breaking The Law" and "Living After Midnight". Both songs have become anthems for the genre and the band quickly became one of the world's top selling metal acts. They even toured with Iron Maiden three times in the early 1980s although both bands became rivals when Maiden's success quickly eclipsed Priest's.

I think one of the best bands to come out of that movement was Saxon; Biff is one of heavy metal's most underrated frontmen and Saxon are most definitely an underrated band. I think if Biff stopped making music (and I hope he doesn't) people would look at Saxon's back catalogue in a whole different light. I remember hearing "Wheels Of Steel" for the first time – it blew my bollocks off! It became the heavy metal anthem for the NWOBHM years. Great albums like »Denim And Leather« and »The Strong Arm Of The Law« have lost none of their appeal even after all this time, more than 25 years. It's a shame Saxon never made it big in the States; even in the mid-1980s with some commercial sounding albums, they were trying to crack America but nothing really happened. The Americans just did not take to Saxon (and Motörhead!) the way they had to Maiden and Leppard. For a long time Leppard and the United States were stuck together like super glue. And it's a crying shame that Saxon have been ignored in the States. But then things happen for a reason and if they had made it big in America they may have imploded and the great albums that they have made in recent years like »Lionheart« may not have seen the light of day.

Speaking of Def Leppard, although I like them, they're not really a heavy metal band and I've heard Joe Elliot say the same thing often with a frustrated tone in his voice. The Americans really took a liking to Leppard more so than the UK and I think Leppard have been slightly resentful about that. Every band wants success in their home country!

The New Wave Of British Heavy Metal didn't last that long; like most movements in music, it was a flash in the pan but its influence on other bands was huge. Look at bands in the States like Slayer, Anthrax and Metallica. Lars Ulrich of Metallica is a famous NWOBHM fan; he collects the records and memorabilia and could probably talk to you for hours about Diamond Head. Metallica have even covered songs by Diamond Head on their album »Garage Inc«: "It's Electric", "Helpless" and "The Prince". I'm sure Brian Tatler was pleased to receive the royalty cheque for that!

Because of tenacious bands like Maiden and Priest, heavy metal became really popular throughout the eighties, like rap and hip hop (unfortunately) is popular now. Suddenly, magazines and fanzines were published and if I could have chosen a time to be in a heavy metal band it would have been the 1980s. Kerrang! had a massive influence on heavy metal, promoting, reviewing and featuring bands of all types as long as they rocked. Whenever there was a retrospective on Priest in a magazine, I'd get a mention or two, which was quite cool.

Judas Priest would feature on the cover of Kerrang! several times over the years and after the release of the successful »British Steel« album they became known as the Metal Gods, named after a song on that very album. They have often said that calling themselves the Metal Gods was not intentional; they simply wrote a song about the fictional Metal Gods and then the critics gave them the title and ever since they have probably never been written about as simply Judas Priest. It's a great marketing tool, that's for sure.

I remember when they released »Point Of Entry« in 1981 and were criticised for sounding too commercial; it was as if they were trying to attract an audience that listened to Toto or Journey. I think Priest have always been brilliant at creating really powerful metal songs that have memorable melodies even when they've been knocked down for it. After that, they released the classic record »Screaming For Vengeance« which features the metal anthems "The Hellion/Electric Eye", "You've Got Another Thing Coming" and the thrash metal monster "Riding On The Wind". There was so much competition in the metal world in the eighties that Judas Priest really had to exhaust their creative tendencies and I suppose »Screaming For Vengeance« proved to the NWOBHM bands that Priest could still come up with the goods.

I kept an attentive eye on the NWOBHM bands and many of the other metal bands in its wake and like every other crazy heavy metal nut I read Kerrang! like it was my personal bible. And to see metal troopers like Maiden having so much success was inspiring but it also made me a little envious.

On a more personal note, it was late '82 and my marriage had started to crumble and my father had been very ill with pneumonia – the disease that had killed my little sister Sheila many years before. I was heartbroken.

He did eventually get over it but it had left him weak and frail and he looked a lot older than his 69 years and one night I got the phone call that everyone dreads: "Your father has been taken into hospital with a suspected heart attack."

I made my way to our local hospital but when I got there they told me he had not been admitted so I rushed around to my parent's house to see what was going on. When I arrived, there was a policeman standing by the doorway and he let me in when I told him I was the son.

When I entered the living room I saw my father lying motionless on the floor with a doctor kneeling over him writing something on a pad. My mother was in the kitchen screaming hysterically and my brother was trying to calm her down.

I knelt down and held him in my arms and kissed his cold forehead, I was too late to say my goodbyes and I felt a lump come to my throat, I ran outside and cried and cried …

I walked back home alone and all the memories of my childhood with my dad and myself came flooding back. I told everyone the terrible news. Looking back, the strange thing about it was that I never comforted my mother but I think I was in a state of shock.

Six months later, my mother moved to Kent to live with my sister and my marriage finally folded.

Just like the song "Crossroads" that Robert Johnson had written, I had arrived at my own crossroads.

It was time to move on … And I decided that my life needed some big changes.

Chapter 6
Travels In Europe (1984-1988)

After a bitter divorce from Linda, whom I had been married to for fifteen years, I decided it was time for a big change in my life and so I moved over to Europe in late 1984. It was a drastic decision but it changed my life.

I spent some time in Yugoslavia – which has now become Croatia – in a small town called Porec where my friend Anita, a singer from Prague, was performing with her Czechoslovakian band through the summer months. I needed to get away from everything back home and take a long break and this was just the place to be: I was with the sea, the sun, the booze and you could eat like a King for only a few pounds.

My first encounter with the ocean was a sore point; I looked at a group of kids diving off the end of an old wooden jetty and I thought I'll have a go at that so I stripped off, ran along the jetty and dived in to the ocean headfirst but as my body slid along the sea floor, I felt a great deal of pain. When I got out of the water I was covered in what looked like black needles under my skin. I had them in my arms, my knees and my feet.

"What the hell is all this!" I shouted.

I hadn't noticed that everyone was being a bit cautious. I looked around and saw that everybody was wearing rubber sandals because the seabed was covered in dead sea-urchins; when they die, their feelers set hard, just like needles. Well, everyone found it funny apart from me; it was never like this at Blackpool, I thought.

I had fun and was relaxed and even got up one night and played with Anita's band, I jammed a couple of blues songs with them, one was the Albert King classic "Born Under A Bad Sign" which was also covered by Cream. And I have to say it felt good to be playing guitar and singing again; I even had a couple of German guys from the audience come up to me later asking for more tunes. It was a great night and I got shit-faced from all the cheap booze. This is the life, I thought.

Anita was a beautiful young woman who I had met some years before and had kept in touch with through our shared musical tastes and she was the attention of all the young men in Porec, especially from an Italian TV producer named Guy. He really pissed me off; he would always interrupt us when we sat down talking and it even came to a head one night when I threatened to hit him for being so fucking rude.

It had been a good time and it left me with some good memories but I felt it was time to move on and my next port of call would be in the South of France staying with my old mate John who I hadn't seen in years. He was living in a caravan at a place called Sete. I have travelled the world over but the South of France made a big impression on me and it's a place where I would like to live in my old age when I retire.

John was a lovely bloke and looked a lot like Frank Zappa; I enjoyed my stay with him a lot over the coming months but it took me a while to adjust to living next door to a nudist colony, and I just wondered what my parents would have thought about all those people wondering round stark-bollock naked. When John was younger he was in the marines but ended up an alcoholic and one night he had no booze so he tried drinking rocket fuel as a substitute. He ended up in a coma for a few days and it left him with a permanent stammer. He was a real character and never touched the demon drink again; he always liked a regular nightcap of a cup of Earl Grey Tea before bedtime.

John had some bad news reach him one day: his mum, who lived back in England, was dying of cancer so he headed back home with me in tow. At Paris, John turned left back to the UK but I went right through Germany and into Holland to stay with my old friend Shaun who made his humble abode in Rotterdam. Shaun was a big fan of Lion and followed us everywhere on our gigs in the seventies when he lived in England; he and his then wife Sue became big friends of ours until they split up and he moved over to Holland. I wondered if their liberal lifestyle had anything to do with that?! I wouldn't see Shaun for over 15 years until he flew over to England to attend the funeral of our mutual friend Cosha Melia; Ian Hill was also at the funeral. It was good to meet up but not under such sad circumstances.

It was here in the Netherlands where I met Inga who I thought was very attractive. Suffice to say we became instant soul mates, she lived in a town in the east of Holland called Enschede, which was close to the German border and this is where I stayed for a while ...

When I was living out of a suitcase travelling around Europe in the mid-eighties, I fancied myself as a bohemian, writing songs and playing the acoustic guitar like Bob Dylan or the famous Belgian gypsy guitarist Django Reinhardt who inspired many guitarist including Tony Iommi. I was bored back home and had nothing to motivate my creative pulses but in Europe, I felt totally free.

I still loved heavy metal even though I couldn't afford to buy the records anymore. And I guess deep down I still harboured the ambition that one day I would make my first album. Through the media I learned that Judas Priest had become one of the biggest selling bands in America. After releasing big sellers like »Defenders Of The Faith« they sold out arenas like Madison Square Garden in New York and had a particularly strong fan base in Southern states like Texas, which was surprising. Those states are famously right winged and you wouldn't think a band with Priest's sound and image would make an indelible impact there in the right way.

I remember one day in 1984, just before I moved to Europe, Kenny actually pulled up next to me in his Porsche as I waited at the bus stop in the pouring rain on West Bromwich High Street. He offered me a ride home; I hadn't seen him for a couple of years and was well impressed with his leather attire and his flash car. He had certainly come a long way since we last played together back in the early seventies. When we arrived back at my place, I invited him in and we sat down with a coffee and talked about the old times and about music. I played him a couple of my new songs on my acoustic guitar; he told me that Priest were thinking of taking a new direction with their next album and using guitar synthesizers and I told him that sounded interesting but I didn't think their hardened fans would appreciate such a dramatic change in the band's music. We shook hands and said goodbye and good luck; I didn't see him again for about three years.

Then, in 1986, Judas Priest released the album »Turbo« (which was originally intended to be a double album called 'Twin Turbos') and my thoughts were correct: it was great to see them experiment and try something new and more melodic but most of their fans were very critical of the album. However, since its release, »Turbo« has become something of a cult classic amongst metal fans but like many fans I prefer their harder, edgier stuff.

The great Texan blues rock trio ZZ Top had huge success using guitar synthesizers on the »Eliminator« album. I think Priest wanted that kind of success but it never happened.

Their success, for some bizarre reason, has never been that of Iron Maiden's and I think Priest really craved a Number One or a big stadium tour. I remember one day seeing a picture of them in some magazine, this was during the »Turbo« era, and it was also obvious how much Priest had become influenced by the bands they influenced; they looked not like a British heavy metal band from the industrial grounds of the Black Country but a hair metal band from L.A. Halford's hair had gotten much bigger and the whole look of the band changed quite dramatically. They still dressed in leather but a more extravagant kind and they looked pampered and quite ridiculous.

The thing is they became so big in the States that their huge stage sets would not fit into the small UK venues like Wolverhampton Civic Hall or even the famous Hammersmith Odeon. Consequently, British fans became pissed off with the band and the music press gave them a bit of a telling off for not visiting ye old Blighty. The were playing venues in the States that held a capacity of 15,000 to 20,000 people so it must have been disheartening to come back home and play to less than a third of that. As well as the States, they toured other parts of the world like the Far East and parts of Europe but in Britain Iron Maiden ruled as the biggest metal band. That must have pissed the band off good and proper, especially as Priest gave them a big help by inviting them on tour in 1980, 1981 and 1982.

For some reason or another, I came to my senses and realized how much I needed to get back into music again. Like I said before, maybe there was a subconscious desire in me to continue to chase my long desired dream? My dream was to make albums that people would enjoy listening to. I wanted to be remembered. Also, I just wanted to enjoy music the way I used to. And so after a couple of years wandering around Europe like a vagabond, I headed back home; West Brom is where I belong. But I couldn't stop kicking myself up the backside for all those wasted years that I had let slip by me. It was now time to catch up on what I had missed. It was at this point that the hard work began, so I eventually decided to go home to England and get back to my music that I was missing now and asked my Dutch girlfriend Inga if she would like to come back to West Bromwich to live with me.

On returning home alone, I bought an old Victorian town house right smack in the middle of West Bromwich and started renovating it. I turned one of the very large bedrooms into a studio with the help of two of my old buddies, Archie Cole and Snowy, who both said they had missed me. It was during the Christmas of 1986 when Inga came over to stay with me but something in me sensed she wouldn't take to living in England.

On her return to the Netherlands she phoned me and after some friendly banter she asked me to live with her. I said I would return and give it another try and so in March 1987, I went back to the Netherlands but this would be the end of our relationship because I just couldn't see myself living in Holland for the rest of my life; although it's a nice country with very friendly people, my heart and soul was back home in England. I also wanted to get my music career back on track.

On my way home, the plane was delayed at Schiphol Airport in Amsterdam because of bad storms over the English Channel so I sat at the bar in the airport lounge to drown my sorrows. It was about a two hour delay so you can imagine how many drinks I had – I almost fell off the bar stool!

It was only a small passenger plane and it was a terrible crossing to Birmingham Airport with the storm still hanging about, so I steadied my nerves with a couple of scotches on the flight. I couldn't wait until it landed in England and when the plane finally did land, I thought it was great to be back home although I staggered through the custom point with a terrible hangover. Christ, I must have looked awful with my long hair and beard, my scruffy rucksack on my back and my old acoustic guitar slung over my shoulder.

"Anything to declare, Sir?" one of the two customs reps said at the desk.

I replied with a simple "No".

"But you have come from a red area of Amsterdam to a green area."

"Well, I haven't been to Amsterdam."

"Do you take drugs?" the rep replied.

And like a moron I said: "Yeah, doesn't everybody?!"

Well, that did it because they searched through all my stuff and then took me around the back for a strip search. It was very embarrassing and when I saw one of the customs people putting on a pair of rubber gloves, I said: "Just try to stick your finger up my arse and I'll deck the pair of you."

They both started laughing and said: "Don't worry, we won't."

After I got dressed and put all my things back in my bag, I wondered off into the dark rainy night on my own to look for a taxi back to my new house in West Bromwich. I stayed on my own for a couple of years but it would be a couple more years until I properly gave music another go ...

Chapter 7
Heavy Thoughts: My Solo Career Begins (1989-2001)

By now, I had started writing songs again with the help of my friend and cousin John Emms who I hadn't seen in years. From this point onwards I basically managed myself although Priest's former manager and my friend Dave Corke was interested in my career and would offer some advice. Dave has always been great to me and I felt shitty that Priest had treated him so badly. I think there's a lot of Judas Priest diehards out there who don't quite realise the importance of Dave Corke in the band's career. It can certainly be said that if it wasn't for him, they would not have made it.

This was also the time I met a woman named Karen, the new love of my life, who would be my rock for years to come. Karen is a brilliant woman who makes me feel good about myself, instils me with confidence and kicks me up the arse when I need to be motivated. She's always there for me and is full of ideas. I've never met a woman like her; we met each other at the right time and I could not have been happier to have found such a wonderful person. I truly believe that we are soul mates. And that is, thankfully, about as emotional as I'm going to get. You're not reading a Bridget Jones novel.

Trust me, I'm not posing for the camera on this one!

John Emms had plenty of experience recording music and he was even a good hand on the business side of things too. We soon got down to work. He was a pleasure to work with and it was not long before I had written about a dozen songs; one of those songs was called "Wasted Years". An apt title on my life, I thought.

"Don't be so hard on yourself, Al", Karen would say.

"I can't help it", I'd reply. "I feel like I've done nothing for the past ten years – just wasted."

"Well, things will change. Just stick at it."

John is a great motivator and he really helped me get my career back on track after all those years away from the business. We even brought in a local heavy metal band to beef up the songs. The band was called Arcana who came from Walsall and featured my young cousin on bass, John's brother Pete, Paul May was the guitarist and co-producer, and on drums was John Brookes. I first met Pete and Paul on one of my many European travels in the eighties. I was in Zurich and ended up drinking in a pub called the Agatoo Place. On stage was none other than an English rock group that featured Pete Emms and Paul May. Anyway, when I decided to invite a band to perform on my new set of demos and eventually my first album, I saw Arcana play at the Portland club in Birmingham and decided that we would fit perfectly together; my bluesy voice would certainly match their hard rock seventies material.

I was really exited about performing again especially with these young musicians who had such great quality and a good attitude towards life and music. Because of my collaboration with those guys, I suddenly had a renewed sense of optimism and energy. I really wanted to make this work and they were behind me all the way, fuelling ideas and working as hard as they could. They had day jobs so it was tough for them to fit my recording schedule into their daily lives but we worked something out and I'm forever indebted to them for giving me a helping hand.

It wasn't long before we had some songs that were good enough to use on my first solo album so I sent the demos off to a contact of mine named Claus Kriebitzsh at an independent label called SPM (a division of Worldwide Records) in Berlin, Germany. I was actually offered record deals by three different companies but about a week after I sent off the demo to Claus; he replied offering me a one year deal, which is what I requested and I also requested that the CD mentions nothing of Judas Priest because I wanted this to be my own venture. I had used up all of my energy and money trying to get a record deal in the 1970s and there I was on my own after years of inactivity and I got myself a record deal. I think a lot of it had to do with my connection to Judas Priest. They were still a big band in Europe and toured the UK in 1988 in support of the album »Ram It Down«. It wasn't their best album but at least they came back to the UK to play some shows after spending most of the past few years in the States and elsewhere. Although I was shocked to hear that they had sold out by recording songs with the eighties pop producing trio Stock, Aitken and Waterman. I don't think a heavy metal band can get much lower than that. I'm glad those songs have never been released. It would be wrong.

And it was really at this point that I started to become known as: 'Al Atkins, ex-Judas Priest singer.' It became both a blessing and a curse but what it meant was that some of the old memorabilia from my years in the band would prove to be quite valuable to serious collectors. In 1993, Record Collector magazine stated that a 1964 Burns guitar that I had used during my tenure in Judas Priest was worth a whooping £1,900! I couldn't believe it when I read that price tag.

Me during the recording of »Judgement Day«, my first solo album in 1989.

I suppose the other positive aspect of being constantly referred to as the 'ex-singer of Judas Priest' is that I managed to make an album and get some press attention in some of the big UK magazines like Kerrang! and Metal Hammer. Some of my demos were reviewed before my first album was released which was rather cool. I remember Garry Sharpe-

Young's review of a demo I sent to him a year before for the page spread Demolition in the magazine Metal Forces. He gave me a rave write-up saying how great the song "Nothing Lost" is. He wrote: "Allan has one of those timeless British voices ala Glenn Hughes or Paul Rodgers that drips with feeling." That line made me chuckle. I grew up listening to those guys and to be mentioned in the same breath as them is amazing but to be compared to them is, of course, very flattering but also slightly embarrassing. They're legends and I'm just a singer from West Brom who can't stick in a nine to five job.

Just before we were due to go into the studio to record the album John Brookes, my drummer, had another offer he couldn't refuse from a band called The Charlatans so he left. He had done some demo stuff at my own studio and was well up for drumming on the album but you don't get many good chances in this business and you have to take them when they're offered to you on a plate. He has done really well for himself with the band (I don't know the record sales) but they have played all the big festivals. John's departure obviously meant I now had to bring in another drummer at short notice and in came a guy named John Anthony. I was really pleased that I was able to find somebody of his talent given the tight schedule that I was working with. Arcana, by the way, had now decided to change their name to A.N.D. and we become known as the collective Al Atkins A.N.D. We became quite popular and got quite a few mentions in the press.

During the making of my first album, I even spoke with old The Shadows' bass player Jet Harris about doing some session work with me but he didn't play on the album; in the end, I think he had other plans at the time but it would have been cool to have him onboard. I think my old mate Bruno Stapenhill would have been jealous about that. He must have been The Shadows' biggest fan when we grew up.

We recorded the album at Outlaw Studios, owned by my old mate Phil Savage and we did it all in about a month. Phil was a lovely guy with a permanent smile on his face but admittedly that was from the weed.

"Are you alright, Phil?" I'd say.

"Yeah mate, I feel good."

I used to spend a lot of time at Outlaw with Phil demoing my own songs and producing up and coming Birmingham bands like Sister Love whose material was always a nightmare to mix because they had two drummers but I always remember one of their songs was called "Hanoi Moon". It was one classic track … at least in my eyes.

We worked our arses off getting »Judgement Day« completed so quickly although it was quite easy to record, and I was really pleased with myself when I played back the album in its entirety. But the production let it down because of our low budget; Paul was a great help as my co-producer and he was always coming up with great ideas on how to make the songs sound better.

"Maybe we can add a guitar to this bit?" he'd say. Or "Why don't we make this bit louder?"

I wanted a big production but it's all down to money and getting the right producer involved but we did the best we could with a small budget and limited technology. We had a few leftover tracks that didn't fit onto the album like "Wasted Years". I was just made up with myself having finally accomplished something that's really important to me and my goals in life. The album cover did go to plan, which I was obviously happy about. The cover was inspired by a bookplate that also inspired Led Zeppelin for their Swan Song record label insignia. I like looking at artwork and decided to use an old painting by the Belgian painter Léon Frédéric, which was originally painted in pink and blue, but I decided to use it in black and white. The cover shows children dying underwater as swans fly overhead. The swans represent the survival of the animal world after the death of mankind which I thought fitted great with my title »Judgement Day«. At the time I wondered if any one else had used this title for a song or album but all I found was an early track by The Pretty Things. But what the hell, at least I had made the bloody thing.

"I've finally done it", I said to Phil on the last day in the studio. "It's taken me all my adult life to make an album and I've done it … At long bloody last."

"Good on you, Al."

"Let's just hope the fans like it. And let's hope we shift a few copies."

»Judgement Day« (SPM 1989)

"Good Lovin' Runs Deep" (Atkins)
"Every Dream" (Atkins)
"Time After Time" (Atkins
"Go" (May)
"Judgement Day" (Atkins)
"I Got Your Letter" (Atkins)
"Nothing's Lost" (Atkins)
"Victim Of Changes"
(Atkins/Halford/Downing/Tipton)

The Band:

Al Atkins (vocals/acoustic guitar)
Paul May (lead guitar)
Pete Emms (bass)
John Anthony (drums)
Mark Presley (Keyboards)

SPM said that they wouldn't mention Judas Priest but without my knowledge they had little yellow stickers made and put them on the cover, which pissed me off. Besides the standard CD release, the first hundred albums were pressed in red vinyl and it got some mixed reviews but sold enough in the first year to break even.

The top English rock scribe Dave Ling gave me a glowing review in Raw: "The songs are generally simplistic, understated and sensitive … Worth hearing. 3/5"

"Atkins' music is rock as opposed to metal, favouring the melodic dynamic approach that fleetingly recalls Thin Lizzy or Led Zep … »Judgement Day« should go far in re-establishing Atkins …" wrote Steve Morris in my local music rag Brum Beat.

My friend Garry Sharpe-Young had »Judgement Day« in his play list in the now defunct magazine Metal Forces; coincidentally »Sad Wings Of Destiny« was also playing in his CD player. Garry also did an interview with me for Metal Forces which was generous of him. I wanted to make a name for myself in my own right rather than riding on the back of Priest's success, but alas, it was proving to be a difficult task because I was forever associated with my past.

Pete Emms, me and Paul May circa 1989.

I was overjoyed that many of the critics complimented my songwriting. I have been writing songs since the sixties and never felt as though people took me seriously, so when the album came out and the reviews followed I was totally stunned but pleased that my lyrics were recognised.

"Time After Time" is a nice song; it's really down to earth and easy to play and there are no drums on it whatsoever which is obviously unusual for a rock album. A lot of these songs were written just after I returned from mainland Europe and I was feeling really introspective and moody, which comes across quite strongly on the album.

The title track is fairly self-explanatory – it's about the ending of the world. Doomsday. Armageddon. Judgement Day. The subject matter is quite clearly grim as it's about death and the decay of the world but I don't think it is as deep as a Bob Dylan or Lou Reed song; I'm a good songwriter but not that good!

"Judgement Day"
(Atkins)

There's a word going round
That the shields are coming down
And the stars in your eyes
Are going to shine once more
There will be a time and a place
For everyone what ever race
No more bonds – no more chains
When the maker comes again

They are calling a judgement day
They are burning down the towers of shame
You can run but you can't hide
Even in the darkness – They are gonna find you

In between the crossfire
And the body burning smell
They will be raising flags of freedom
They will be raising all hell
Casting out the demons
The madmen and the thieves
Today's the trial of the high priest
Today's the last besiege

    Another emotional song is "I Got Your Letter" which is a really personal one for me. The song is about a girl I knew who died from cancer but she didn't tell me she was dying. I wasn't sure whether to add it to the album because it is a very emotional one to sing. It came out really well after we'd played it back in the studio so I decided to add it to the final mix. It's probably the most meaningful song I have ever written and still to this day I'm really proud of it.

    "Nothing's Lost" is a complete contrast to the previous songs; it's really heavy and hard hitting. It's only a short lyric but I like it.

"Nothing's Lost"
(Atkins)

Sleep little baby and don't you cry
'Cause time will mend your broken dreams
And you will find that when your love runs dry
Nothing is ever what it seems
You find that life goes on and on and nothing changes
You'll find that dream you had before and nothing's lost

Tomorrow – tomorrow is another day
Tomorrow – tomorrow another love will come your way
And when that cold hard door shuts right in your face
Another opens up for you to take its place
You find that in your life you're not that lonely stranger
You'll find that dream you had before and nothing's lost

    The final track is a known classic. I decided to record "Victim Of Changes" because everyone told me that it'd be cool to hear how I'd sing the song but I think my version is heavier than Priest's because they added the slow bit in the middle. I don't think the rest of the album is really related to my version of the song but I think all eight tracks are very compatible. I tried to make the album modern and heavy whilst capturing the true spirit of classic hard British rock which is what I grew up listening to and it's the kind of music I played in Priest and Lion during the 1970s. Melody is a really important part of a good hard rock album and so we tried to make some memorable melodies. A lot of modern rock or metal bands these days don't realise how important a good melody is to the shape of an album.

Generally speaking, I was really happy with »Judgement Day« and my favourite songs on the album are definitely "Nothing's Lost" and "I Got Your Letter".

I was just glad to see something of mine available to purchase in the shops although it was quite difficult to find. Most of the big stores in cities like London and Birmingham stocked it. If only we had the internet as a way to sell records back then, it would have probably sold a lot more. I think more than anything else the release of »Judgement Day« proved that despite the negative things people had said about me I could make a career for myself in this business. It gave me a major boost of confidence and I felt that I could carry on.

About one year after the release of my »Judgement Day« album, I was contacted by another Berlin based independent label called Green Tree Records (a division of TRC Distributors). They asked me if I would like to record an album for them because they liked my first solo album very much. Of course, I agreed and was ecstatic that I had been offered another record contract. However, they only wanted me for a one-off album like the previous deal I had with SPM and again I told them I didn't want any mention of Judas Priest on the cover of the album at all. I wanted this to be an AL ATKINS album not an AL ATKINS: THE EX-JUDAS PRIEST SINGER album.

I recorded my second album, »Dreams Of Avalon«, at Outlaw Studios and again used various musicians who were available at the time. I suppose it took around two months to record so it was slightly longer than my first album. I sang and played all the acoustic guitars and used three bass players: John Wylde, Pete Emms and my old pal Bruno Stapenhill. On lead guitar I had Paul May, on drums Pete Rogers and on keyboards Neil Price and Colin Orr from Janus. Janus was a cult progressive rock band who were massive in Europe with an album called »Grave Digger« and Colin was their leader, I suppose. We met up via SPM when they re-released their album. Paul May eventually played guitar on Colin's newly released stuff. I also invited a woman called Linda Upthegroove (yes, that's her proper surname) to sing backing vocals on "Run River Run". She was singing in the rehearsal rooms next door to the studios and I just asked her one day if she could do some backing vocals on "Run River Run" and she willingly obliged. It was great to have such a strong cast on board and to have a female backing vocalist was something totally new to me. I used to be quite sexist, especially in the seventies, and would not allow women anywhere near the band as we rehearsed and geared up for a gig but as I got older I became more laidback. I was always focused on the music and didn't want distractions but Linda was there as a professional. She was great to work with, really nice and friendly.

The album title »Dreams Of Avalon« came from an idea that two of my dear friends Archie Cole and Kevin Hill had. They said I should write about a battle, any battle, and I thought it was a good idea so I scribbled down some lyrics and eventually came up with the music for the song "Dreams Of Avalon". I thought it would make a good name for an album, too. Unfortunately, Kevin died a few years ago from cancer so »Dreams Of Avalon« serves as a reminder of what a good friend he was to me.

"Dreams Of Avalon"
(Atkins)

In the mist across the mountains camp fires
Burned all night
The Battle of two nations was building to a fight
One held a sword of steel, one wore the hood of doom
And the rivers will run red soon

In the eastern morning sun they gathered up their arms
To the pounding of a drum together they did march
'Till they faced the Celtic warrior across the water side
And soon the DREAMS OF AVALON will die

This island of mystery this land once so free
Was torn by the enemy, beaten by the sea
And the hopes now of paradise on earth have gone by
And soon the DREAMS OF AVALON will die

    I'd amassed lots of demos by now so I had lots of songs to choose from by the time it came to recording »Dreams Of Avalon«. It was basically a case of what best suited the album. I decided to use the previously leftover songs "Left Out In The Cold" and "Coming Thick And Fast" as they didn't really suit the material on my first album. In fact, I had to rename "Left Out In The Cold" because Priest have a song on their »Turbo« album called "Out In The Cold" so I added 'Left' to the title. I didn't want to get into any legal trouble! It's basically a love song and as I wrote the whole album with an acoustic guitar, this one sounded really well.
    »Dreams Of Avalon« was released in 1991, and similarly to »Judgement Day«, the only thing I didn't like about the album was the production – it needed to be much bigger and smoother. I thought it was time to leave Outlaw Studios for any future recordings; I had done two albums there and felt it was time to move on. So that was the last time I worked with Phil Savage and I haven't seen him in many years. Coincidentally, at the time of writing this book my local newspaper the Express & Star ran a front page piece about Phil and his Outlaw Studios; there was a picture of him in the article and he hasn't changed one bit. What he's doing now is interesting: he runs a production company called Major Key Studios and also works in partnership with Wolverhampton University working in music production and music management. He has also taken over the running of part of the Public Gallery – which is a new building in the Centre of West Bromwich costing over £50 million – that works on recording, film and theatre productions. I wonder if he still smokes joints every day? I must meet up with him at some point. He played an integral role in the evolvement of my solo career and as such he certainly deserves a few pints at my cost.
    The cover artwork for »Dreams Of Avalon« was terrible. I wanted to use a picture by the famous painter Rossetti, which depicts a dying King Arthur surrounded by his weeping queens. But we had to use that picture on the back of the album and a bland picture of me on the front which was done by artist and bass player John Wylde and his collaborator

»Dreams Of Avalon« (Green Tree Records – 1991)

"Dreams Of Avalon" (Atkins)
"Eastern Promise" (Atkins/May)
"If You Should Leave" (May)
"Coming Thick And Fast" (Atkins)
"Run River Run" (Atkins)
"Victim Of Love" (Atkins/May)
"Sacrifice" (Atkins)
"Left Out In The Cold" (Atkins)

The Band:

Al Atkins (vocals/acoustic guitar)
Paul May (lead guitar)
Pete "Blade" Rogers (drums)
Neil Price (keyboards)

Guest Appearances:

John Wylde (bass on "Coming Thick And Fast" and "Victim Of Love")
Bruno Stapenhill (bass on "Sacrifice")
Colin Orr (voice on "Eastern Promise" and keyboards on "Sacrifice")
Linda Upthegrove (vocals on "Run River Run")
Pete Emms (bass on "Left Out In The Cold")

Dawn Cox. The green and brown colours were awful, so bad you couldn't read the writing. Yuk! The photography was done by John England and the layout and design by a company called SPM Art Factory.

I listened to the album recently in preparation for this book and it hasn't dated too badly. A quick run through the album reveals some really strong melodies, even if I do say so myself. I wanted "Dreams Of Avalon", the first track, to begin slowly like when soldier's head to battle before hell breaks loose and the fighting begins. After the drums kick in, the melody gets heavier but it stays as a mid-paced song which I think adds to its power, like soldiers' footsteps thumping on the ground. "Eastern Promise" is a faster song with good use of keyboards from Neil Price; it's only a short song but it was a good chance for me to rock, although I think we could have made the chorus more memorable. "If You Should Leave Me Now" was written by Paul May; I think it's a wonderful ballad like some of Phil Collins' best work. It's a really romantic song with some good guitar work courtesy of Mr. May and I sound quite emotional, which my wife likes a lot.

A stand out song on the album is "Coming Thick And Fast" which has just been added to my latest live setlist and we may re-record it again at some point in the future. I think it's a killer seventies style hard rocker.

"Coming Thick And Fast"
(Atkins)

I looked through your window
There was nobody home
But I need you tonight
More than I've ever known
All week I've been sold out
All day I've been used
Hard times are coming so thick and fast
I got no time to lose
If the heat doesn't get me then the pressure will
I feel like I've been running so long baby down a one way hill
If I fall and nothing changes, then I don't know where I stand
'Cause I've tried but you know I feel inside, I'm just a losing man

I stood in your doorway
A lonely shadow in the night
I looked all around me
At the city lights
I just don't feel a part of this
I'm up against the wall
Hard times are coming so thick and fast
I don't feel nothing at all

Well I feel on the outside and just can't get in
I wonder where I went wrong all this time and wonder where I've been
Everyone's coming at me and there's nowhere to hide
But I feel no emotions, I feel nothing inside.

"Run River Run" is a hard hitting song and I love the chorus; it's really catchy and Linda's backing vocals add a bit of sex appeal. "Victim Of Love" is a power ballad which all rock albums should have. I like a lot of Bon Jovi and some of the heavier eighties power ballads and I wanted to make my own version although I doubt you'll see me advertised on the next power ballads compilation. Perhaps it could have had more beef to it but Paul's guitar and John Wylde's bass adds some strength.

However, I still think my favourite track on the album has to be "Sacrifice", the one Bruno played on and Colin Orr added keyboards.

Thankfully, Bruno was available and I hadn't settled on one particular bassist to play on all the songs so I asked him if he'd like to contribute to the album. I decided to add his talents to the song I liked the most. It was great to work with him again after all those years. It's amazing to think that the last time we worked together was in 1978.

"Bloody hell Al", he said to me as he walked into the studio. "It's been a long time, hasn't it mate."

"Yeah, it has and we don't look a day over 20!"

I remember that we went out to the pub for a drink and had a good chat about the old days. Bruno still likes a cold pint (as do I) and it was like old times. With Bruno living at the other end of the country, we only kept in touch by phone and rarely met up so it was really pleasing to us both that we had the chance to hook up together in the studio and go for a pint.

"Sacrifice" came about after watching a wildlife TV programme. A baby gazelle had just been born but within minutes of its birth it was eaten alive by a pack of hyenas before it could even stand. You may laugh at me but I really felt terrible watching its death and it made me think about life in general and some of the atrocities in this world from the animal chain to the human race and why innocent little children have to suffer at the hands of paedophiles and murderers.

"Sacrifice"
(Atkins)

So this is innocence – so this is how all life begins
So lost in ignorance – held before the world and all its sins
Their fate just changes overnight – they sense the love but there's no sight

(Chorus)

No danger signs – no nothing at all
All love is blind – no feelings they fall
No fear or fright – they hold out their hands
By the knife – their futures are planned

So much for innocence – so this is how their lives must end
No sign of deliverance – we turn our heads and just pretend
Their fate it changes overnight – they sense the love but there's no sight

(Chorus)

There's a hole in their day where love holds no price
Their's a hole for their life – sacrifice
There's a piece of the heart where love holds the key
To liberty
There's a look in the eye there's a chill in the voice
It's a kill without feeling – sacrifice
Well I cry for the freedom – the love and the choice
In this cruel world – sacrifice

"Left Out In The Cold" closes the album; it's a bit like Magnum meets Saxon which sounds like an odd mix but if it works. It's a good song to finish the album but I think the production could have been better.

When the album came out, the reviews were pretty good so I was happy enough. Steve Morris wrote a pleasing review in the Birmingham music magazine Brum Beat: "Judas Priest founder Atkins returns with his second solo set and an album whose production values reflect the experience of the first and the confidence borne of that record's euro success. Atkins is no metaller. Rather he's hard rock or what might have been called progressive once upon a chemical dream. He tends to build an acoustic base on which he lays textures with hard guitars and drums and bass … Melody insinuated by a better than average voice."

I think he was right about the sound of the album; it's more hard rock than heavy metal, like a lot of the stuff the Scorpions did in the seventies but that would soon change. I wanted my music to get heavier; there's a lot of competition out there so I need to make a noise.

In 1992, my old label SPM released an excellent album called »Buried Together« which featured four songs by Glenn Tipton's former outfit The Flying Hat Band and four songs by the progressive band Antrobus. After entering a new decade, classic rock and heavy metal was considered to be dead. Grunge music had killed the genre I love. Sure, some of the Seattle grunge bands like Soundgarden and Pearl Jam sounded heavy metal and they made comments to the media about how much they adored bands like Sabbath, Priest, Zeppelin and even Budgie, but people were quick to separate them from more commercial bands like Van Halen, Def Leppard and their sort who craved for attention and mega-stardom. Heavy metal was huge in the 1980s so it was a shame that Nirvana and their peers put an end to it all. This meant a lot of bands went bust; some of the bigger bands struggled to sell tickets and albums. Priest toured the States at one point with Alice Cooper, Motörhead, Metal Church and Dangerous Toys and it was reported that they struggled to fill arenas and that was probably because there wasn't a taste for metal the way there had been in the previous decade.

Grunge was basically American alternative rock with a gritty combination of punk, heavy metal and rock. Guys like Kurt Cobain were pissed off at people and the world so their lyrics were filled with angst and rage. And like punk there was a sociological side to grunge, which brought a massive cultural change. Obviously, I'm not an anthropologist or a social commentator but I could see how much grunge effected young people. Anybody could see that …

But at the same time as grunge some bands proved to be indestructible. I was glad to see Metallica riding on a storm of success with the release of what has become known as »The Black Album«. That's a fucking beast! Although many argued that they had sold out to MTV and adopted a more commercial sound after teaming up with the famed producer Bob Rock (hey, Bob – I'm available!) Lars Ulrich said they would never make a music video but they soon changed their minds. Money talks!

AC/DC had made a comeback of sorts with an album called »The Razor's Edge« which includes the brilliant song "Thunderstruck". I think they had a big problem trying to follow in the footsteps of »Back In Black« which, let's face it, is one of the great rock albums of all time. Most of their albums with Brian Johnson after »Back In Black« are not that great although he is a brilliant Northern, working class singer. I don't think the Young Brothers could have picked a better singer to replace the late great Bon Scott.

Sadly, one of my favourite groups – Queen – lost their singer in 1991. Freddie Mercury died from an Aids related illness. In '92, the rest of the band got together a terrific line-up that included Def Leppard, Metallica, Guns 'N' Roses, Extreme, Robert Plant and Roger Daltrey to perform at a tribute concert held in his honour at a packed Wembley Stadium. I saw footage of the gig on TV and it looked like a great night. It was a celebration of Freddie's life, music and rock in general.

Another one of my heroes, Noddy Holder, waved goodbye to rock and roll in '91 when he left Slade for good; he took a career change and become a TV and radio personality. The band is still touring with another line-up that includes Dave Hill and Don Powell but it's just not the same without Noddy.

So, yeah, the nineties was a pretty dull time for genuine hard rock and heavy metal.

1992 was the year that Rob Halford officially announced that he was leaving Judas Priest to explore new musical directions and territories for a while. Supposedly, he let the band know of his decision via fax which, to be honest, sounds quite shitty. When I found out he had left the band I just couldn't believe it. I thought Priest was his life and he would stay with Glenn, Kenny and Ian forever. It just goes to show how topsy-turvy bands in general are.

I was surprised more by the timing of his departure than anything else. Rob left the band after the infamous court case which gave them a lot of press attention and that always sells records. They had also just released one of the best albums of their career – »Painkiller«. When I first heard »Painkiller« I thought it was an absolute monster; full of really powerful riffs that screamed like dying children even some good melodies in songs like "A Touch Of Evil". It's one of my favourite Priest albums. After a couple of disappointing runs, »Painkiller« proved that the band could still come up with something worthwhile and memorable but all that meant nothing when Rob left. But it's all part of the band life, you have to expect these things to happen. From what I read in the press at the time, it sounded like Rob was battling with his own demons which we all have and we all struggle to cope with. I can empathise. Unfortunately for him, he had to do it in the media spotlight.

Rob kicked off his solo career by forming Fight with Priest drummer Scott Travis and some unknown musicians from his adopted home of Phoenix, Arizona. Since Priest, as a band, decided to spend most of their time in the States (as well as owning homes in Spain) during the 1980s, Rob probably felt at home there; the freedom, the culture and sheer bulk of America suits his personality and his creative side. When he quit Priest he also changed his famous image which was another major shock for fans. He left his leather, chains and biker's hats in his wardrobe and started wearing kakis, baggy t-shirts and even a baseball cap. What the fuck?! The press in the UK certainly wasn't generous towards Fight and I think it was a struggle for Rob to be taken seriously. Having said that, good on him for having the confidence to explore his passion. His desire to drive down new avenues of taste makes him a more interesting artist; there aren't too many people out there with the talent and believe in themselves to try that.

Fight was an interesting band although the material they made was not a patch on any of Priest's best work. Fight's first album »War Of Words« had some really heavy moments like "Into The Pit" but it sounded like Rob had been listening to a lot of Pantera and thrash bands like Annihilator. There's not a great deal of melody there for fans of vintage Priest but there are some brilliant riffs. I don't think that album deserved the panning it got. Personally, I thought it was a great album and I loved "Nailed To The Gun". Rob sounded really energetic and youthful.

Even though at this point I had two studio albums under my belt, we actually didn't play any live shows together and that's because I didn't want to. I hadn't played any gigs in the UK since the days of Lion; the last gigs I played where in Europe during my travels over there. I had different ideas on how to construct my new career. What I really wanted to be was just a songwriter so doing the solo albums was a bonus to me; A.N.D played some gigs though, most notably with the Tamworth based band Wolfsbane, led by Blaze Bayley who temporarily joined Iron Maiden in 1994. And by that point Wolfsbane had built up a good reputation having released a handful of recordings, most notably their self-titled album in '94. They'd even worked with the famed producer Rick Rubin. I was really pleased for A.N.D. when they told me about supporting Wolfsbane and they also played on the same bill as Priest's old rival Budgie who were still going strong after all those years. They've had their fair share of troubles like all bands do but they've kept going strong and even supported Ozzy in 1984. The sad thing is they've never been taken that seriously and neither have they had the kind of success they deserve.

And so with more lyrics to use, it was soon time for my next studio opus. With two albums under my belt, I was gaining momentum and confidence and wanted to keep on the move. My wife Karen is really supportive and has always been there for me. She's my muse, somebody I look to for help and guidance. As a songwriter, she's inspiration for some of my lyrics. I like to observe things and people and write down what I see.

A couple of years later, I approached David Howells at Gull Records in London (the original Priest label) with a handful of more songs that I had just written; he made me an offer to record my third solo album for his label. In 1994, I entered Stairway Studios in Walsall to record what was to become »Heavy Thoughts«.

Basically, David asked me to do a 'Priest connection' album, not like my first two albums, released by German companies. I was a bit unsure at first because it's not the sort of thing I wanted to do. Judas Priest was in the past and I knew I'd come under fire for it but as there was nothing else on offer I gave it some serious consideration and accepted David's idea. He wanted me to make it a much heavier album too. I'd found a box of old Priest cuttings and lyrics and thought I could use them for my next recording venture.

I came up with the idea of calling the album »Heavy Thoughts« because that was the name of the last tour I did with Judas Priest way back in 1973. Dave Corke, our manager, put the title 'Heavy Thoughts' on posters with a black and white shot (which was not very flattering) of Priest and plastered them everywhere. He asked me to write a song with that title. I started to write down some lyrics about someone's heavy thoughts on religion and how he wanted to become a born again Christian but it could never be. We never got to rehearse the half finished song because; as you know, I left the band. So I only got to finish it when I recorded this album. I also used an old poster of the band as the centre artwork in the CD packaging.

"Heavy Thoughts"
(Atkins)

You went in search of excellence
Somewhere you lost your way
You saw yourself not in the distance
But in the light of day
Some men find it – some men don't
Some they tried to take your soul

And when you walk among them
That's when it starts to show

(Chorus)

That's when the nightmares start
You walk with total strangers
You search inside your heart
But nothing ever changes.

You went in search of providence
But fell on stoney ground
You went to listen to the words of wisdom
But never heard a sound
Some men hear it some men don't
Some they try to take your soul
And when you talk among them
That's when it starts to show

(Chorus)

Your fate is out your hands/Your destiny in joy or sorrow
You can't control life or command/What waits for you tomorrow.

You went in search of mountains
But found yourself in the valley of shame
You tried to hide behind the face of Judas
And never take the blame
Some men hear it – some men don't
Some they try to take your soul
And when you walk among them
That's when it starts to show

(Chorus)

So we hit the studio in 1994 and our sound engineer Paul Hodson, who was great to work with and went on to play keyboards with Magnum for a while, played keyboards on some of the tracks and also sang some of the backing vocals. We made a demo and sent it off to various magazines to drum up some early promotion. When I sent the demo to More Than Music Magazine in '94 one reviewer wrote: "This eight track demo is full of great rock songs, heavy and blistering guitar solos, and a powerful rhythm section from Paul May and Pete Emms: Al proves with this record what a great musician, songwriter and singer he is … This is one of the strongest hard rock CD's from 1994!"

Wow! That was pretty cool, I thought. I've not even completed the album and already I was getting some really good reviews.

"Just look at this", I said to my wife with the review in hand. "This is just bloody brilliant."

"That's why you should keep at it Al. There's obviously people out there who pay attention to you and like your music."

I wrote six tracks on the album and a favourite of mine has to be "The Deepest Blue". I wrote the lyrics to that song not long after my divorce and when I first started to write the music my thoughts were: "I can't write a song with just two chords all the way through." It was a haunting vocal melody and was based around the words, not the music and I couldn't break the chain of the melody. When I played it to my guitarist Paul May some time later, he said it sounded great and helped me with the arrangement when we came to record it and I was very pleased with the result. One music critic said it sounded like a song The Doors would have made into a classic track. It has one hell of a good guitar solo in the middle which I absolutely love; still to this day I think it is a fantastic song and one I am most proud of.

"The Deepest Blue"
(Atkins)

Into the deepest blue – into a chilling cold
Into a room of silence – into a timeless low
Into the longest night – into a world unknown
Where you can lose the spirit and you can't feel the soul
Into a troubled heart – into a worthless time
Beneath the ruthless moon you lie.

Into a wanting torn between the hurt and you
Can't stop the longing – into the deepest blue
Into a savage land faced by the naked truth
Can't stop the longing – into the deepest blue

Into a shallow hope – into a fading fire
Can't face this fate without you – into a cruel desire

My other favourite lyric off that album is probably "Little Wild Child" which, as you can probably tell from the title, is semi-autobiographical. I suppose a lot of people can relate to this song, most of us were wild children. Like the lyrics, the melody is quite robust and I tried to put a lot of anger in my voice to give some meaning and power to the story I'm trying to tell.

"Little Wild Child"
(Atkins)

Crazy like a dog in a thunder storm
Wild like the wind in the night
He was born to run ain't nobody's son
Little wild child
Raging like a bull in a hurricane

Can't seem to hold him down
Got life by the throat speeds 'til it chokes
Little wild child
Kicking like a colt in a cyclone
Untamed and out of control
He's a law to himself, don't need no-one else
Little wild child

You can't sympathise – there's no disguise
You can see it in his eyes – kids gone wild
Holds no regard – considers no one
He's got a heart of stone, he's well left alone
Little wild child

I even asked Kenny Downing if he would like to put some guitars down on a song or two, and one day he turned up and helped with some of the production side of things but declined to play guitar when he found out it was for Gull. I guess he still had antipathy towards the company after all those years but I accepted that. It would have been good to work with him again though! And I would have got less criticism from die-hard Priest fans.

I also recorded the "Caviar And Meths" song in its full format because Priest fans had always wondered what it sounded like after the band cut it short on their »Rocka Rolla« debut album. We used to end our gigs with that song; it was a long loud climax. I changed a few things around and brought it more up to date and also asked Kenny and Ian if I could have the rights back to the song; they both agreed in writing. I also asked David for a better publishing deal on the song and he gave me that too. I was happy with the way things were working out. Gull Records wanted to release the original version of "Caviar And Meths" but they couldn't find the master tapes so the version that is on »Rocka Rolla« is significantly shortened. An unknown song called "Ladies" was also intended for Priest's first album but again they couldn't locate the master tapes. The same thing happened to the "Mother Sun" demo right before Priest left Gull for CBS. "Mother Sun" has since become a cult song even though it's never actually been released; the band played a nine minute version of "Mother Sun" at the Reading Festival in 1975.

One thing I didn't want to do was use drum machines, which David had requested I use and I didn't want to record a random classic song that everyone was familiar with. Both ideas had us scratching our heads in bemusement for a while. I honestly don't know why Dave wanted me to record such a song unless he had a single release in mind. Then Paul May came up with a great version of the Everly Brothers song "Price Of Love" on which we used a horn section and female backing singers. It's a dark and moody song which fitted perfectly with the other songs we had recorded although I was still dubious about using a song originally made by the Everly Brothers. Thankfully for us, David loved our version but I wasn't convinced this album was going in the direction I originally intended it to go. In the end, I had to agree with David and use the Everly Brothers track on the finished album. But I insisted that if it was going to be a celebration of Judas Priest and what I did with them from 1969 to 1973 then the album must be HEAVY METAL, most certainly heavier than my first two albums. I didn't want to have it any other way.

Other songs on the eight track album include "Turn Around" which begins with a melodic Jimmy Page style guitar piece before the band kick in. It's a good ballad but as the second track I think it should have been moved further along the album. "When Love Steals The Night" is mid-paced with a quality riff that powers the song from beginning to end. "A Void To Avoid" is faster and heavier and I sound like I'd been smoking more than usual before my vocals were recorded which always makes a good effect. And again I think that track has a strong melody.

The »Heavy Thoughts« album was finally released towards the end of '95; it was very low-key and didn't even get released in the UK. I got some press but not a great amount. I did manage to receive some decent reviews though, which always helps shift records.

Ray Dorsey wrote in the American fanzine Chaos Realm: "While you can walk into any store and easily grab Glenn Tipton's lousy excuse for an alterna-metal solo CD, this third masterpiece by Priest's original crooner is not even out in the US. Then again, trendy America doesn't deserve music this good. Much like Al's first two efforts, »Heavy Thoughts« is a massive study in '70s style hard rock … his vocals a wonderful, rich and soulful tone delivering songs that those into the first two Priest LP's would worship."

I think the album's production sounded pretty good and I thought it sounded quite commercial but again I never liked the cover just as I didn't like the artwork on my second album. What I had in mind for the cover artwork was a picture of Auguste Rodin's statue: The Thinker dressed in a biker's leather jacket and sunglasses. David had other ideas and commissioned Blaize Thompson, who is a very well known London artist, to paint it but I thought it looked like me having a dump. How embarrassing! But on the plus side the noted rock journalist Garry Sharpe-Young wrote the sleeve notes for me and managed to put my career into perspective in a few hundred words.

»Heavy Thoughts« (Originally released by Gull Records in 1995. Re-issued by Market Square Records in 2003)

"Heavy Thoughts" (Atkins)
"Turn Around" (May)
"Price Of Love" (Everly Brothers)
"When Love Steals The Night" (Atkins)
"A Void To Avoid" (Atkins)
"The Deepest Blue" (Atkins)
"Little Wild Child" (Atkins)
"Caviar And Meths" (Atkins)

The Band:

Al Atkins (vocals)
Paul May (guitar)
Paul Hodson (keyboards)
Pete Emms (bass)
Gerwin Morris (slide guitar)
Debbie Hunt/Karen Blaylock (backing vocals)

I remember when the album came out, hardened Priest fans accused me of overstating my importance in the band and criticised me of abusing my connection to a legendary British heavy metal band. But despite my initial feelings, I didn't think there was anything wrong with being nostalgic. I wrote some of the Priest's earlier songs and worked my arse off for four years trying to get the band somewhere so I should get some sort of credit. Okay, I may not be as flamboyant as Rob Halford and I'm certainly not as good a singer as he is – our voices are totally different – but I do have a role in the history of the band, it's just that a lot of people don't know about it because as far as they are concerned Judas Priest has only existed since Rob joined. Even when they have mentioned my name, they have been reluctant to elaborate on my role and they haven't really acknowledged any of the other past members like Bruno and Ernie. I've never wanted to have a slinging match with the band over this because I think they're a great bunch of guys and incredibly talented but I don't think they should criticise me for wanting to make a living through music.

Thankfully »Heavy Thoughts« got a proper album release in 2003 after I signed a deal with Market Square Records; the album was distributed through KOCH International. The re-issue has two bonus tracks: "Cradle To The Grave" and "Sentenced". They were basically demos Simon Less and myself had been working on. We later recorded them properly and used them again on my last album »Demon Deceiver« because I liked them very much.

It was Gull's fault that »Heavy Thoughts« never got a decent release back in '95 and I suppose I wasn't shrewd enough business-wise to make the release happen. I heard through the grapevine that Gull Records allegedly ceased to be a record company when Priest's management threatened to sue them for exploiting the band with the first two albums back in the seventies. David Howells told me »Heavy Thoughts« was to be licensed and distributed by another company, which I thought was strange but he never told me why.

I got some really good reviews on the re-release and the album sold quite well in the Far East: One reviewer wrote on Hard Roxx Online: "An outstanding vocalist who just happened to make the right moves at the wrong time ... This is metal forged in Britain's industrial heartland. No frills, no airs and graces, just heavy rock and battered love songs, brooding soundscapes and a world that never changes. Good stuff."

The respected website Get Ready To Rock declared: "Those expecting a Priest-like offering may well be surprised. If you didn't know his past, you wouldn't pigeon-hole Atkins in the Priest more-metal-per-minute bracket. With a cracking good band, this is essentially eighties power rock given an updated twist but sounding quite AOR and American in places."

Rockezine was really generous: "For people who don't know this album, you won't be surprised. It's exactly how you expect it to be. Great sound and fine music, all in the vein of early Judas Priest ... Although the original CD was released in 1995 most tracks sound remarkably fresh ... Atkins seems to be breaking with his bluesy emotional approach and goes for a more straight rock approach instead. Not a wise decision because these songs are rather mainstream."

At the time of the original release of my »Heavy Thoughts« album, heavy metal and good old fashioned British hard rock seemed to be nothing but a distant memory. The big magazines weren't as popular anymore and bands of the eighties had disappeared. You just didn't see bands like UFO in the charts anymore and you definitely didn't see the likes of Slade, a band you just couldn't escape (nor would you want to) in the seventies. Brit pop was the big thing with bands like Oasis who just seemed to rip off Beatles tunes.

Looking back, I suppose one of the great British rock and roll bands of the nineties was The Wildhearts led by the invincible Ginger, a frontman cut in the same vein as Lemmy; hard core rock and rollers who live and breathe the music and everything that goes with it. I really admire people like that who are completely consumed by their art. (The Wildhearts haven't had an easy ride despite some successful singles). They are one of those bands that seem to miss out on major success. Other British rock bands that never quite achieved the success they should have got are Thunder, Little Angels and The Almighty. Thunder, for example, are still going strong and filling arenas all over the country. Danny Bowes has a really powerful voice and the guitars of Luke Morley can be quite seductive (there's a word you won't hear me use very often). They've made some truly great ballads in their time as well as some powerful blues rock numbers like "Dirty Love". Their love of the blues inspired them to release an album called »Robert Johnson's Tombstone« (again, this proves that Johnson's legacy is unmatched) and on the back of that they did a major UK tour including playing a slot at the »Monsters Of Rock« Festival alongside Deep Purple and Alice Cooper.

What I didn't like about the more mainstream, upcoming bands was how they completely ignored a good guitar solo and a chunky riff. Bands became too self-conscious. Alice Cooper got it right when he said the last American band to have memorable guitar solos was Guns N' Roses. Slash, like his idols Brian May and Jeff Beck, loved to create a melodic, harmonic guitar solo and his contributions to rock music are immense. Everybody knows "Paradise City", "November Rain" and "Sweet Child O' Mine". Isn't it weird that Stoke-On-Trent of all places is famous for producing Slash and Lemmy. Now, that's just weird.

I think if I had released my solo albums at the height of rock's popularity, I may have sold more copies because in the nineties rock was unfashionable. Even Mötley Crüe, one of the loudest and crudest bands of the past decade, were nobody's after the grunge thing. Vince Neil was replaced by John Corabi and suddenly Mötley Crüe's popularity quickly slid down a slippery slope and they split up briefly only to re-unite and have more line-up troubles.

Even Bon Jovi had taken some time out in the early 1990s although considering just how huge they became after the »New Jersey« album; I think they would have been untouchable anyway. When they released »Keep The Faith« in the early nineties, they were one of the most popular bands on the planet which is odd considering how much grunge tried to destroy pampered bands like Bon Jovi. I think the thing with Bon Jovi is that they appeal not only to rock bands but to pop fans and stay-at-home mums. They've taken a lot of stick for that and these days, like Bryan Adams, they've become a little bit middle of the road but they're still hugely popular and fill stadiums everywhere so they must be doing something right. But boys, stay away from country music, please! It's really not that cool.

I take a lot of inspiration from Alice Cooper who despite the passing fickle trends in rock never slows down. How does he do it? Is he human? Or is that a silly question? He carried on touring and released an excellent album in the 1990s called »The Last Temptation« and even appeared in movies, most famously the hilarious comedy »Wayne's World«. Its creative artists like Cooper that will always have a strong and loyal fan base wherever they go because they work really hard and always seem to give the fans what they want.

Perhaps one of the biggest surprises in the rock world during this period was the comeback of Meat Loaf, a man larger than life. The sequel to »Bat Out Of Hell« was easily one of the biggest hits of the decade and it spawned the mammoth hit single "I Would Do Anything For Love (But I Won't Do That)". It was a bit too dramatic for my tastes but it was great to see a classic rocker doing so well despite all the hit backs he's had in his career.

I still listened to my old records for inspiration; I still adored bands like Cream, Zeppelin and Sabbath. They were unique and groundbreaking but they were in the past. What rock fans had to do was to seek out those smaller bands that big record companies wouldn't pay attention to. The fact is, there is a whole world of music outside of what's sold in the big music shops like HMV and I suppose in a small way I'm part of that world.

In 1993, there was a knock on my door and my then four year old son Joe looked out of the window shouting: "I think Batman is here!" When I opened the front door I was shocked to see it was Kenny Downing. I hadn't seen him in ages but I admit that he looked younger than he is. All those tours of America had paid off rather well; he'd stayed in good shape.

"I have a gift for you", he said.

"Come in", I replied.

Joe, by the way, was referring to Kenny's car which was a black Porsche with 'KK1' on the number plate. Kenny gave me a double vinyl album and video called »Metal Works '73-'93« which I thanked him for. They must have got tired and bored of trying to replace Rob that they decided to bring out an album of old songs but I must admit I liked it very much. I think they picked some brilliant songs for that compilation, including some of the lesser known material like "Blood Stone" and "Devil's Child". Some time later, I phoned him and asked if he could let me have a CD version and he said he would give me six copies, if I gave him the album back because there was just a small amount pressed. I declined his offer. It was a desperate time for them and they needed as much press coverage and sales as possible.

Fast forward to 1997 and I paid Kenny a visit at his home, Astbury Hall in Bridgnorth. It must be worth millions! I pulled up at these huge electronic metal gates and spoke to him through an electronic speaker and I said it was Tatter. The gates opened up and I drove down to the main door where Kenny stood in a posh looking black silk Japanese dressing gown. We shook hands and he invited me in for a coffee.

I looked out of the huge bay windows across his lake and said: "How much of this land do you own?"

He passed me some binoculars and said: "How far can you see?" How times had changed from those heady days back in the seventies when his arse was falling out his tatty jeans and we drove up and down the motorways gigging for a few pounds. What I can say is, Kenny you have worked hard for what you have got and deserve every penny you have earned in the music business … I'm still fucking jealous though.

In 1996, metal fans saw Tim Owens join forces with Judas Priest after a lean spell without Rob at the helm. I never thought I'd see the day when Judas Priest hires another singer other than Rob. When Rob left them, I thought that it would finish them off for good; how could anybody replace him? I heard that Sebastian Bach was on a short list but there's no way he would have fitted in with them. I heard from a very reliable source of mine that Ralf Scheepers of Gamma Ray was in the running for the job but he seemed more concerned about money and apparently lacked a sense of humour. He now fronts the brilliant Judas Priest inspired metal band Primal Fear.

It took them years to find their man in Tim Owens who I thought did a brilliant job holding the band together. He deserves more credit that he got.

Tim was the second American to join the band. I think they should have stayed as a completely British band; not that I have anything against Americans; it's just that Priest have always stated the importance of being a British band. When Steve Harris was on the hunt for a new singer to replace Bruce Dickinson in the nineties he was adamant about hiring somebody who's native. I think Tim, who was nicknamed "Ripper" by the band, did a brilliant job. Christ, I remember thinking that this guy must have one big pair of balls to take on such a tough job. He has a great voice and after meeting up with him backstage at the Birmingham Academy when Priest played during the »Demolition« world tour I found him to be a really nice bloke too.

Tim's rise to fame from being in a Judas Priest tribute band called British Steel to actually fronting the band was turned into a Hollywood film called »Rock Star«. It's an incredible story and I didn't think something like that would happen again until Journey hired Arnel Pineda from the Philippines. Journey main man Neal Schon saw some footage of Pineda on YouTube and hired him as a successor to Jeff Scott Soto.

I think when Rob left, Glenn became the Steve Harris of the band; the leader of the pack. Glenn also took over the reigns as the lead songwriter and became a sort of co-manager with Jayne Andrews. Every band needs a leader, somebody to make all the important decisions which sometimes includes sacking the manager. Glenn's a strong character and had made a huge impression on the band as soon as he joined back in the early years. Glenn co-led the band with Rob, so when Rob left he took charge.

Kenny is more interested in playing good riffs and getting the girls, Ian stays quiet, much like John Deacon in Queen but Glenn likes to make some of the important decisions. Indeed, taking on the role of band leader is a very difficult task and you can be blamed for taking the band into the wrong direction and you can distance yourself from the fans.

Throughout the nineties there was a famous war of words between Rob, who is based in America, and his ex-band Judas Priest who stay in England. Fight were not doing too well and they struggled to shift records and ticket sales were low. It must have been uncomfortable for him to not sell out relatively small places like the London Astoria 2 after having headlined gigs at Madison Square Garden more than once in the previous decade. Fight finished after just two albums and an EP.

Priest, meanwhile, were also struggling to fill the more prestigious venues. Even with their reputation and with a new, younger singer they still suffered from weak albums sales of their first album of new material since 1990. They were no longer signed to the prestigious American label CBS (a division of Sony) which showed how dramatic their temporary fall from grace was. When »Jugulator« came out in 1997, it didn't please fans and critics the way everybody hoped it would although I admit that I liked it because I really like Tim's voice. But I have to say that Priest just didn't sound like Priest even though Kenny and Glenn found a singer that resembled Rob. I was happy for them that they still continued to keep the flame burning despite all the arguments and bitterness after Rob's departure.

Slowly, but surely, I was building a good reputation for myself. I was finally getting some sort of recognition not just as a heavy metal singer but as a songwriter. I was featured in a lot of rock/metal magazines and fanzines, especially abroad in Europe, Japan and even America.

It was hard trying to make some sort of living as I didn't have a day job and relied on money from my albums and on the frequency of my royalty cheques from Judas Priest. But

I have managed to survive; I just couldn't stand the thought of going back to a job that I know I'd hate so I have always been good with money never being too flamboyant or frivolous.

The idea for my next studio opus came from Garry Sharpe-Young who had become a friend of mine after being very generous towards me giving me lots of press coverage in magazines like Metal Forces. Garry had written for a few rock magazines in the UK and abroad and I remember the first time I met up with him in Birmingham to do an interview. I think it must have been in 1990 and he took a liking to me and wanted to help me in any way he could. Garry was also a great artist and ran a company with Priest's old drummer John Hinch. The company was called Pagan and they made brooches, buckles, badges and all sorts of gothic/devil related items for sale. They once gave Rob Halford a full length black leather coat covered in their merchandise back stage at one of Priest's concerts and I watched him pose with it on while Garry took some photos. Garry did another interview with me the following year at a house in Birmingham which was rented out by UFO and that was the first time I had met up with the band. He went to management taking care of the metal band Marshall Law before he emigrated from Nottingham to New Zealand where he runs the successful website Rockdetector and writes god knows how many books on metal.

Back in the mid-nineties, Garry suggested that on my next album I should record all the songs I had written with Judas Priest between 1969 and 1973 as well as my early demos. To be honest, I thought this idea sounded too much like a cash-in situation similar to »Heavy Thoughts« but even more prominent and if I had wanted to do something like that I would have done it years before. But having said that the idea to record all those old songs like "Winter", "Never Satisfied" and "Victim Of Changes" really appealed to me, and to re-record the obscure demos of "Holy Is The Man" and "Mind Conception" sounded like a challenge too.

One day I had a call off from Garry saying ex-Tygers of Pan Tang vocalist Jess Cox (now manager of the Northern metal record company Metal Nation Records) wanted to offer me a deal using Garry's concept. They had a good pedigree working with nearly all the NWOBHM bands and it sounded just like the company I was looking for, so after a few phone calls Jess and myself thrashed out a deal which suited us both.

Now, luckily or unluckily, whichever way you look at it, Dave Holland, the former drummer with Judas Priest, was doing a lot of session work with the likes of the Tony Iommi-Glenn Hughes project and various other musicians and he became available to play on my new project too. I asked Dave Holland to play drums on my new album because I thought it would give it some more interest to all the keen Priest fans out there. I knew Dave from years ago, our paths had crossed a few times and we got on really well together and by god he was a great drummer and his time keeping was as good as any drum machine. Dave has worked with lots of great artists over the years and had a strong reputation.

(I have to say that during the writing of this book, Mel Galley, Dave's former Trapeze band mate, had died of cancer. He passed away on February 7th, 2008. My local newspaper, the Express & Star ran some articles about his battle with cancer. His buddy Glenn Hughes flew over from California to see him in his final days. That's very sad news; Mel was a great guitarist having also played in Whitesnake although he never made the big time.)

I remember Dave telling me that he decided to leave Judas Priest on two accounts: one being his aging mother and his sister who had Multiple Sclerosis so he decided to stay at home in Northampton and look after them. The other reason was that after all the years he had played drums for Priest (1979-1988), they still wouldn't make him a member of the band and they just paid him a set wage which really pissed him off. I think it would piss me off too! After a few vodkas he would tell me some unbelievable stories but I couldn't prove them to be true. This problem is the band distance themselves with all past members, it's as if all of us never existed. Dave actually told me he was set up but we will never know.

At the time there was a rumour that Dave was pushed out of the band because his drumming style was less technical than Les Binks, his predecessor. Dave's drumming was perfect for the kind of metal Priest wanted to make in the eighties and that's probably the reason why he was hired in the first place. They had moved from the darker edged stuff of the past decade and as they entered the 1980s they decided they wanted to crack America with more accessible and anthemic metal, hence the likes of "Living After Midnight" and "Heading Out To The Highway".

There was a bit of controversy surrounding Dave's role in the band during an American tour in 1986. A Kerrang! scribe wrote a review of the band's gig at the L.A. Sports Arena in May with support from Dokken. This particular writer saw another drummer, Jonathan Valen (formally of Legs Diamond), under the drum riser. Valen played drums alongside Dave Holland during that entire North American tour. Needless to say, the band were not too keen about this little bit of exposure and in interviews they were actually quite mean towards Valen who only seemed to be doing what he was obviously hired to do. I don't think the band have been too complimentary of some of their past drummers.

Anyway, I booked us into Mad Hat studios just outside of Wolverhampton to record my fourth album with Mark V. Stuart at the mixing desk who is Magnum's sound engineer.

Coming out of the studios one day was Marshall Law and I got talking to Andy Pyke, their vocalist, about Dave and myself recording a new album and Andy, who is a massive Priest fan, asked if he could help out with any vocals. Of course, I said yes, because to me it was just a fun album to record so I welcomed him on board. Marshall Law were also signed to Neat Metal too so there were no contractual problems to overcome.

For this album I tried something slightly different: Paul May wrote an instrumental called "Metanoia", which I think sounds great amongst the heavy rock songs and I would do something similar on my next album. Instrumentals can work really well or they can nose dive. I think Paul nailed it down and came up with something exciting and original.

»Victim Of Changes« (Neat Metal – 1998)

"Mind Conception" (Atkins)
"Holy Is The Man" (Atkins)
"Never Satisfied" (Atkins/Downing)
"Meltdown" (May)
"Winter" (Atkins/Downing/Hill)
"Metanoia" (May)
"Caviar And Meths" (Atkins)
"Black Sheep Of The Family" (Hammond)
"Victim Of Changes" (Atkins/Halford/Downing/Tipton)

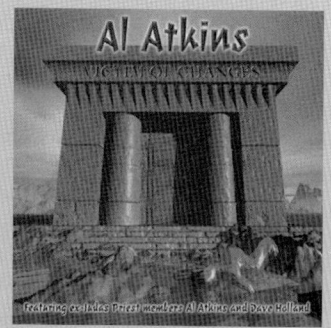

The Band:

Al Atkins (vocals)
Paul May (guitar)
Pete Emms (bass)
Dave Holland (drums)
Andy Pyke (additional vocals)

Yet again I was really pissed off with the album cover. Basically, the cover of the »Victim Of Changes« album, designed by Andy Warwick, was thought up by Neat Metal Records and when they first sent me a copy I threw it across the room in anger.

"Look at this fucking shit!" I screamed to myself. "This is not what I wanted. No fucking way."

I rang the company to tell them what I thought about it: it is basically a rip-off Judas Priest's classic »Sin After Sin« album but Jess Cox wouldn't listen and said it would make a good talking point. I didn't see it that way and thought it would anger the band and their fans. It's one thing to record some of the old songs I co-wrote with them but to rip off an album cover of their's I had nothing to do with is entirely different.

"I can't believe another album of mine has another dodgy cover. They can just never get it right", I later said to my wife.

"Try not to get so angry about it", she'd say.

"I can't help it. They've fucked up another cover of mine. Why can't these people get it right?"

However, my dear friend Beverley Stone has some old photos of me and Priest through various line ups and I used some of those on the back of the album and in the booklet. I gave her a copy of the CD as a thank you.

»Victim Of Changes« was released in 1998 and was very well received by all the rock/metal press worldwide and started selling by the thousands.

And I was totally surprised that just recently it started selling quite well in the Japanese market, which is where Judas Priest made a large impact in the late seventies. I know that Japan has a surprisingly big market for classic rock and heavy metal with magazines like Burrn! paving the way. And how many artists have released live albums or DVD's recorded at the famous Budokan Hall in Tokyo.

The album probably got the press reviews of my career, so I couldn't argue with that. I've got a big stack of press cuttings, here's what some of them say:

Joe Geesin wrote in Record Collector: "A very interesting cover version is Quatermass' 'Black Sheep Of The Family,' a highlight of the album. Some solid songs in the (old) Priest vein that fans will probably enjoy."

Dave Ling wrote a rave review in Classic Rock: "This collection of full-blooded hard rock tunes proves that ... he was definitely a skilled enough writer."

As well as being included in the Snakepit playlist, I also got a pretty cool review. "The quality of the material is pretty good", wrote Frank Stöver, "always above the average and definitely interesting, no matter if you're a Judas Priest die hard or not."

Brett Claxton wrote in Powerplay: "From the opening galloping riff of 'Mind Conception' to the last strains of the classic title track, all these songs show that not only is (was) our man Al a songwriter par excellence, but he has also lost nothing in the vocal department either ... Definitely a very pleasant surprise from Neat Metal."

I got 8/10 in Hard Roxx, which was just great. Matthew Honey wrote: "What gives the album credibility however, is the quality of the songs which if you ignore the Priest connections are actually rather good … With no wimpy ballads to interrupt the flow 'Victim Of Changes' is a full on metal racket …"

I was even happier that the celebrated Canadian metal author and historian Martin Popoff also gave me 8/10 in Brave Words & Bloody Knuckles. "Al's voice is in fine street-powered form, his band of Birmingham vets squarely exhibiting depth and metal soul … there's a bunch of cool metal originals here."

I also got a lot of press in foreign magazines; I couldn't' even read the bloody reviews but at least I got mentioned. I've got reviews from France, Japan, foreign editions of Metal Hammer and other magazines in Germany and even Spain. It all helped to spread my name.

I think at that point »Victim Of Changes« was by far my most accomplished album and it was great to work with Dave Holland and Mark Stuart.

By the time my latest album had come out, Rob Halford's career hit an all time low. After dissolving Fight, which I thought was a good band, he teamed up with Trent Reznor on a joint project called Two. Reznor is famous for his band Nine Inch Nails and for working with Marilyn Manson and at the time I remember thinking: "Christ, what's Rob up to now?"

It was a bit of a weird project and they only released one album which is called »Voyeurs«. The »Voyeurs« album focused on homoerotic themes and he even hired a porno director to make a video to his single "I'm A Pig".

I don't think anybody was interested in hearing any more from Two. Rob had completely lost his famous connection with heavy metal and gone down an industrial metal path which his fans were not too happy with. I think Rob's fans had a feeling he was going to distance himself from metal after he told Metal Edge in 1997 that "metal is dead and I'm done with it." Those words have come back to haunt him and won't go away. After spending most of his adult life telling everybody that he is obsessed with metal to declaring the death of metal was pretty extreme. I was totally shocked when I heard about that and thought Rob must have been on something when he said it. I think the whole metal world was taken aback when they heard about Rob's comment, so when he released the Two album a year later it seemed like the final nail in his coffin. Of course since then, he has said it was a stupid thing to say. But Rob is a very talented artist and an intelligent guy so it's no surprise that he had some tricks up his sleeve to reignite his flagging career and all major artists have down periods.

But if that comment wasn't enough, he finally admitted to the public he is gay. Just weeks before the release of the Two album in 1998 he appeared on MTV and spontaneously admitted his sexuality. Everybody close to him knew about his sexuality and you don't have to be his best mate to know he swings the other way. Judas Priest must be the heaviest but campiest band in the business and Rob was never seen with a woman on his arms and there are no stories of backstage antics with groupies which is quite odd for a heavy metal band especially during the eighties. The fact that he never affected his career or Judas Priest's goes to show that people assumed he is gay anyway. Who knows what would have happened to Judas Priest if Rob "came out" in the 1980s at the peak of their success. The Americans would have not taken to kindly to that; they didn't appreciate Freddie Mercury's campness in the video to "Body Language", so Queen's career in the States during the 1980s took a massive nose dive, and the video for "I Want To Break Free" did not do their career over there any good either. And even though Rob's admission was spontaneous, it was still rather well timed; his career was on a downhill slide anyway so there wasn't much damage to be done. In the cutthroat and masculine world of heavy metal it' still a brave move and I think it probably made him feel a hell of a lot better after it. Good on him, I say.

Believe it or not, in 1999 Lion reformed to play »Fill Your Head With Rock 3« at Gilberts in Birmingham. It was fantastic to be back on stage with Harry Tonks, Pete Boot and, of course, my good mate Bruno Stapenhill. We played a few numbers and we did a great version of "On The Wheel". And to be honest, it was as though we'd never been away from each other; it was a blast from the past. We also played "Journey" and it sounded great; as did "Stranger To This Country", which is an old blues song that I wrote many moons ago. I blew the cobwebs out of my old blues harp and George Northall got up and jammed with us on his sax. In the audience were a lot of old friends who we hadn't seen for years and most of my family were there for support.

But the only reason why we reformed was to raise money for Pete who has Parkinson's disease. Pete set up a foundation called »Fill Your Head With Rock« which raises funds to help him cope with Parkinson's; he also has a website at www.fillyourheadwithrockinternational.com. Even Mick "Zoom" Hughes took a break from Metallica to do the sound mixing. This gave me a kick up the backside and I started to plan what all my friends had been asking for years: "Why don't you go back on the road and play live music again?"

At the same time Rob's career was on the slide, Judas Priest's career with Tim at the helm wasn't doing too well either, which I thought was a real shame. I remember having a conversation with my wife about this. We were both gutted that Priest were no longer the big heavy metal success story.

They'd changed record companies and released »Demolition« in 2000 which many fans consider to be one of their worst albums but again I quite like it largely because of Tim's brilliant voice. A lot of criticism aimed at the album focused on Glenn's songwriting which some thought was clichéd; I would have liked to have seen Tim contribute more to the songwriting because he has talent in that area too but it appeared that Glenn and Kenny were too possessive over him and wouldn't let him contribute any lyrics. And similarly to »Jugulator«, their second album with Tim focused less on the twin-guitar brilliance of Tipton/Downing and more on creating a heavy sound which was cool with me but not so cool with a lot of hardcore Priest nuts who basically want to hear a rehash of »British Steel«.

I think Tim was really great at singing the old Priest songs just as much as the new stuff. They'd already released a killer live album called »'98 Metal Meltdown« although I think Tim does a little bit too much screaming on it. You can hear Tim blast through two discs of vintage Priest; stuff like "Metal God", "Grinder", "Painkiller" and "Hell Bent For Leather". It must have pissed Rob off good and proper! Tim is an incredible singer and many have argued that his voice is even better than Rob's but something like that is always debatable. Don't forget that Tim is much younger than Rob and I very much doubt that anybody is a better singer than a young Rob Halford. I think they both have very special voices that some of us would kill to have. They were born lucky, I guess.

I think Tim copies a lot of stage moves from Rob and if you watch the DVDs he doesn't really control the crowd the way Rob does but I guess that's down to experience. Rob is like Freddie Mercury, Bon Scott and the other all-time rock greats; he's got so much energy, passion and charisma and it comes across on stage at every gig. To have a rapport with thousands and thousands of people is something to respect even if you don't like the music. To have the balls to do that, to sing in front of an arena packed with fans that have paid a lot of money deserves admiration.

Chapter 8
Living In The Shadow Of The Past: Embracing The Priest (2002-2004)

During and after the release of the »Victim Of Changes« album I did lots of press, including two appearances on German and American television. I was interviewed for about 20 minutes on MTV and was asked a lot of questions about the early years of Judas Priest but it got cut to about two minutes in the end and it covered more about Rob's sexuality than music but at least it got my name around. But all that got me thinking about the past. Most people are only interested in my history with Priest and no matter how much I had tried to distance myself from it when I started to make my solo albums I realised that I would never escape my past no matter how much I tried. Judas Priest is a part of me. Full stop. Some people hate me for using the band's name to make a career for myself, yet I do have a strong, albeit small fan base around the globe. In this business you have to take people's criticism no matter how much they may hurt you. At first, it really bothered me that people took the piss out of me for covering songs like "Victim Of Changes" but now I don't care. Life is too short. I've learned to embrace the Priest!

When my »Victim Of Changes« album was released in 1998 it brought some interesting opportunities. I took a rest after its release to think about my future and the amount of press I did just killed me. Dave Holland and myself saw a gap in the market for us both to record another album and after we had done lots of interviews together to promote »Victim Of Changes«, record companies had badgered us to stay together. We were offered new deals and different names were being thrown around such as Judicator and Steel Force but eventually we settled for just plain Atkins/Holland. I think Glenn Tipton and Jayne Andrews would have thrown a fit if we had called ourselves Judicator especially after Priest had released the »Jugulator« album. It was only tongue-in-cheek but I wanted to try it, except I was concerned about any legal implications. I used to ring Jayne Andrews sometimes regarding Judas Priest; we didn't have any arguments but she did stand in the way of everything I asked of her, so now I don't bother with her at all.

Dave and myself had several meetings in London and one record company wanted us to record the next album using top names like Don Airey, The Moody Blues' Justin Hayward and even Glenn Hughes on bass. What a great project that could have been: Al Atkins, Dave Holland, Glenn Hughes and Don Airey! Such a project would have been a dream come true for me.

Neat Metal Records, the label that distributed »Victim Of Changes«, had been sold to Sanctuary Music Group, which I thought was great news. Now my album will be on a much bigger label! It could get a better distribution deal and more press! The first track that they released was inevitably the "Victim Of Changes" song, which was put out on a four CD box set called »Rock Of Ages« which featured some massive name stars like Gary Moore, Bruce Dickinson, Diamond Head, Geezer Butler's band G/Z/R and even Rob Halford, to name a few. And it got me thinking about how much this would change my life. At last, this was the break I have always wanted! To be included on the same CD as those guys is just an honour and I can't say anything more than that!

»Rock Of Ages« (Sanctuary Records – 2002)

1. Gamma Ray – "Lust For Life"
2. Celtic Frost – "The Heart Beneath"
3. UFO – "Too Hot To Handle" (live)
4. Diamond Head – "Am I Evil?" (live)
5. Moody Marsden Band – "Fool For Your Lovin" (live)
6. The Quireboys – "Seven Days"
7. Wolfsbane – "Protect And Survive"
8. G/Z/R – "Drive Boy Shooting"
9. Ugly Kid Joe – "Sandwich"
10. Thunder – "Pilot Of My Dreams"
11. The Almighty – "Do You Understand"
12. W.A.S.P. – "K.F.D."
13. Al Atkins – "Victim Of Changes"
14. Stratovarius – "Black Diamond"
15. Halford – "Resurrection"
16. Bruce Dickinson – "Bring Your Daughter To The Slaughter"
17. Megadeth – "Mechanix" (live)

Yet again, my luck didn't hold out because in 2002 Dave Holland was accused of sexually abusing a young student of his; he had been giving drumming lessons to this kid and things got out of hand. After his career in Judas Priest came to an abrupt end he reunited with Glenn Hughes and Mel Galley for a short lived Trapeze reunion in the early nineties but after that he became a drum teacher and set up a shop in Northampton to support his income.

Apparently, the student in question was 17 years old but with a mental age of a child. When the police raided Dave's cottage they apparently found sex tapes, pornographic magazines and sex toys. His trail began in January 2004 at Northampton Crown Court. The following month he was found guilty and sentenced to eight years imprisonment with a £10,000 fine and that no doubt has put an end to his career. The press absolutely annihilated him and I found the whole thing to be really unsettling.

I remember thinking how much more Judas Priest would want to distance themselves from Dave after the court case. Their press statement read: "We are as shocked as everyone by this news. However, we would like to point out that Scott Travis is Judas Priest's drummer and has been since 1989. We haven't had any contact with Dave Holland at all since we parted company with him over 15 years ago."

Putting Dave's court case aside, you can see how much Priest want to erase past members from the band's history. The last line that statement says it all: "We haven't had any contact with Dave Holland at all since we parted company with him over 15 years ago." How one person can go from being a hard working member of the band for a decade to being a total nobody is incredibly offensive. It's pretty obvious that they have treated their drummers like objects! Scott Travis' career seems secure but so did Dave's in the mid-eighties.

Tony Iommi also famously distanced himself from Dave. In 1996, they worked together on a project that also included Glenn Hughes and Don Airey. The product of those sessions was released by Sanctuary in 2004 as »The DEP Sessions«. Bootlegs from those sessions had been in circulation for years as »The Eighth Star«. On the official release, Dave's original drums were replaced by Jimmy Copley who now plays drums in Magnum.

My last telephone conversation with Dave was an emotional one. He was adamant of his innocence over the whole affair and told me not to believe a word of all the accusations that were being thrown at him. To be truthful, he did sound very sincere to me. My next call was from my friend Ian Hill who said that if the British press should call me about Dave I should just say "No comment" and put down the phone.

Due to Dave's imprisonment my album got shelved because of his terrible publicity and, of course, all the record deals inevitably got cancelled too. One minute you're on a high and the next you are on a downhill slope but that's the roller coaster ride that rock and roll sometimes throws at you. Sanctuary has since been sold to Universal Records in a reported £45 million take over bid so we will have to see, if »Victim Of Changes« ever sees the light of day again. But some good news is that my version of "Victim Of Changes" is being featured in a new movie that's being made in America. The writer of the film is Lee Finn who comes from Memphis. It's a horror movie called »Juggles« and has recently been bought by a Hollywood producer/writer so you might see it on DVD soon. There will also be a song on the soundtrack by ex-Maiden nutcase/singer Paul Di'Anno. Just kidding Paul … you're not that crazy!

Some people would have quit by now. Christ, some would have quit years … no, decades ago. I've had a hell of a lot of knock backs in my life but I have continued to follow my dream despite knowing that I will never be rich and make it big. Why do I do it? I love the music. Ever since I heard Eddie Cochran and those great American rock and roll singers of the fifties I've never wanted to do anything else. Some people could say I've wasted my life following a dream that has faded after each passing year. My retort to that is: I have lived a bloody brilliant life and met some incredible people and most importantly I've had a laugh. I don't want to leave this earth knowing that I haven't made a contribution. I wasn't going to give up after the failure of Atkins/Holland. I had another plan up my sleeve …

Rob Halford had spent the past couple of years working hard trying to regain some lost respect. To everybody's surprise, he made an astonishing comeback. After the failure of his album with Trent Raznor, he was literally forced to have a major re-think about his career and it seemed that the only thing he could do that would save his career would be to return as the Metal God. Rob and his manager John Baxter hooked up with the metal producer Roy Z who is famous for his work with Bruce Dickinson of Iron Maiden. They also formed a new band and called it Halford, which is hardly surprising.

Halford's first release was the bloody brilliant »Resurrection« album in 2000. I was absolutely blown away by that CD and it showed the world that Priest needed him more than he needed them. It was released at the time as Priest's »Demolition« CD I remember that critics pitted them against each other in the press. By all accounts, both albums didn't actually sell all that well, certainly not compared to their heyday, from »British Steel« to »Turbo«. It was certainly interesting to see how both albums differed from each other. The critics made out that »Resurrection« was the "best Priest album Priest never made" which hit the nail on the head. I think it was a very wise move that Halford did; it was such a shame to see how much damage his career had taken in the previous decade. He's a metal guy and despite what he told Metal Edge, his best music is with Priest.

»Resurrection« has lots of great songs with strong melodies, twin-guitar attacks and tremendous vocal power. Songs like "Made In Hell" really struck a chord with me; basically it's a history of metal and Rob does a fine job summing up heavy metal music. I also liked "Silent Screams" and "The One You Love To Hate", his duet with Bruce Dickinson. What about that for a collaboration? Two metal giants unite! Halford went on tour for the first time in ages and it was really great to see him getting a lot of good reviews for his gigs. He even toured the UK with Iron Maiden and that was definitely a treat for hardcore heavy metal fans. Rob actually played at the local famous JB's nightclub in Dudley but it sold out before I could get a ticket and I was also busy doing my own thing on my other dates, so I missed him during that particular road jaunt.

After »Resurrection«, Halford's second release was »Crucible« which I liked less but it still had some really heavy moments in it. It was a much darker album, a bit weird in parts but I liked the songs "One Will" and "Betrayal". I think in some ways it was a more mature album that harked back to late seventies stuff like »Sin After Sin« because of it's gothic nature. Halford hit the road again but after the release of this second album the band went quiet. I wonder why?

I think that was a good period in Rob's career and suddenly all the old metal heads started to take notice of him again. It was almost like he was some kind of a forgotten legend. He's like some sort of superhero like Batman or Superman because as soon as he puts on his famous leather and silver studded costume, he automatically commands the stage and the people around him bow down to his feet in awe. That's something you don't see happening with every other metal singer. Those of you who were not around during the early years of heavy metal probably don't get what I mean, but those of you who are as old as me will understand completely.

Thankfully, after the grunge period in the early nineties metal had become popular again by the time Rob Halford had made his highly-publicised comeback. By the turn of the millennium a style of metal called nu metal had become huge, not by the eighties standards, but big enough to get people back into the music, so you can't really argue with that.

Nu metal merged rap and urban music with metal, which goes all the way back to Run DMC's duet with Aerosmith on "Walk This Way" and of course there was Anthrax's great duet with Public Enemy on "Bring The Noise". I'm a fan of any band that tries something different. Look at Sabbath, the music they made when they first started out was totally different to what was going on around them. So bands like System Of A Down, Mudvayne and Disturbed helped to bring metal back to the masses.

What was cool about this was that those guys, along with other nu metal bands such as Linkin Park and Limp Bizkit, got the young kids listening to the bands that influenced them, namely Metallica and before them Motörhead and Sabbath, amongst many more. Korn are a really great band and I listen to them a lot and that's because my son Joe (now 18 years old) plays their music all the time and he got me in to the aforementioned nu metal bands. Joe keeps me interested in the current scene. Because I'm a rocker at heart I rarely tell him to "turn down that bloody racket" like some parents do. I think I'm a cool dad.

"Turn that song up. I can't hear it!" I'd shout to Joe.

"Dad, my CD player can't get any louder than this."

Everybody seemed to be into rap and all that shit so it was great to see an uprising of ass-kicking metal bands. Some of them haven't stood the test of time but the more talented ones like Korn and Linkin Park are still going strong. A lot of them sold out huge arenas all over the world and had hit albums in the States and Europe but like any movement, it didn't last long and a lot of the snotty music critics thought nu metal was a joke. Hell, if it gets the kids listening to Priest and their like, then I'm up for it. I bet there were loads of kids out there who strapped on guitars or started playing the drums and formed bands after seeing the rise of Korn and Linkin Park. So tell me why is that such a bad thing? They may not be playing what Judas Priest or Sabbath used to play but it's still metal. They're still riffing. Music evolves. Rock and roll music has gotten louder, faster and more aggressive but it's still the basic guitars, drums, bass and vocals.

As I've just said, the best thing about current trends in metal is that the upcoming bands talk endlessly about their respect for vintage British metal bands like Sabbath. There was a brilliant tribute album to Black Sabbath released about ten years ago called »Nativity In Black«. It featured all sorts of great bands like Biohazard, Sepultura, White Zombie and even Bruce Dickinson. After years of struggling with different line-ups (led by my ex-IMA agent Tony Iommi) Sabbath had become really popular again after their first reunion gig at the Birmingham NEC in 1997. Their success in large part was due to the respect they command from young bands. When the reunion was announced everybody when crazy trying to get a ticket. It was like the second coming and it was really thoughtful that the band chose the NEC rather than an American arena to play their first reunion gigs. Since then the reunion gigs have rolled on. But like everybody else I'd love to hear a new album.

A sequel to »Nativity In Black« was released a couple of years later and that one featured System Of A Down, Machine Head, Megadeth, Slayer and even Busta Rhymes, the rapper. I guess Sabbath really have proven how much music can transcend genres. God bless 'em, as Ozzy would say.

Looking at how much metal and hard rock had changed over the years, and how popular bands like Sabbath and the classic Priest line-up had become again, I felt that it was about time I got my arse into gear. I decided that I should go back into the studio to record another album.

I left the Dave Holland issue in the past; he was always a nice guy to me and I'm not going to knock him. My first four studio albums were hard rock albums with lots of melodies, some acoustic moments and some ballads but I wanted to make a heavier album. I wanted to make something very British, something hard hitting but melodic and exciting. There was a lull after the »Victim Of Changes« album and the failure to get the Atkins-Holland project going frustrated me but this time I was determined that I would make the best album I possibly could at this stage in my life. I was still writing songs at home but it was a struggle trying to look after my family, pay the bills and write songs all at the same time. Whoever said being a songwriter-singer is glamorous is wrong. I have a normal life, I just get to make music and meet some really cool people at the same time. I was still using my home studio and whenever I got a minute I was always jamming, making demos and creating new ideas for use on an album. I'm still like that.

"Al, your dinner is ready!" my wife would shout to me.

"I'll be down in a minute; I'm just putting the finishing touches to this song", I'd say back. Of course, it would be about another hour and my dinner would be cold and my very understanding wife would have to re-heat my food.

The thing is when I'm working on some new music my mind is completely consumed by it. It's weird, it's like I'm in a different world and I forget that I have a family and that the world is still in motion. But that is the power of rock and roll; you're supposed to forget about real life.

I had briefly parted ways with Pete Emms and Paul May my bass player and guitarist, respectively. Pete went on to form and front his own band called The Vaseline Rats (who would record three demos in 2003) and Paul decided to carry on under the A.N.D Band and later, The Temple Dogs. They both converted to Christianity and we had different ideas on how to do things. What I needed was a new band but until that could happen I adopted The Vaseline Rats as my back-up band for a while. I also carried on with my songwriting for my next solo project. It was a slow process but slowly I was picking up the pieces and moving forward.

For a few years now Rob Grohl – Dave Grohl's uncle – of R.G. Promotions in New Jersey had asked me to guest on some of his American rock festivals but I always refused until 2003 when he said I could take my own band over there and he would also set up some other name players to join us too. The other player was none other than ex-Iron Maiden and Praying Mantis guitarist Dennis Stratton, so this time I agreed to Rob's request. This opportunity was too good to turn down. I've always been a big fan of Dennis; he's an underrated guitarist and a damn nice guy.

> I've since become good buddies with Dennis so I'm more than pleased that he'd like to add a few words ...
>
> Dennis Stratton: "My first experience with Judas Priest was when Iron Maiden supported them on tour in 1980 and we never got to close to them but many years later I got to meet Al Atkins, their original lead singer. We hit it off straight away. He's a lovely geezer with a great voice and it's a shame he wasn't on that tour in 1980, I think I would have enjoyed it a lot better."

However, despite how elated I felt after being offered to play in the States, I was hit with some bad news: in November '03, I lost my dear friend and webmaster Michael Liljhammer from Sweden who was a massive Judas Priest fan. On my new website we keep a history section which chronicles everything I have ever done, it's quite brilliant and it was all set up by Michael (R.I.P.).

This would be my first tour since the Lion days. I was a bit nervous about the prospect of playing gigs abroad but I soon realized what I had missed: the excitement, the madness, the buzz and obviously the fans. The only thing that will stop me playing live again would be my health but I soon got back into the swing of things and it felt like it's the old days again. But I never realised how hard it would be trying to do everything myself which is what I did at first: writing songs, managing the band, getting all the gigs and rehearsing, writing this book and doing interviews for worldwide rock magazines but it felt great to be back.

So in March 2004, I set off to the States with Dennis and my new band: Pete Emms, drummer Adrian Badland and South African guitarist Mike de Jager from The Vaseline Rats; he has been in the country for about six years and it was Pete who introduced us. We were also joined by NWOBHM hero and Neat Metal director Jess Cox (ex-Tygers Of Pan Tang) to play some East Coast gigs which included two festivals.

Left to right: Bassist Pete Emms (The Vaseline Rats), drummer Adrian Badland (ex-Ainsley Lister Band), guitarist Dennis Stratton (ex- Iron Maiden), singer Jess Cox (ex-Tygers of Pan Tang) and me.

I had been to the States before but this would be my first time playing there so I was excited about trying something new. I remember the flight over to the States. We had a laugh and took over the plane; you could probably hear us in the first class area! We talked about rock music on the eight-hour flight and that's it, just music. Dennis worked out a setlist of old Judas Priest and Iron Maiden songs, which Rob Grohl had requested for us to play. Rob is a big metal fan and likes a lot of British bands especially the classics like Priest, Maiden and Sabbath. I have nothing but positive things to say about Rob. He is a fantastic New Yorker and can be very loud and intimidating but he gets the job done. I was always glad to be on his side and he treated my band like kings and has a heart of gold and would make a very good manager. He boosted our confidence and has a great sense of humour.

I really enjoyed the songwriting and recording side of music but had missed the buzz of playing live and being on the road again and was really looking forward to the tour.

"I can't wait to kick their arses", I said to Mike on the flight over to America. "They're not going to know what's hit them. I've got loads of energy for this."

We kicked off under 'The NWOBHM All Stars' banner at a club called Boomerz on Seminole Boulevard in Tampa, Florida. Even though I wasn't actually involved in the NWOBHM era I just couldn't say no to that gig. The Americans idolize British bands and a lot of the thrash bands from years ago like Metallica are huge fans of the NWOBHM. It was a good opportunity for me and my band to spread out wings and make some new fans but we played without Dennis because he was too pissed. To be honest, the American audience gave us a mixed reception on our first gig but I thought the actual venue was amazing. The setlist was some old songs like "Victim Of Changes", "Never Satisfied", "Black Sheep Of The Family" and new songs like "Cradle To The Grave". The Maiden songs were "Running Free" and "Sanctuary".

We then did some sightseeing and two days later we played Florida's first metal festival »Sun And Steel« at Pinellas Expo Centre which was spread across two days and featured 40 bands including some great names like Deicide, Obituary, Trivium and Testament. We were second off, top-billing to Obituary but sadly the place has since burnt down.

Apparently, there were some arguments between Obituary and the concert promoter Jack Koshick. After the festival, Obituary actually made a public press statement about what they saw as a poorly organised event with too many bands and they fell out with Koshick over money. Thankfully, there was no financial trouble in our camp; we were treated well enough and with respect.

One band we hooked up with and became good friends with was the Austrian band Spearhead. What a really great bunch of guys! It was important for us to play the »Sun And Steel« festival because we stood alongside younger bands who really fired us up and made us play faster and harder. A lot of the audience was young and were into thrash/death metal so maybe we were out of our depth but when we hit the stage we surprised the lot of them and I think we won some of them over and didn't go down too bad. We weren't just a bunch of old farts from England! But I got the feeling that some of them went to the festival just to meet up with Den and myself to get our autographs and photographs with us backstage just because of the Maiden and Priest connection.

Of course, I was shattered after the gig but hung around to catch some of the other bands in action. I'm a fan of Testament and a lot of the thrash bands of the eighties, so it was a privilege just to be sharing the same bill with them.

We then made our way up the East Coast and finally finished playing at the two day »Metal Meltdown« festival in New Jersey in a smaller venue which held around 2.000 people. We played alongside even more great bands like Raven and Seven Witches. What a great bill! We actually played second down the bill under the great Symphony X and fired up by an intense audience we were terrific. It was easily our best gig.

We decided to cross the Hudson River and visit NYC. Driving through the Big Apple in a white stretch limo was a great feeling; it's probably the first and only time in my life when I've felt like a true celebrity. Believe it or not, it was my first visit to New York and it definitely wouldn't be my last. I have actually been back twice since then. I just love the place and the buzz of it all. I even miss the smell and the noise. It's a crazy place and I thought the way New York is depicted on TV and in film is just a cliché but it's real: there are hot dog stands everywhere, drivers go through red lights, taxi drivers beep their horns constantly and it's very fast-paced.

On returning home to England after an amazing trip, Dennis and myself decided to get together again under the name of The Denial but alas it was an ill fated project. We both had too many commitments of our own to work on. Dennis was waiting to see what the reaction would be to the Praying Mantis greatest hits CD and if the band would get back together. As for myself, I had decided to get some material together to write this book and I also needed to go back into the studio to record some more songs which I had written and had been promising myself for that past couple of years that I would get a bloody album together. What can I say, I'm a diligent worker.

Metal fans were not surprised (me included!) when Rob Halford re-joined the mighty Priest which was announced in a press statement in early 2003. I saw a bit of the coverage on TV. The band had re-issued all of their CBS/Sony albums which got them major press attention and I think it did them the world of good. After years of relative obscurity and a lack of mainstream success and recognition they were finally getting the sort of reviews they deserved.

Each CD – from »Sin After Sin« to »Painkiller« – came with bonus tracks and it certainly seemed that the critics who had given them digs during their heyday were now committed fans; they were probably totally surprised that Priest's music is a lot better than they have been given credit for. This kind of thing happens all the time; it's one of the reasons why record companies continue to re-issue CDs and greatest hits packages. AC/DC re-issued all of their albums not long after and it got them some major press and really good reviews. Priest also released a huge CD/DVD box set called »Metalogy« which features some of my songs on the first disc. It's a really cool set designed with silver studs on the sides. It's filled with some of the greatest heavy metal you are ever likely to hear and, of course, it includes the classic "Victim Of Changes".

Suddenly, Judas Priest were everywhere: on television, in all the major rock magazines and even in the newspapers. It just goes to show that Priest needed Halford. They obviously had to sack Tim Owens who went on to join Iced Earth, a brilliant American metal band. From what I gather, Tim and Priest are still friends, which is cool. Sadly, Iced Earth main man Joe Schaffer sacked Tim in 2007, replacing him with the band's previous singer. This completely shocked all Iced Earth fans. But as I write this book it has been announced that he is to collaborate with the great Yngwie Malmsteen on the guitarist's new album after finishing his run with singer Doogie White.

Tim is also busy with his own band Beyond Fear who released a great debut album a couple of years ago. I can't wait to hear from them. I don't think people have treated him as well as they should; he's a better songwriter than people give him credit for and I hope he does really well with his band.

So Priest – that's Rob Halford, Kenny Downing, Glenn Tipton, Ian Hill and Scott Travis – hit the road in 2004 playing festivals all over the world, except, it has to be said, in England. They co-headlined Ozzfest in the States with a reformed Black Sabbath. From what I read at the time, it seemed that Priest upstaged Sabbath. As you know, I love Sabbath especially the original line-up but these days Ozzy really struggles on stage; sometimes you just can't understand what he's singing, he doesn't make any sense and mumbles his way through a gig which is really sad. I don't think the TV show he was involved with has done a lot of good to his heavy metal reputation either. Priest included lots of well known songs in the setlist for that tour; it was basically a greatest hits package so I was eager to hear what "Victim Of Changes" sounded like. Rob is still a great singer despite the passing years and the riff to the song is unmistakable. I think it lasts for around six to seven minutes on stage.

Chapter 9
Demon Deceivers: Al Atkins & The Holy Rage (2005-2009)

The trip I made to the States last year really invigorated me and even though what could have been a great project between me and Dennis Stratton, didn't work out (there's still time!), I had other ideas.

Entering a brand new year, I decided that this time around my latest album would be financed by myself so that I would own all the rights to it. Not only is this financially more lucrative (providing it sells and is made for relatively low costs) but it also means that there is no bullshit involved with a record label. I can pretty much do what I want. A lot of singers do this and even filmmakers; George Lucas paid for the »Star Wars« prequels knowing that We would make even more money in profits. Of course, I didn't expect my CD to sell millions, maybe small thousands, but I just liked the freedom of it. I also decided that I would take control of the album's artwork which as you know has been a cause of contention between me and the record label on past albums. I would license the album myself for worldwide distribution. It was about time I got down to some hard work in the studio! I titled my new album »Demon Deceiver«.

My good mates Pete Emms (bass) and Mick Hales (drums) gave my new recordings a robust backbone. I also had guest appearances by name guitarists and friends who I had met over the years. My friend Dennis Stratton was booked into the studio one day to lay down a riff on the album but in the end he never played on it because during a weekend gig in London a PA speaker fell over and injured his shoulder.

I used the brilliant guitar riffs of Brian Tatler from the legendary NWOBHM band Diamond Head, who's classic song "Am I Evil?" has inspired many famous metal bands. There were talks between Brian and myself about me taking over vocals with Diamond Head after Sean Harris left the band but I think he had made his mind up to appoint the younger

Ex-Iron Maiden guitarist Dennis Stratton and me in a couple of publicity shots.

Nick Tart. That's when I asked Brian if he could play on one of my songs "Blood, Demons And Whiskey" and he agreed – it was a great session. Like myself, Brian is a Black Country lad so we got along great.

One of the other famous guitarists that I collaborated with was the talented Simon Lees from Budgie who in my mind is one of the best guitar players to come out of the UK and was once voted 'Guitarist of the Year' by Guitar Magazine. He's one of the best I have ever played with. At one time, I asked him to play in my live band but Budgie offered him a better pay packet. "Demon Deceiver", the opening instrumental by Simon which features myself reciting an old poem by Lionel Johnson, was going to be a very short introduction piece to the album and I was going to fade it after a minute or two. But why would I cut it short before we even get to Simon's awesome guitar playing towards the end? So I just left it as it was. I was made up with that intro.

> *Simon has been a good friend of mine for more than ten years. He's constantly full of ideas and is a really respected guitarist in rock/metal.*
>
> Simon Lees: "The music business is full of people who talk a lot and achieve nothing. Everybody has grand dreams 'We can do this, we can do that, it'll be fantastic ...' and more often than not these dreams end up unrealised. Al Atkins is one of the few people I've worked with who actually gets things done. He's a 'do-er' rather than a 'talker' and this was obvious from the first time we met. I was fortunate to have been involved in recording tracks on both the »Heavy Thoughts« album and »Demon Deceiver« and each session was light hearted and damn good fun. One of Al's many assets is his ability to communicate his ideas clearly, so I knew immediately what type of thing he wanted me to play. Al's energy and enthusiasm for music is infectious and as a performer he still kicks ass! I'm proud to have worked with a guy who is still one of metal's all time greats."

»Demon Deceiver« was recorded over the next year at Mad Hat Studio's in Wolverhampton with Mark V. Stuart and Sheena Seer at the desks apart from the one song "Drown", which was recorded in Kansas in America and featured Johnny Lokke (of the band Kansas USA) and myself doing an unlikely duet.

The story goes that a few years ago Johnny Lokke asked me to sing with him in an album called »The New Breed – Bound By The Thread«, which also features Stefan Leibing of Primal Fear and Chris 'Wah Wah' Watson, the guitarist from Black Rose. The money from the album sales was given to Johnny's drummer Scot who unfortunately had a motorcycle accident. The track Johnny and I sang together was a song called "Drown", which I absolutely loved and I asked him if I could put it on my new album. The sound of it differs form the rest of the songs on my album; it's a lot more melodic and mid-paced but I think it works okay.

> *I don't know Johnny Lokke that well but what I can say is that he's a really great guy to work with. I'm more than happy that he can contribute a few words to my book.*
>
> Johnny Lokke: "I met Al Atkins back in 2004 when we worked together on the song 'Drown' on my CD »The New Breed – Bound By The Thread«. My drummer Scot Goacher had just had an accident and had broken his hip in three places and was left bedridden. That meant his income was gone, and his bills were piling up. I decided to do a benefit CD

for him, and so I quickly wrote ten songs and had some friends that Scot and I had jammed with in previous bands come by to play on it. When it came time to add some finishing touches, I had some of my buddies like Stefan Leibing from the band Primal Fear and Mike Campese, who is a great fusion player from New York, jump in and throw down some guitar solos. I actually had the project almost done when I stopped by a friend of mine's house and he was reviewing one of Al's CD's – »Heavy Thoughts« if I remember correctly – for an online publication. I had never heard Al before that and I was completely blown away. I ended up sitting there and listening to the whole CD, and thought to myself: 'Man, I'd like to get him on my CD.' My friend must have known what I was kicking around, because he looked at me and said: 'You should try and get Al on your CD. I interviewed him and he was a really cool guy.'

I thought that there was no way, but later that night I decided to give it a shot anyway, and sent Al an e-mail explaining the situation and sent him a couple of songs to listen to. Much to my surprise he e-mailed me back right away and said he'd love to do it. How great is that? He didn't know Scot or I from Adam, and he agrees to go into the studio and record a cut for us. That's pretty killer. Anyway, a couple days later I get this big, booming vocal back that I didn't have to do a thing to, and it was phenomenal. I still try and keep up with Al and see what he is doing, and I hope I can repay the favour to him one of these days. I can't wait to work on another project together."

I used a Priest connection again; I decided I wanted to re-record "Victim Of Changes" using my new band: Simon Lees, Mick Hales, Pete Emms and with help from guitarist Chris Johnson. It's probably the most powerful version of the song I've ever done. I also chose to re-record "Dreamer Deceiver", which is one of my all time favourite Priest songs. »Sad Wings Of Destiny« was a great album and I think a benchmark for Judas Priest and all their later recordings that followed and I wanted to make my on special version of the song.

I think my favourite set of lyrics from this particular album has to be in a song called "Bleeding". I wrote this song after reading about a married couple in their fifties; she had got MS and her husband, who looked after her, was told he had only got three months to live because of cancer. They had no children and no one to turn to so out of desperation he killed her by cutting her throat and then tried to stab himself to death but failed so he eventually hung himself. It's a very powerful story and I knew it would make a good song. I'm drawn to people and real life situations, that's what I prefer to write about. Although I like fantasy and unrealistic tales I think that at the end of the day my best lyrics are about everyday events and the people in them.

"Bleeding"
(Atkins)

Out of the shadows steps hell's confusion
Life has no meaning there's no solution
Out of this madness of anger and sorrows
No deals with the darkness for there's no tomorrows
And I'm reeling and I'm seething
And I'm screaming and I'm bleeding

Out of this hatred of life all around me
There's no one to turn to but soon we are both free
Out of this chaos of no mind or reason
Questions unanswered silenced and beaten
And I'm calling to our needing
Now I'm crawling and I'm bleeding

Maybe heaven holds the key, maybe hell just waits for me
Don't want to wake up in the darkest night
Maybe my father will guide the light
Never meant to see you hurt, never meant to 'cause you any pain
Sorry words for what they're worth
So many dreams were all in vain

The heaviest song on the album is probably "Cradle To The Grave". Although it's only a short set of lyrics the band sounds fantastic. There's a great bass line, strong riff and good chorus. The premise of the song is simple: it's about an imaginary person who through his life is held captive by the devil but one day hopes to be set free.

"Cradle To The Grave"
(Atkins)

It's such a sad situation, all my life has been a long temptation
Hell's rebel held by vengeance, they say one day that I will pay the penance
Servant of sin, dark of the day, Iron Mountains couldn't stand in my way
No tears have fell but got to tell, it's been one long nightmare ticket to hell

(Chorus)

From the cradle to the grave – between hell and high water
And the challenge that I crave – is to free me from this deed.
Message longer, mission stronger, no break no sense in this hunger
Twisted mind, one of a kind, thoughtless, restless, speeding blind

(Chorus)

The album title, »Demon Deceiver«, came about after I had some artwork painted for me for my next album by my good friend and artist Andy Robinson. His painting depicted a black angel looking into what looks like a sea of molten lava. I thought it was a fantastic piece of work and had already chosen to record "Dreamer Deceiver" on the album. This is where it may get confusing because I then decided to change that title around to "Demon Deceiver", which is the opening track on the album, while the Priest-Atkins song "Dreamer Deceiver" closes the album. Then I saw that Priest had a similar idea with an angel on their front cover of »Angel Of Retribution«. There's no way I could have released an album with that cover at the same time as Priest's highly-publicised comeback CD. I would have got absolutely slated. It was a weird

An early design for my album »Demon Deceiver«. This was scrapped when Priest released »Angel Of Retribution«.

coincidence so I had to change it. Maybe I'll use it on another album but not for a while.

There were so many players that appeared on my album, I was going to call it 'Al Atkins & Friends' but with a title like »Demon Deceiver«, it sounded too tame, so one drunken night I decided to subtitle it »The Sin Sessions«. I think it's a good title and very fitting for the album's content and the demons involved in its making! (Just kidding guys …)

I finished the album in September 2006, which was later than planned but I wanted to spend a lot of time and energy on it.

I was happy to see that Judas Priest's comeback album »Angel Of Retribution« was released in 2005 to rave reviews, although many critics attacked the lengthy song "Lochness". On the whole, I really like the album; it reminded me of old-school metal with a modern production. It was good of them to mention the old days and even Holy Joe on the arse-kicking screamer "Deal With The Devil" and I also really like "Judas Rising". It was so great to hear Downing/Tipton open a song with a powerful duel guitar riff. That album represents vintage Priest and the artwork was really cool, too similar to their early stuff like »Sad Wings Of Destiny« which I'm a great fan of. The album was a worldwide hit and it even reached the Top 40 in the UK and the Top 20 in America. A major coup for the band is that they re-signed to Sony who were great in terms of giving the band lots of publicity.

Throughout 2005, Judas Priest toured the world taking a number of successful bands with them as support, including the Scorpions, Whitesnake, Anthrax, Baron Rojo, Hatebreed, In Flames, Paradise Lost, Queensryche and Rob Zombie. Priest finally did a major tour of the UK which included two sell-out nights at the Hammersmith Odeon in London. I got to see them at the Birmingham NEC and even got to meet up with the lads backstage after the gig. I just said hello to Kenny and Glenn and shook hands with them. It was funny because some old geezer fan of the band recognized me with them and said he remembered seeing me singing with Priest all those years ago. I was flattered by it. Andy Pyke from Marshall Law was also backstage and he came up to me for a chat and some other young fan of Priest's came up to me for my autograph. I told Ian what an awesome show it had been and said hello to Scott Travis as well. I didn't see Rob at all backstage, which was a shame because I wanted to tell him how much I enjoyed the gig.

Again, they got lots of great reviews and released a live DVD recorded in Japan. Rob looks as though he's put on a bit of weight and he's not as mobile on stage but his voice is still really powerful. How anybody can sing like that in their fifties is beyond me! They included some new stuff in the setlist for this tour and continued, much to my pleasure, to play "Victim Of Changes". I think of all the countries they played during 2005 they went down a storm in America; their biggest fan base has always been the States and this time around they played some really big venues over there. It was great to see them back in the big venues again, that's where they belong. A band that has worked so hard in their career, which going back to 1969 has lasted five decades now, deserves all the success they get.

How great would it be to have my band, Tim's band and Judas Priest as headliner in a one-off gig? We could bill it as a 40th anniversary event: '1969-2009: PRIEST THROUGH THE PAST.' It'll never happen but it's a nifty idea if I do say so myself and I know Tim wants to do something like that but the ball is in their court. If we did a concert uniting the lot of us together we could play material right from the beginning to Priest's latest CD and give the material some meaning and depth. And if the gig was held in Birmingham, we'd be sure to get a good turnout and lots of publicity. (As it goes, I'm currently planning a Judas Priest convention for some time in the not too distant future).

Judas Priest had previously been given the 'Metal Guru' award at the Classic Rock magazine 'Roll Of Honour' awards but another fitting tribute to the band was their inclusion in the 'V.H.1 Rock Honours' in Las Vegas in May 2006, which I watched on the TV when it was first aired. The ceremony also featured fellow British legends Queen and Def Leppard and the American glam rockers Kiss. In a tribute to Priest, Godsmack played a blinding medley of vintage heavy metal: "Electric Eye"/"Victim Of Changes"/"Hell Bent For Leather". Priest blazed through "Breaking The Law" and "The Green Manalishi (With The Two-Pronged Crown)" and then Rob rode on stage on a Harley before the band broke into "You've Got Another Thing Comin'".

I think by this point Priest had come full circle; they've had their fair share of ups and downs but after 30 years they were finally getting the sort of recognition they deserve and what's crazy is that there are literally thousands of teenagers listening to Judas Priest right now and wearing the t-shirts. Of course that meant the future would bring new challenges for them and it remains to be seen whether Rob will stay in the band. Like all talented and innovative artists they push themselves and try different things, sometimes it works and sometimes it doesn't, but the important thing is to keep trying and one day you'll hit the right button. The best thing they can do is to keep touring and recording while they've still got the energy and enthusiasm. Hell, I've had my ups and downs too but I'm in a good position now.

I had signed a one-off distribution deal with a Swedish company called Diesel & Glory. They wanted the album out earlier but decided that they had too many albums on their schedule so they held it back which meant I had more time to work on the recordings. Diesel & Glory specialise in releasing and re-issuing classic British rock and have even revamped Priest's first two albums. They have also released the latest album »Violent New Breed« by Randy Piper's new band Animal, formerly members of W.A.S.P.

I had early press copies of »Demon Deceiver« available for the end of 2006. When the box of CD's arrived at my house I just couldn't believe how good they looked. I was happy with the artwork by Al Barrow of Generic Designs and after playing it on my CD player, I was very happy with the sound and overall production. It's easily the best album I have done.

»Demon Deceiver« (2007 – Diesel & Glory)

"Demon Deceiver" (S. Lees)
"Money Talks" (Atkins)
"Blood Demons And Whiskey" (P. Emms)
"Drown" (J. Lokke)
"Sentenced" (Atkins/Emms)

"Victim Of Changes" (Atkins/Halford/Downing/Tipton)
"Bleeding" (Atkins)
"God Help Me" (Atkins)
"Cradle To The Grave" (Atkins)
"Dreamer Deceiver" (Atkins/Halford/Downing/Tipton)

The Band:

Al Atkins (vocals)
Pete Emms (bass)
Mick Hales (drums)
Simon Lees (guitar)
Mike de Jager (guitar)

Guest Appearances:

Paul May (guitar)
Brian Tatler (guitar)
Chris Johnson (guitar)
Johnny Lokke (vocals and guitar)
Lon Weaver (guitar)
Jeff Gragg (bass)
Dan Dreher (drums)
Adrian Badland (drums)

    To gear up for the album's release we played some shows during the winter. I decided to tentatively dub ourselves 'The Al Atkins Band.' We played a handful of gigs in the Midlands but I have to say the most special place we played was JB's in Dudley. JB's has always been a favourite gig to play and the band went down really well with the audience who came from near and far to see us. Old friends turned up, like Trevor Lunn, Priest's old roadie from the seventies, and Ernie Chataway, the original Priest guitarist who I hadn't seen for about 20 years. I just couldn't believe how much Ernie had changed. I didn't recognise him at first. And we even had four guys from Germany come over to see us.

    We decided to open our set with a cover of the Priest classic "Metal Gods" but our version is different from Priest's original cut. My voice has definitely changed over the years as I've gotten older. I have been compared to Paul Di'Anno on several occasions but I don't know about that anymore. I was brought up listening to Paul Rodgers whose style I like very much. And then it was Robert Plant and later with David Coverdale but I don't think I sound like any of these. Years of cigarettes and whiskey have given me my own personal voice although I have now have given up the nicotine which has affected my vocal chords.

    I tend to work with different musicians on the road and for those gigs my live band consisted of: bassist Pete Emms, guitarists Mike de Jager and Chris Johnson and my young drummer Alex Reynolds. Alex is the powerhouse behind the band and already has experience playing across the pond. His drum kit was bought from Jason Bonham and Alex is going in the right direction in following in Bonham's footsteps.

I haven't known Chris Johnson all that long but he has become a good friend of mine. I'll let him tell you about our friendship.

Chris Johnson: "I met Al a few years back at a family function. It turned out that Al Atkins was my wife's uncle. A lot of things happened over those few years but basically I ended up recording on »Demon Deceiver« and eventually became a core member of the band. However, it was amazing how much history we had without us knowing each other. My uncle (Nick Bowbanks) was a lighting guy for one of the early line-ups of Judas Priest with Rob Halford so I had met the guys many times in the Yew Tree estate near West Bromwich where they grew up. I found out many years later that Nick was also Rob's partner for four years. When he tragically died, Rob dedicated Fight's »A Small Deadly Space« to my uncle Nick. I remember clearly when Glenn Tipton sat me on the top of my grandmother's fridge and him showing me the E chord. It seems odd that my life musically came full circle and I now play for the founder of the band. What is there to say about Al? Well, he's an amazing vocalist, songwriter and a very good friend. I am one lucky guy."

Holy Rage guitarist Chris Johnson.

I pasted a note on my website about my adventures in 2006. It was a topsy-turvy year. Unfortunately, my mother passed away and of course it's always sad when a relative dies but she lived a life and I'd like to think she was pleased with what I had achieved.

Obviously, it pissed me off that my album was delayed for several months but that is the nature of the beast. It also meant that the live dates that we had planned to play in Europe had to be delayed until the album's release so we could do lots of promotion and give justice to its release. To be honest, I couldn't wait until the year was out; I was gearing up for the New Year and hoping that 2007 would bring happier times.

January 2007 saw the release of my eagerly awaited fifth solo album which I was very pleased with. My co-writer Neil Daniels was generous with his review in Fireworks: The Melodic Rock Magazine.

Once again Dave Ling gave me quite a good review in Classic Rock saying: "Full credit to Al Atkins … The gruff-voiced singer's fifth solo album has more in common with the rudimentary yet principled working man's metal of a band like Demon …"

The website Metalrage said: "Highlights definitely are the stunning guitar work which can be heard on almost every song, and the ending track: a very nice cover of Judas Priest's 'Dreamer Deceiver.'"

Paul Williams wrote on the website Hard Rock House: "This is old-school British metal in the style of early Priest, Diamond Head and many others in the NWOBHM genre. It's all

The Holy Rage: Alex Reynolds, Chris Johnson, me and Scott Dallow.

very well played … There is absolutely nothing wrong with this album … excellent modern production job and some of the best guitar work I've heard in ages …"

Lords Of Metal, a popular online music magazine, said »Demon Deceiver« is "filled with timeless, well prepared hard rock." The reviewer also wrote: "The ten songs are well written (55 minutes of music), they are played properly (the solos earn some attention here), and Al Atkins provides with his dark and powerful voice the correct vocals to the album."

Gary Hill said in his review in Music Street Journal: "Overall this is a very strong disc, with no bad tracks … If you like classic metal you should give this disc a chance."

Rock United: "The entire album oozes of denim, leather and classic heavy metal. Indeed Al Atkins goes for the jugular, staking his claim for pole position in the metal race with a pretty solid release that delivers classic heavy metal for the classic heavy metal fans. Solid indeed and definitely worthy of a test run on your stereo. 7/10."

To coincide with the delayed release of the album, I decided to issue a promotional DVD produced by MpegUK Ltd. The DVD is called »The Sin Sessions« and features videos to three tracks from the new album: "Demon Deceiver", "Cradle To The Grave" and "Victim Of Changes". I didn't have much money to spend making the DVD so we had to improvise. The video to "Cradle To The Grave" for example is a montage of clips of me and the band in New York during out first visit there in 2004 as well as shots of us in the studio and on stage. The video for "Demon Deceiver" is basically us in the studio and I decided to use a live performance for the video to "Victim Of Changes". I've never done a VHS or DVD before so it was something new for me and you can still buy it from www.guitaristtv.com and www.mpeguk.com. »Guitarist TV«, by the way, is Mike de Jager's pride and joy. He set up the world's first broadband guitarist TV channel in June 2006 with help from the legendary Joe Satriani. And since then it has gone from strength to strength and I urge all guitarists to check it out.

Upon the release of »Demon Deceiver« I decided to make some big changes. It was a new year, new album and I felt that if I was to continue in this business I would need to make some adjustments. I chose to re-name the band The Holy Rage so from now on we're called Al Atkins & The Holy Rage. I wanted a double barrel sounding name like Judas Priest or Black Sabbath and one day I was reading about the Iraq war in the newspaper and it said something about a holy rage and I thought it was a great name for a band and everyone agreed. The Holy Rage sounds very powerful representing anger and energy, which are common traits of heavy metal. And I wanted to have more fun on the road and felt that a change of name would be like a change of pants, it'd make you feel more comfortable. Before Christmas, Pete Emms decided to leave the band for good. He wanted to pursue his side-project The Vaseline Rats and I wish him all the best with that. They're a funk-rock band and have just finished making their first album. So the new line-up featured Chris Johnson and Mike de Jager on guitars, Scott Dallow on bass and Alex Johnson on drums. I was extremely happy with my new band but it took some time for Scott to learn the songs and that's because we have an extensive setlist. He's done a great job though and I think he's a great bassist.

The other exciting piece of news is that we'd signed a new deal with Moser Custom Guitars in California which we will be forever grateful for. And I can tell you that Mike and Chris could not have been happier with their new custom made axes. We made a good friend of Rondz from Aberdeen, Scotland, who is the main distributor for the guitar company in Europe.

We also signed a deal SSG Artist, Management and Publishing Company in Finland. It was about time I off-loaded all the managerial work and business side of things to the professionals. After all the gigs that we had played over the past couple of years, and with more gigs in the pipeline, I simply couldn't do everything on my own. It is way too much work. We also got a deal with CMM promotions who got us lots of press in Germany; »Demon Deceiver« really took off there. And my Asian associates were doing lots of promotional work for me and the band in Japan. Later on in the year we would also signed up with Rob Grohl's music agency R.G. Promotionz in New Jersey, USA. How cool is that?

> *Rob Grohl is a really good guy and has helped me enormously over the past few years so it's a privilege to include a few words from him.*
>
> Rob Grohl: "Al is a true genius. He was the founder member of the all time great heavy metal bands – Judas Priest. His 'Victim Of Changes' and other greats set the precedence for all to follow. I have had the great honour of having him grace our shores two times: once as a member of the 'N.W.O.B.H.M. All Stars' with Dennis Stratton and Jess Cox at the Florida and New Jersey metal festivals and then with his new amazing band The Holy Rage, recently in Los Angeles. I am looking forward to be working with them again soon …"

We kicked off the year's live events with a gig at JB's in Dudley and we even secured a residency there. Scott came through his debut gig with flying colours. After so many rehearsals and social activities (i.e. going to the pub) Scott was really fitting into the band although he wouldn't let us get him pissed!

We held the first UK Moserfest (sponsored by Moser Custom Guitars) at JB's and Ronz, who plays bass and sings, came down from Scotland with his rock band Fubar. Also on the bill with us was power metal band Sixpounder who hail from Northampton. My young nephew opened the night with his one man band act Mitchell Monster and god has this kid got talent! He plays a mean guitar; he has already appeared on TV and radio and he writes all his own songs and he is still only 15 years old. With his long blonde hair and good looks, he reminds me of a young K.K. Downing in the making.

"How the hell have you gotten so good?" I'd say to him. Every time we'd meet up I'd get increasingly amazed at how much his talent has grown. Of course, there's a lot of talent in my family!

Paul May's band The Temple Dogs were also on the bill and we finished the night with Paul and Mitch joining us on for a grand finale. The guitar sound was simply incredible on the night. I had been suffering from a cold the previous few days but I soldiered on. After a slightly croaky start my voice got stronger and I had an absolute blast.

It was a great night and the beer flowed and conversations did not go dry (nor did our throats!). We took loads of pictures and many of them are on my official website. I made some new friends and had a laugh which is what the event was about.

Another great gig was held (again) at JB's as special guests to the revered Warrior Soul fronted by main man Kory Clarke. He got Warrior Soul back together to tour the UK in support of the re-issues of their first few albums.

It was a good gig but I didn't get much out of Kory. I asked him about Judas Priest but apparently he was not that influenced by them; when he started out has a drummer in New York he was in to Jazz/Fusion music. Kory is a cool guy, very easy to like.

I've got a cool picture of me and Kory backstage which was quickly put on my website. Warrior Soul even got a full score review in Kerrang! I thought we kicked arse that night too but we didn't get a mention in the review. I didn't realise just how strong their fan base is here in England; there was a good mix of people in the crowd that night.

I was on a high after the UK Moserfest, our gig with Warrior Soul and all the good reviews my album received and having a new band made me feel young again but I had a little setback in March after K.K. Downing spoke to »The Classic Metal Show«. He was basically criticising me for calling myself the 'original Judas Priest singer.' He said that it's ridiculous that I should say stuff like that because I haven't been involved with the band for over 30 years. He also mentioned Dave Evans, formally of AC/DC and Paul Di-Anno of Iron Maiden. I felt quite angry about his comments and wrote a response on my website.

I said: "As for myself using the Priest name is verging on ridiculous, let me just say (and my memory is still good) it was me who gave you the 'Judas Priest' name in the first place and it was me who co-wrote those early songs like 'Winter,' 'Never Satisfied' and 'Victim Of Changes,' to name a few, that helped you get a record deal. I've never asked you for a thing over all those years and I have respected Priest for all the hard work you have done and the brilliant records you have turned out, show a little respect back, please ..."

I don't think I have ever overstated my role in the band; I'm simply trying to make a living. I don't think Kenny realises that not every singer is a millionaire and can afford to live in a mansion and drive fast cars. In a way I can understand where he's coming from because Judas Priest is his band now and has been for 30 years but there are people out there who are interested in my music and what I've got to say about the early years. I'll never understand how they love their tribute bands but not their past members!

I think from now on I'm just going to ignore those kinds of criticisms. The fact is I'm too old to give a shit any more. I just want to play gigs, make music and have a laugh with my band. It's really great because they're all younger than me I can still outdrink them! I set up a Myspace page with the help of Chris Johnson who also does a brilliant job running my website. You should check it out at: www.myspace.com/alatkinsholyrage. There's loads of cool footage, tour dates and reviews. Myspace seems to be the most popular way of promoting yourself these days and I need as much promotion as I can get; it's not as if I'll be appearing in Mojo or Q magazines any time soon. I'm not really into things like Myspace and Facebook but if it sells my music and helps me get some new fans then I'm all for it.

Lots of great things continued to happen during 2007. I got The Holy Rage signed to Dave Clough's UK music agency Extreme Music and we got endorsed by Marshall Amplification. Our first gig with Extreme Music was scheduled for December with local gigs planned a bit sooner.

But before the gigs started to flow, I went on a week's holiday in October with my family to North Africa. We actually went to Tunisia on the coast and it was absolutely brilliant. I even went camel riding! George Lucas filmed »Star Wars« in Tunisia and over the years it has become a really popular holiday destination. It was very hot and you have to haggle with the market owners because they don't have fixed prices. An English pound is worth a lot of money to them.

When I arrived back home it was time to get back to the music as well as doing interviews for magazines and continuing work on this book. The first gig we had planned was on November 25th at JB's as special guests with Skid Row, the famed US rock band. They were still touring on the back of »Revolutions Per Minute«, which was produced by the super rock producer Michael Wagener who produced their first two albums »Skid Row« and »Slave To The Grind«. Wagener is probably one of the best producers in the business; he is famous for his work with the Scorpions amongst many others like Mötley Crüe, Ozzy, Dokken, Megadeth, Extreme and Great White. Now that is one enviable CV! Skid Row split up and the 1990s and reformed with Johnny Solinger who replaced the great Sebastian Bach. I only got to meet drummer Dave Gara and I found him to be a decent bloke. I've got a cool picture of us together. It's not like the old days; I am now always armed with a camera to back up my stories. They mainly stayed on the tour bus outside JB's until they made their entrance so I didn't get much chance to have a chat with them. Thankfully, JB's was a full house and Skid Row were on fire that night. It was an awesome evening!

Well, that was it for 2007, a brilliant year with so many positive things happening to the band. It confirmed my belief that I am doing the right thing and no matter what shit some people have to throw at me about stuff that I've done in the past, I know that I do have a fan base not just in the Black Country but other parts of the world like Europe, Finland, Japan and even the United States. Chris, my guitarist, was asked to play a show in Scotland. It was an outside festival and attended by a staggering 20,000 people.

It was time for a break and with the Christmas period approaching I told the lads to take it easier because it looked like we would have an even busier year in 2008. Needless to say we hooked up over Christmas for the usual festive shindigs, in other words, a trip to the pub for a long drinking session that ended with us struggling to walk home in a straight line. Rock and roll!

Judas Priest certainly kept quiet during 2007. They had already announced a year before that they were going to record an ambitious concept album about the 16th century French prophet Nostradamus. I'm not sure if that's what their fans want so early into their reunion period. I think it would have been much better for them to make a straight forward heavy metal album similar to »Angel Of Retribution«. Rumours were flying around that it would be a double CD set so perhaps it is intended to be their attempt at being taken seriously by the music establishment, who often look down at heavy metal bands like Judas Priest. They announced plans to tour in 2008 to promote the release of their latest album which had taken a lot longer to record than they anticipated.

On the other band, Rob Halford formed a new company called Metal God Entertainment and re-issued his solo albums on i-Tunes and even released some of the underrated Fight material. He brought out a collection of his best solo material on the excellent »Metal God Essentials: Volume 1 CD« which contains my song "Never Satisfied" on the bonus DVD. When »K5: The War Of The Words Demos« was released on CD in late 2007, a lot of the critics pointed out that those songs were not nearly as lame as they remembered.

Rob is not the only member of the band to have explored a solo career. Glenn Tipton has two albums to his name: »Baptizim Of Fire«, which features Cozy Powell, John Entwistle and Don Airey and »Edge Of The World« which is credited to 'Tipton, Entwistle & Powell.' Both albums have a slightly confusing history but they were issued in remastered form with bonus tracks about a year after »Angel Of Retribution« came out. Glenn is a talented guy, so when Judas Priest was out of action in the mid-nineties he wanted to explore his creative side as a solo artist. Personally, I'd like to see Ian doing some solo work. I know he's got it in him. He probably prefers the security of a band but he's a hell of a bassist and could probably make a killer album with the right producer.

My son and me in our back garden at home.

Rock and metal had come back into business in a big way by 2007. There were many interesting young bands causing shockwaves in the rock world, including the progressive rockers The Mars Volta and Coheed and Cambria, both of whom hail from America. Again, my son Joe gets me interested in all these bands.

An entertaining story is the rise and quick demise of The Darkness, a British band with close similarities to Queen but Justin Hawkins' ego became a little too much and the band folded only to resume work as the Stone Gods without J. Hawkins. Give me Queen any day ...

Maybe the resurgence of rock had a lot to do with the spate of reunions. A shed load of classic rock bands have reformed in the past couple of years, including The Police and Van Halen; Black Sabbath reformed with Dio working under the name Heaven & Hell and even members of Queen went on the road with Paul Rodgers.

Rock festivals became successful again, the most prominent being »Ozzfest« in America, »Sweden Rock«, »Wacken Open Air« in Germany and »Download« in the UK which is held at the prestigious grounds of Castle Donington. »Monsters Of Rock« was resurrected in 2006 at Milton Keynes Bowl but it was a one-off.

These days I listen to anything from Skid Row to Slayer and when I'm playing a gig you'll even see me wearing a Slayer t-shirt on odd occasions.

There was no better way to kick start 2008 than with a gig at The Knitting Factory in L.A., California on January 4th, playing alongside the Taz Taylor Band with Graham Bonnet, the excellent American thrash metal band Imagika, the San Diego death metal band Immolated Seraphim and the Californian band Jugular with the incredible bass player and our good friend Monster.

After a long flight we had an awful time at JFK airport in New York. We had to leave all our equipment at the airport due to the absolute incompetence of baggage handlers so we could catch our connection flight. It didn't turn up until ten minutes before we were due on stage the following night! We were really angry about that and it was not a good way to start the trip, which we had all been looking forward to. I love going to New York but the customs procedure at JFK is a joke. By the time we got to L.A. we were shattered and not ready to play a gig the following day but we had to forget about that, it's not good to go on stage in a band mood. Of course, beer is the best medicine to kill any bad feelings or emotions!

We held meet and greets during the soundcheck and had some really good conversations with our American fans and the other bands on the bill. We had a right laugh speaking with Monster – what a great bunch of guys! We took lots of photographs and had a good time. For me, I could not have been more honoured to be on the same bill as Mr. Graham Bonnet, a fantastic singer who has fronted such great bands as Rainbow, Michael Schenker Group, Impellitteri and Alcatrazz. Of all places, Graham is actually from Skegness in Lincolnshire but is now based in Southern California, so he is a local lad over there. He's worked with guitarist Taz Taylor and his band for the past couple of years and they are great on stage, really tight and melodic. I guess, like me, Graham will forever been remembered by his past so I think we have some common ground. Taz is also a great guy, he's from Walsall and when I first met his wife, she said: "With that accent I know where you're from." She's from West Bromwich, so the three of us got along great.

Dave Grohl's uncle, Rob, took us all on a sightseeing trip around Hollywood and L.A. which was very generous of him. We also met up with Skid Row at the Rainbow Rooms but we didn't hang out with them because the jetleg had almost knocked each of us unconscious. Those few days in Southern California were almost surreal and as with all my trips to the States, I had a great time even if I have to endure the flight and the crappy customs procedures.

Since our trip to the States there's just Chris Johnson on guitar now. We're rehearsing with him and he sounds fucking awesome. He's a brilliant player. And now there's a slot for guest players, which is especially good, if we do any big gigs or tours in the USA so then we can bring along Dennis Stratton or Simon Lees, but who knows what's going to happen? The one thing with a four-piece is: it's what you see, is what you get. There's no bullshit.

Chris Johnson and me on stage at JB's in Dudley.

In March, »Demon Deceiver« was finally released in Spain via Goimusic, and the following month it was released in Japan through Asian Alliance. The album picked up a lot of press on the international market which is great for me and the band.

As a band we've spent a lot of time together this year, getting ourselves in shape and working on the setlists and so on. We rehearse just twice a week if we are not playing regular gigs at The Mad House in the centre of Birmingham. It's run by Shy bassist Roy Davis and his wife Jackie. Not long ago he held a recorded interview at The Mad House for Sky TV, which included Pete Way (UFO), Blaze Bayley (ex-Maiden), Brian Tatler (Diamond Head), Bob Catley (Magnum) and myself. I was quite flattered to be asked to do it in such great company. And on April 7th, I was interviewed on a new Birmingham based radio show hosted by Roy. I played three of my all-time songs, so I chose Cream's "White Room" and I talked about their influence on my career. I also chose Deep Purple's "Mistreated" and Priest's "Painkiller". Three songs from my latest CD were aired and the station had loads of texts and e-mails coming in with people saying they wanted to buy the book. I have been invited on again when this tome finally comes out.

In terms of our recent live sets we usually play around one hour and 15 minutes but we can for play longer, it just depends on what the gig promoter requires. Sometimes when we play a festival, they only allow you 45 minutes and that goes for most bands on the bill. We're playing some pretty big venues in the Midlands and elsewhere. I have set standards for the band; I know we'll never fill Wembley Arena but can play to packed houses. I'm just really pleased that my fans have stuck with me through thick and thin.

Our setlist in early 2008 ran as follows:

"Drown"
"Blood Demons And Whiskey"
"A Void To Avoid"
"Never Satisfied"
"Money Talks"
"On And On"
"Coming Thick And Fast"
"Cradle To The Grave"
"Little Wild Child"
"Rock And Roll"
"Victim Of Changes"
"Metal Tyrant"

We have definite plans for the future. In May, we will be helping out my old mate Pete Boot by performing at his charity event »Fill Your Head With Rock« at Gilbert's in Birmingham. It's basically a two day festival to help him raise money usually for Parkinson's disease but this year it's for a charity called Acorn. Pete is recognised around the world for his charity commitments and he has received letters from the Queen herself about his good work. He has made friends from all over the world who also have the disease such as the film star Michael J. Fox and Bruce Springsteen's manager Bob Benjamin who himself now organises concerts in USA and Pete even travels out to America to help him.

In July, our California guitar company Moser Custom Guitars will hold the second Moser Festival; this time it will be held in Aberdeen, Scotland, and be aired live on radio. We will also be taking part in the first-ever all-day festival at JB's playing alongside ten other bands including Requiem and Blaze Bayley. And then in August we will be on a tour of the East Coast of America with Graham Bonnet's band Alcatrazz. Our first gig with Alcatrazz will be at The Haunt in New York; it looks like a nice place with a 850 capacity.

Japan would be really cool place to visit especially after what Dennis Stratton told me about the numerous occasions he's played there with Praying Mantis. Our next priority is to get another recording deal and put out a Holy Rage album. I am already writing songs now; one is called "Kingdom Of Hell" and it's shaping up to be a strong song. Another one is called "Power And The Glory", which I think will be a killer on stage.

I firmly believe that from 2008 onwards things are on the up for Al Atkins & The Holy Rage, and this is just the beginning of what I hope to be the best musical experience of my life …

Epilogue
What More Can I Say?

So there you have it, my story so far and what a ride it's been. Writing this book has been a therapeutic experience and at times a very emotional one. Now that it is finally finished, I could not be happier and I am glad that I'm able to share it with you. Never have I had to be so introspective and never have I gone into so much detail about my childhood, my family and my music. It's a weird feeling having so many words on so many pages, knowing that they tell all the stories of my life. Writing an autobiography is a vain thing to do but it can be a valuable tool to those who read it. Some of you might like my many nostalgic reminisces and anecdotes, I certainly enjoyed writing them. Then, many will be keen to learn about the genesis of Judas Priest – the world's greatest heavy metal band. It was a crazy time with lots of stories to divulge and it was a pivotal moment in popular music with the rise of heavy rock bands like Zeppelin, Purple and Sabbath.

Unlike a lot of my peers, I clearly embraced heavy metal. I've never forgotten what it was like to listen to Robert Johnson for the first time or what it was like to see Cream on stage but music evolves regardless of its style. The blues has stayed with me but ultimately HEAVY METAL took over my life and things, of course, changed. I've never had the chance to speak about all the music I like, usually if I'm talking about music with my mates, we'd get pissed after an hour and conversations tend to get rather complicated and incomprehensible.

You'll hear more from me in the future; hopefully you will be able to purchase an album by my new band The Holy Rage in your local High Street music store but right now you can buy it via your home computer. We're already planning our first album under our new moniker so watch this space. Or if you fancy travelling to the Midlands, you will probably be able to catch us live at our favourite joint JB's in Dudley.

Lastly, I would like to thank my wife Karen and the rest of my family and all my friends for their help when compiling the research for this book. I have made a lot great friends in the music business over the years but there are still a few back stabbing Judas' out there who have tried to put me down. I guess I'm a lone wolf; I've always managed to survive and have learned how to deal with people. At the minute, my career is going according to plan and things will only get better for The Holy Rage. I'm the happiest I've ever been. Above all else though, I would like to say a big thanks to Neil Daniels for all the hard work he has put into writing »Dawn Of The Metal Gods« with me.

I wonder what my hero Eddie Cochran would think of heavy metal? Maybe something like: "Well, I'm glad Iron Maiden named their mascot after me!" Lemmy said if Cochran was alive today he'd be playing this shit. I agree, completely.

The End

Appendix 1
A Personal Tribute To Judas Priest

Red, White & Blue, Birmingham NEC, March 19th, 2005

The Priest is back! Surely any metal fan familiar with such a famously iconic phrase cannot help but raise a smile when Rob Halford shouts it out to an arena packed with thousands of crazed and sweaty metalheads. During those tough early years when I was in the band we only ever dreamed of playing to so many fans in such a huge arena such as the NEC in Brum.

With their famous Flying V Guitars strapped around their upper bodies, K.K. Downing and Glenn Tipton – when posed together on stage – are as equally iconic as Rob. Hell, if that doesn't raise the hairs on the back of your neck, you need to grab a six-pack out of the fridge, lock yourself up in a room, switch off the phone and play »Unleashed In The East« non-stop until you have been converted. Kenny has come a long way since I hired him back in 1970; Christ, he couldn't string a note together in those days but now he is a true professional and has been for decades.

The phrase became even more powerful when the self-proclaimed Metal God rejoined Judas Priest in 2003 and re-claimed his rightful role in popular music; I was more than pleased to see that happen. And the roaring phrase that is "The Priest is back!" became even more emotional when Judas Priest – a Midlands band through and through – headlined their first ever gig at the Birmingham NEC, one of the biggest and most famous concert arenas in the country. And I was there! I even met the band backstage at that very gig and shared some mutual reminisces.

Unbelievably, it had taken them their whole career to achieve it. Heavy metal was back with a bang in the Midlands, its home territory. Although Halford had played there with his own band in 2000 whilst supporting Iron Maiden (at that point they'd just reunited with the equally talented Bruce Dickinson), it was not the same. He wanted to headline a gig at the NEC as a solo artist or one day back in Priest, not under another artist's steam. It's great that my son Joe is into heavy metal because I get to tell him all about the great bands like Maiden and Priest and, in turn, he can keep me updated with modern bands.

Like a posse of cowboys being welcomed home as heroes after a long and bitter fight against renegade Apache Indians in the Wild West, Judas Priest, fittingly attired in black leather and shining black leather boots, strode back home to the Midlands with their guitars strapped around their shoulders, ready to celebrate their return by blowing half of Birmingham away with some of the greatest heavy metal ever made. Rob Halford, the strong charismatic John Wayne type of figure and his group of dedicated but equally important sidekicks were back home to celebrate heavy metal.

Like me, they are born and bred musicians from the Midlands. They took their music, British heavy metal, around the world and helped define the genre and have become legendary because of their undeniable passion and talent. And like the great historical figures of the West, they too have become heroes in their own right and on this night ... it showed. As soon as the arena lights went down in the NEC, thousands of local and even international metal fans in the audience cheered and clapped for the band. But in particular those fans from the Midlands could raise a pint for their boys – despite the band's success in America and elsewhere, the locals hadn't been forgotten. Try to picture it vividly in your mind's eye: the many smiling faces, the euphoria, the sheer joy of such a momentous moment. It was spine-tinkling stuff and it made the locals as excited as over-eager kids on Christmas morning.

"I can't wait for this gig. It's been a long time", said one guy waiting in the queue outside the venue. "There's nobody like them", said another fan.

On March 19th, 2005, Halford and the rest of the band – Kenny Downing, Glenn Tipton, Ian Hill and American Scott Travis – gave an extra boost of energy and passion into their performance. After all that time apart from each other when Halford was doing his solo stuff and the rest of the band was working with Tim Owens, they were not going to give a half-arsed gig on this evening; that's not their style, regardless of the exact location of the venue.

As the recorded tape of "The Hellion" started playing from the speakers, an electric eye – held up high on a raised platform – stood still as the centrepiece of the stage and rumbled aloud with flashes of light. When the band walked onstage and blasted out "Electric Eye" the crowd went absolutely berserk. The crazy fans in the mosh pit headbanged with enough force to clear the local pharmacists of aspirin. It seemed to take a while for Halford to make his appearance in the retina of the eye but as soon as he sang the lyrics to that immortal song, it was like 1986 on the »Turbo: Fuel For Life« tour all over again.

The Metal Gods were proud to be back in the UK and happy to be back flying the flag for British heavy metal in their native region of the country. They ripped through classics like "The Ripper" and "Metal Gods". Obviously, my highlight of the evening was to see and hear them play "Victim Of Changes" the song I co-wrote and ended up recording myself a few times over the years, most recently on my critically acclaimed album »Demon Deceiver«. They gloated in the anthemic singles "Living After Midnight", "You've Got Another Thing Coming" and "Breaking The Law". And they enjoyed a return to lesser known songs like "I'm A Rocker" and "Hot Rockin".

As for the new stuff from their well-received comeback album »Angel Of Retribution«, well, songs like "Deal With The Devil", "Hell Raiser" and "Judas Rising" fitted perfectly with the golden oldies – they could have been written and recorded 20 years ago and featured on albums like »Screaming For Vengeance« and »British Steel«. So, yes, I have followed their career over the years.

Halford looked a little different as he returned to the Priest fold. You can hardly claim he has grown old gracefully. That would be too bloody boring. He is barely recognisable compared to the photos of his earlier years in Priest. His bald but tattooed head made his appearance rather more prominent but his voice still carries its familiarly unique range, which no other singer has ever bettered. No one in popular music can demonstrate such an unbelievably vast vocal range and power. Rob and myself are totally different singers. A self-proclaimed diva like Mariah Carey can hit the high notes but she has about as much soul and passion in her voice as those irritating, fake pop stars that forever seem to be making dull appearances on prime time Saturday night TV; for them it's all about fame and money but not for the Priest – it's the music that matters.

Rave reviews followed that evening's gig with the likes of Kerrang! and local news papers in the region heralding their return. The rest of the tour went down equally well, with many of the UK shows being sold out – decent sized venues too. They added second nights in Manchester and London.

For the past 30 years, Priest had been all over the globe but on this occasion they were back home in the centre of England. It took them over a decade of starvation and heartache but pure sweat and graft finally delivered them success even though they've never been quite as popular as Maiden or Kiss.

After such a momentous night, Priest certainly deserved their inclusion in a special issue of Kerrang! titled 'The 25 Most Important Rock Bands In The World: 1981-2006,' which obviously celebrated Kerrang!'s 25 years in the music publishing business. The Metal Gods were polled at Number 13, one position below the great American alt-rock band Korn. Within 25 years Priest produced classics »British Steel«, »Screaming For Vengeance« and »Painkiller«. Each album was represented on this special night in Birmingham, 2005.

Their popularity lays particularly in America although they do have a loyal and dedicated fan base here in the UK, albeit a much smaller one, which is why their headlining gig at the Birmingham NEC was so special to their legacy. Halford had always wanted Judas Priest to headline a gig there. It took them a while – the best part of four decades, actually – but they did it and, of course, good things come to those who wait.

On the night, they were proud of themselves and rightly so, wouldn't you be? The Birmingham gig, hell, the whole tour just made me wonder about my role in the band all those years ago when we were literally starved for food and cash and played to equally poor people in local venues that served cheap ale and grubby food; I remember playing gigs at the Hippodrome Theatre, West Bromwich Town Hall, Liverpool Town Hall, Stafford Hall, Quaintways Chester, Kinetic Circus and Brum Art College, to name a few. I used to think there has to be more to life than this. I remember one time driving the few miles to Birmingham from West Bromwich and our van broke down in the rain; it was a bloody nightmare, I kicked the front wheel and nearly broke my foot. The rest of the band were really pissed off too but we needed the cash so we couldn't walk away from the gig. When we got there it was almost packed and we went down well. Looking at the people smiling as they watched us play reminded me why I have to stick at this job.

"This is what I'm meant to do", I said to the band after the gig. "This is my destiny."

And so this book is my collection of memories from that important period in Judas Priest's history way back when. Every musician has his own stories to tell but I have the privilege of telling the world about mine. You can pay me a visit at www.alatkins.com.

Appendix 2
Judas Priest Line-Up History
(1969-1973)

When I was in Judas Priest I had the privilege of singing alongside several talented musicians; here is a complete list of those players ...

Mark I – 1969-1970
Al Atkins (vocals)
Bruno Stapenhill (bass)
Ernie Chataway (guitars)
John Partridge (drums)

Mark II – 1970-1971
Al Atkins (vocals)
K.K. Downing (guitars)
Ian Hill (bass)
John Ellis (drums)

Mark III – 1971-1972
Al Atkins (vocals)
K.K. Downing (guitars)
Ian Hill (bass)
Alan Moore (drums)

Mark IV – 1972-1973
Al Atkins (vocals)
K.K. Downing (guitars)
Ian Hill (bass)
Chris "Congo" Campbell (drums)

Appendix 3
Judas Priest Tour Dates
(1969-1973)

For the four years I fronted Judas Priest we played anywhere we could, including some quite big venues. The most memorable tour we did was around Scotland although it's memorable for all the wrong reasons. During research for this book I uncovered some new dates through an ex-roadie and friend of mine.

This is a list of most of the concerts the first four versions of Judas Priest played.

1969 UK Tour

November 25	The George, Walsall (England)
December	Beginning of a three week tour of Scotland including dates in: Aberdeen Dingwall Fort William Lossiemouth (Two nights at a Naval Base) Nairn Forres Inverness Dundee

1970 UK Tour

January	End of Scottish tour
February	Masonic Hall, Walsall (England)
February	Community Centre, Wednesbury (England)
February	The George Hotel, Walsall (England)
March 8	Club Westbourne, Edgbaston (England)
March 9	Rugby Club, Shrewsbury (England)
March 11	Old Swinford Hospital School, Stourbridge (England)
March 13	Moor Farm Inn, Nottingham (England)
March 15	Hereford Town Hall, Hereford (England)
April 20	Youth Centre, Cannock (England)

1971 UK Tour

March 16	St. John's Hall, Essington (England)
April 7	Burntwood, Bath (England)
April 16	Three Mile Oak, West Bromwich (England)
April 20	Youth Centre, Cannock (England)
April 21	Masonic Hall, Walsall (England) (Support to Black Sabbath)
May 1	Dudley Tech, Dudley (England)
May 8	Technical College, Walsall (England)
May 21	The Plaza, Old Hill (England)
June 1	Henry's Blues House, Birmingham (England)
June 18	Coppertops, Worcester (England)
June 19	Three Mile Oak, West Bromwich (England)
June 25	The Plaza, Old Hill (England)
June 30	Lafayette Club, Wolverhampton (England) (Support to the Chicago Blues Band)
July 2	Three Mile Oak, West Bromwich (England)
July 5	Central Hall, Birmingham (England)
July 10	Dudley Tech, Dudley (England)
July 12	The Gunn Inn, London (England)
July 26	Quaintways, Chester (England) (Support to Status Quo)
July 30	The Plaza, Old Hill (England)
August 8	Clouds, Derby (England)
August 14	The Village, Coventry (England)
August 21	Cavern Club, Liverpool (England)
September 2	Kinetic Circus, Birmingham (England) (Support to Graphite)
September 16	(Unknown venue and location) (Support to Supertramp)
September 17	Coppertops, Worcester (England)
September 24	Cleopatra's, Derby (England)
October 1	Angel Underground, Nottingham (England)
October 2	Kings Head, Stafford (England)
October 3	Kinetic Circus, Birmingham (England)
October 4	Borough Hall, Stafford (England) (Support to Thin Lizzy)
October 6	The Yeoman, Derby (England) (Support to Slade)
October 9	Kinetic Circus, Birmingham (England) (Support to Rory Gallagher)
October 13	Yew Tree Centre, Walsall (England)
October 15	Community Centre, Newport (Wales)
October 16	Community Centre, Newport (Wales)
October 17	(Unknown venue), Bristol (England)

October 21	La Café des Artistes, London (England)
October 22	Rose and Crown, London (England)
October 29	Zeppelin Club, Merton (England)
November 5	The Temple Club, London (England)
November 7	The Pheasantry, London (England)
November 12	Three Mile Oak, West Bromwich (England)
November 24	The Belfry, Birmingham (England)
December 3	Bromsgrove College, Bromsgrove (England)
December 5	Catacombs, Wolverhampton (England)
December 17	Distractions at the Bear, Burntwood (England)
December 24	Henry's Blues House, Birmingham (England)
December 28	Stoneground, Manchester (England)
December	Carven Club, Liverpool (England)
December	Cleopatra's, Derby (England)

1972 UK Tour

January 1	Hucknall MWC (Miners Club), Nottingham (England)
January 2	Gold Diamond, Nottingham (England)
January 3	Youth Wing, Penarth (Wales)
January 4	Bristol Legion, Cwmbach (Wales)
January 6	Youth Centre, Kincardine (Scotland)
January 13	Pavilion, Cheltenham (Scotland)
February 5	Underground Club, Worcester (England)
February 6	Magnet Club, West Bromwich (England)
February 9	Yew Tree Centre, West Bromwich (England)
February 17	Henry's Blues House, Birmingham (England) (Support to Trapeze)
February 18	Two J's Club, Essex (England)
February 20	Club Horn Hotel, Braintree (England)
February 26	The Greyhound Club, London (England)
February 28	Quarthouse, Chester (England)
March 4	Dudley Tech, Dudley (England)
March 9	Samantha's Blues Club, Leeds (England)
March 11	Manchester Centre, Manchester (England)
March 12	Bangor University (Arts Festival), Bangor (Wales)
March 13	City University, Northampton (England)
March 24	Glen Ballroom, Llanelli (Wales) (Support to Wild Angels)
March 28	Rock City, Northampton (England)
April 5	Top Rank Suite, Doncaster (England)
April 12	Dix Club, Wolverhampton (England)
April 19	Palace Lido, Douglas (Isle of Man)

April 20	Youth Club, (Unknown location) (Wales)
April 24	Dix Club, Wolverhampton (England)
April 28	Fag Club, Wigan (England)
April 29	Wellington Hall, Shropshire (England) (Support to Spirit)
June 9	College of Education, Swansea (Wales)
June 13	Ceda Club, Birmingham (England)
June 14	Ceda Club, Birmingham (England) (Support to Dr. Ross)
June 17	Laney Ballroom, (Unknown location) (Wales)
June 20	Cleopatra's, Derby (England)
June 21	The Red Lion, Northampton (England) (Support to Atomic Rooster)
July 11	Dudley Tech, Dudley (England)
July 12	Yew Tree Centre, West Bromwich (England)
July 13	Farafe Hotel, (Unknown location) (Wales)
July 15	Walsgrove Hotel, Coventry (England)
July 21	Lafayette, Wolverhampton (England)
August 1	Henry's Blues House, Birmingham (England)
August 4	Dudley Tech, Dudley (England)
August 20	Moor Farm Inn, Nottingham (England)
August 27	(Unknown venue), Nottingham (England)
August 31	Mandy's, Coventry (England)
September 7	Town Hall, West Bromwich (England) (Support to Gary Moore)
September 8	Plough and Harrow, Nottingham (England)
September 15	British Legion Club, Nottingham (England)
September 17	Moor Farm Inn, Nottingham (England)
September 24	Kinetic Circus, Birmingham (England)
September 28	The Babalou Club, Liverpool (England)
September 29	The Fighting Cocks, Mosely (England)
September 30	County Cricket Club, Northampton (England) (Support to Curved Air)
October 1	Angel Underground, Stafford (England)
October 2	King's Head, Stafford (England)
October 4	Borough Hall, Stafford (England)
October 5	Marquee, London (England)
October 6	The County, Northampton (England)
October 6	The Speakeasy, London (England)
October 7	Plough and Apron, Nottingham (England)
October 8	The Spectrum, Stockport (England)
October 9	Hotel (Unknown venue), Workington (England)
October 10	Angel Underground, West Bromwich (England)
October 10	(Unknown venue), Birmingham (England)
October 13	Pyramid Club, Liverpool (England)

October 13	Cavern Club, Liverpool (England)
October 14	Uniforum, Bradworth (England)
October 21	Cavern Club, Liverpool (England)
October 23	Quarthouse, Chester (England) (Support to Status Quo)
October 27	Fag Club, Wigan (England)
October 29	Brumling Budgie Club, London (England)
November 3	The Penthouse, Bridlington (England)
November 5	The Temple, West Bromwich (England)
November 13	The Top Rank, Doncaster (England)
November 20	Seven Stars, Haywood (England)
November 27	The Plaza, Old Hill (England) (with The Flying Hat Band)
December 14	Fantasia, Northampton (England)
December 16	Boat Club, Nottingham (England) (Support to the Alex Harvey Band)
December 21	Wellington Arms, (Unknown location) (England)
December 26	Henry's Blues House, Birmingham (England)
December	Catacombs, Wolverhampton (England)
December	Spectrum, Stockport (England)
December	Fantsia, Northampton (England)
December	The Speakeasy, London (England)
December	Café Des Artistes, London (England)
December	Pedugh, Harrow (England)
December	The Pheasntry, Chelsea (England)
December	Zeppelin King, (Unknown location) (England)

1973 UK Tour

January	Seven Stars Club, Haywood (England)
January	New Windmill Hall, Essex (England)

»Heavy Thoughts« Tour

February	Three week tour of Scotland (No available dates)
February	(Unknown venue), Manchester (England)
March	St. Georges Hall, Liverpool (England) (Support to Budgie)
March	(Unknown venue), Southport (England)
April	(Unknown date) College of Art and Food, Birmingham (Support to Budgie)
April 12	Dix Club, Wolverhampton (England)
April 15	Hippodrome, Birmingham (England) (Support to Family)
April 29	Wellington Hall, Shropshire (England)
May	(Unknown venue), Morecombe (Cancelled)

Appendix 4
Miscellaneous Tour Dates

It would be impossible to compile a list of every gig I have ever played; this is merely a small list of the more memorable gigs/tours I've played since I left Judas Priest.

Lion

1975	(Exact date unknown) The Marquee, London (England)
May 16, 1976	Barbarella's, Birmingham (England)
May 23, 1976	Coach and Horses (Unknown location) (England)
May 31, 1976	Crown and Cusion, Birmingham, (England)
June 18, 1976	Penny Farthing Club, Ulverston (England)
June 19, 1976	Black Rock Club, Matlock (England)
June 25, 1976	Polytechnic, Stoke-On-Trent (England)
June 9, 1976	Kendal Arts Centre, Kendal (England)
June 10, 1976	Staging Post, Leeds (England)
June 11, 1976	Half Way Hotel, Barnsley (England)
June 16, 1976	Reden Diamond Club, Sutton (England)
August 2 1976	Crown and Cusion, Birmingham (England)
August 4, 1976	Load Star, Blackburn (England)
August 6, 1976	Pencil, Retford (England)
August 7, 1976	Oswald Hotel, Scunthorpe (England)
August 13, 1976	Trent Bridge Inn (Unknown location) (England)
August 19, 1976	Seven Stars, Haywood (Unknown Location)
August 20, 1976	Penny Farthing Club, Ulverston (England)
August 21, 1976	Lion Club, Warrington (England)
September 1, 1976	Bogarts, Birmingham (England)
September 3, 1976	Reden Diamond Club, Sutton (England)
September 4, 1976	Black Rock Club, Matlock (England)
September 5, 1976	Lake Land Lounge, Accrington (England)
September 7, 1976	Top Rank, Cardiff (Wales)
September 21, 1976	Tiffany's, Scunthorpe (England)
September 6, 1976	Craigland's Complex, Leeds (England)
September 28, 1976	Tiffany's, Scunthorpe (England)
October 6, 1976	Rebecca's, Birmingham (England)
October 9, 1976	Samantha's, Leek (England)
October 10, 1976	Boat Club, Nottingham (England)
October 13, 1976	Bogart's, Birmingham (England)
October 15, 1976	Boat Club, Nottingham (England)
October 17, 1976	Rebecca's, Birmingham (England)
October 21, 1976	Bank House, Worcester (England)

October 30, 1976	Bradford University, Bradford (England)
November 6, 1976	Imperial's, Nottingham (England)
November 7, 1976	Coach and Horses, (Unknown location) (England)
November 10, 1976	Laffaette, Wolverhampton (England)
November 18, 1976	Seven Stars, Haywood (England)
November 20, 1976	Three Mile Oak, West Bromwich (England)
November 26, 1976	Penny Farthing Club, Ulverston (England)
November 27, 1976	Galaxy, Burton (England)
December 9, 1976	Bradford Principle, Bradford (England)
December 10, 1976	Florde Green Hotel, Leeds (England)
December 11, 1976	Hadden Hall, Leeds (England)
December 12, 1976	Pencil, Retford (England)
December 13, 1976	Dolly Grey's, Wakefield (England)
December 16, 1976	Underground Club, Blackburn (England)
December 18, 1976	Black Rock Club, Matlock (England)
April 1, 1977	Royal Albert Hall, London (England) (Nah, just kidding …)
June 3, 1999	Gilbert's, Birmingham (England)
	»Fill Your Head With Rock« Festival

The Holy Rage

April 3, 2007	JB's, Dudley (UK) (with Kory Clarke/Warrior Soul)
July 15, 2007	»Moserfest«, Dudley (UK)
November 25, 2007	JB's, Dudley (UK) (with Skid Row)
January 4, 2008	The Kitting Factory, Hollywood (US) (with Graham Bonnet and Taz Taylor)
May 25, 2008	»Fill Your Head With Rock« Festival, Wolverhampton (UK)
June 28, 2008	»Rock & Metal Fest«, Dudley (UK) (with Blaze Bayley)
August 14, 2008	Robin 2, Wolverhampton (UK) (with Diamond Head)

Appendix 5
Full Career Discography

I don't have an extensive body of work largely because I have spent most of my professional career on the road. This is a complete list of my solo material. More information is obtainable at www.alatkins.com.

Judas Priest

Demo Recording (1969):
"Good Time Woman"/"We'll Stay Together"

Demo Recording (1971):
"Holy Is The Man"/"Mind Conception"

Lion

Demo Recording (1975):
"On The Wheel"/"Journey"

Solo

»Judgement Day«
Release Date: 1989
Label: SPM
Track Listing: "Good Lovin' Run's Deep"/"Every Dream"/"Time After Time"/"Go"/"Judgement Day"/"I Got Your Letter"/"Victim Of Changes"

»Dreams Of Avalon«
Release Date: 1991
Label: Green Tree
Track Listing: "Dreams Of Avalon"/"Eastern Promise"/"If You Should Leave Me"/"Coming Thick And Fast"/"Run River Run"/"Victim Of Love"/"Sacrifice"/"Left Out In The Cold"

»Heavy Thoughts«
Original Release Date: 1995 via Gull Records
Re-issued Date: 2003 via Market Square
Track Listing: "Heavy Thoughts"/"Turn Around"/"Price Of Love"/"When Love Steals The Night"/"Void To Avoid"/"Deepest Blue"/"Little Wild Child"/"Caviar And Meths"/"Cradle To The Grave"*/"Sentenced"* (* Bonus tracks on the re-issue)

»Victim Of Changes«
Release Date: 1998
Label: Neat Metal
Track Listing: "Victim Of Changes"/"Never Satisfied"/"Black Sheep Of The Family"/"The Meltdown"/"Winter"/"Metanoia"/"Mind Conception"/"Holy Is The Man"/"Caviar And Meths"

»Demon Deceiver«
Release Date: 2007 (Advance copies made available in 2006)
Label: Diesel And Glory
Track Listing: "Demon Deceiver"/"Money Talks"/"Blood, Demons And Whiskey"/"Drown"/"Sentenced"/"Victim Of Changes"/"Bleeding"/"God Help Me"/"Cradle To The Grave"/"Dreamer Deceiver"

Multimedia

»The Sin Sessions« (DVD)
Release Date: 2007
Label: Independent/MpegUK Ltd
Track Listing: "Demon Deceiver"/"Cradle To The Grave"/"Victim Of Changes"

Appendix 6
A Q&A With Al Atkins & The Holy Rage (2008)

I thought it would be cool to include an interview with me and the guys; after all, they play an important role in my life.

What is the best gig you've played so far?
Al Atkins: The best gig with my present line up would be The Knitting Factory, Hollywood; we don't get to play in L.A. everyday so it was a great experience for the band but one of the most memorable gigs would be going back to the seventies playing alongside Thin Lizzy at The Borough Hall in Stafford when I fronted Judas Priest.
Scott Dallow: All of them … Every gig I have played with the band has been such a great experience. Every time we play we get to meet such great people, making every gig one to remember.
Alex Reynolds: It's got to be The Knitting Factory in L.A. for me, the crowd was crazy and the other bands were all great. Even the airline losing all our gear on the way over and having about ten hours sleep in five days didn't seem to matter!
Chris Johnson: Hollywood without a doubt. Meeting up with Graham Bonnet and Skid Row was cool. Great bands, great guys. But the burgers ... Oh god, how I miss the burgers!
Do you have any backstage rituals?
Al: No, not really.
Scott: I don't really have any backstage rituals as I prefer to spend most of my time at the bar meeting new people and having a beer with the guys.
Alex: Well, apart from when I'm warming up I don't tend to stay backstage. I love live music so I normally watch the other bands.
Chris: The two beer rule. I never go on stage without a couple of beers, or in the case of »Moserfest«, which is just a massive jam: four beers, a bottle of Jägermeister, five gins and whatever else I can grab.
Do you have many arguments with each other?
Al: Again no, we all get on really well: Chris, Alex and Scott are three of the nicest guys I have ever met. There are no egos and no bullshit with them, what you see is what you get.
Scott: All the time … about whose turn it is to fetch the beer. Seriously though, everyone in the band has become such good friends and we are having to good a time to argue.
Alex: No, we don't really argue because we're all pretty laid back and just happy to be making music together.
Chris: Nah. Especially since we became a four-piece. The atmosphere has been really good. Everyone is relaxed and confident; unless someone gives me the attitude, then I just threaten whomever with one of my Moser guitars. Scary stuff that is.
How do you arrange the setlist?
Al: The band usually leaves that up to me, and it's one of the many jobs I like doing, sorting out the setlist, the guest list and so on.
Scott: I leave that to Al, as he seems to always find the right balance for the song order.
Alex: I don't organise the setlist – I leave that to Al.

Chris: Although Al is always open to suggestions, we really leave that to his experience. If we do make suggestions he just threatens to sack us, it works well that way.

What do you do after a gig? Go to the pub?
Al: Usually, that's a good idea.
Scott: I'm always hungry after a gig, so like to eat and then have a couple more beers.
Alex: Depends where we are. Some good food and plenty of beer is top of the list after a gig. I only ever have one beer before I play so I'm usually playing catch up.
Chris: All the guys are very sociable, admittedly me more than the others, so yeah, we always have a few beers.

Do you have a favourite venue to play?
Al: It has to be JB's, we play there on a regular basis and we have had some great nights either topping the bill or opening up for bands like Skid Row. Sam cooks up a lovely curry and fills the dressing room fridge up with free beer, what more do you want?
Scott: JB's in Dudley always feels like home to me, so I love playing there. It's always a great night and a chance to catch up with close friends.
Alex: Well, JB's has been our regular haunt, but personally I like playing smaller venues. The atmosphere is so much better when it's up close and personal, both as a musician and a fan. So places like the Moles club in Bath or the Little Civic in Wolverhampton are my favourite.
Chris: I think variation is the key for me. I like visiting different places and meeting new people. My personal favourite town is Aberdeen. The band will play there in June for »Moserfest« 2008. I really want to get the guys in my adopted local pub run by the coolest woman Laura, (the Saltoun) and see how long it takes for one of them to fall over drunk. Great fun.

How long does it take to set up the gear before a gig?
Al: How long is it to plug in a microphone?
Scott: A couple of minutes tops, I use Trace Elliot amps that always sound perfect as soon as they are thrown on stage.
Alex: Bloody ages! Who'd be a drummer, eh?
Chris: My gear is great. I use a GT6 into a Marshall stack. It really is plug and play. Eight minutes max.

Do you get nervous before playing on stage?
Al: Never ... The stage is my second home. I've been doing it too long now to get nervous.
Scott: I never get nervous before playing, I'm to busy having a great evening. I have to rely on the guys to grab me and throw me on stage at the right time.
Alex: No, but I find it really difficult to sit still. I have to go for walk or something. I suppose I'm still just excited to get on stage.
Chris: May I refer your honour to the question about backstage rituals?
I did used to get very nervous; however, on New Year's Eve in 2007 I played for 20,000 people again in Stonehaven with my best Scottish mates Fubar. I had to learn a two hour set in four days of partying and one or two rehearsals. I will NEVER be nervous of a gig again.

Have you ever played to a hostile crowd?
Al: Not with this band, but there's still time.

Scott: Never. We all like to have as much fun as the people who come to see the shows. When everyone is having a laugh you never get any hostility.

Alex: No, we've never had a hostile crowd I can think of. I've seen a few in my time though. Daphne and Celeste at Leeds festival was one of the funniest things I've ever seen, they must have lasted five minutes ...

Chris: Never. We are a really approachable bunch of guys with great attitudes. The songs are great and we rock. Simple.

What is Al like to work with?

Scott: It never seems like work when you are playing with Al. We all enjoy the music we play. I very much like the way that Al never sees any of the music in black and white. He is always looking for that grey scale effect adding lighter and darker shades to the songs.

Alex: Al is really down to earth and easy to get on with. He speaks his mind – if something's crap he'll say so. Its refreshing really, I've worked with a few singers and songwriters who are absolute nightmares.

Chris: Crap. He is nothing but a miserable old git! No, seriously, not only am I related to Al but he is also a great friend. I would do anything for the guy (apart from fix his damn computers, the man is cursed). He is superb and I am honoured to be in his band.

What shows have you played outside of the UK?

Al: Shit loads, but only the L.A. gig with this band as yet.

Scott: I have always played in the UK before joining Al. It has been a great experience to learn that other countries love rock just as much as we do.

Alex: Just L.A. with Al, I've toured in Texas before too, with a different band. We're due back in the US soon.

Chris: I have played all over the UK but never had the pleasure to play overseas and when Al said we were doing California I was well up for it.

It was an incredible experience and I can't wait to play the USA again. I miss the burgers. May I take this opportunity to say that USA beer is horrible apart from Samuel Adams?

How long do you usually play for on stage?

Al: One hour to an hour and 30 minutes

Scott: Usually 90 minutes, it never feels that long though. They say time flies when you are having fun...

Alex: It's always at least an hour, up to about an hour and a half. Anything less isn't fair on the fans, it's really disappointing when you see a band headline with a half hour set.

Chris: It does depend on the gig. We have a cut and long set. If we are headlining then we usually do 90 minutes.

What are rehearsals like?

Al: Too fucking loud.

Scott: We always look forward to rehearsals, we like to play loud and have a good workout. There is always a laugh to be had if someone gets something wrong or breaks something.

Alex: Loud! We work pretty hard, try to get through the set as if it was a gig and then concentrate on any problem areas. But its always fun.

Chris: Always good. As I said the band enjoy each other's company, we are always laughing about something. Usually Alex tries to kill at least one of the band members with a laser-guided drumstick so that does keep us on our toes.

What's the best cover version you've played to an audience?

Al: "Metal Tyrant" always goes down well.

Scott: We don't do many cover versions live, but we do enjoy jamming out "Metal Tyrant" by Seven Witches. "Rock And Roll" by Led Zep also went down a storm in L.A., the crowd went wild.

Alex: I really like "Metal Tyrant" by Seven Witches, If only I could play it properly ...

Chris: That's a tough one. We do not usually do covers. I think it would be "Rock And Roll" by Led Zep.

What sort of reaction do you get when you play "Victim Of Changes" and "Dreamer Deceiver?"

Al: I've played that song in my setlist with different line up's for years and it always goes down great with whatever crowd you play it to.

Scott: "Victim Of Changes" always seems to go down well and has always been a great song to play. The newer version is played slightly faster and has great attitude.

Alex: "Victim' Of Changes" always goes down well, it's a great track. But I've never played "Dreamer Deceiver" with Al unfortunately.

Chris: In Hollywood, the crowd went nuts. The songs are always received well but American crowds seem to enjoy the songs a little more for some reason.

What kind of crowds do you play to?

Al: Mad, totally mad, the old rockers in the audience are the worst.

Scott: The best kind ever ... The people who come to see our gigs are fantastic. They are all like-minded people who we very much enjoy spending time with. They can always find us at the bar. We have all made the best friends ever doing the shows we have done. I especially enjoy crowds that join in and have as much fun as we do.

Alex: A pretty good age range – we get people that remember the early days of metal and kids that are just discovering it for the first time.

Chris: All sorts, young, old, senile, nuns. Who cares as long as they enjoy the show? I prefer crowds that are in your face, right up close. Big festivals are great, but not personal ,you know ... If I get chance to highfive someone mid-solo then I am happy.

Acknowledgements

There are lots of people I have worked with over the years and I simply can't name them all here.

For the record, I'd like to thank the following people: Alex Reynolds, Archie Cole, Armin Kramer, Beverley Stone, Bruno Stapenhill, Chris Johnson, David Corke, David Howells, Ernie Chataway, Express & Star (my local newspaper), Ian Hill, Jack Ballas Jr., Joe Atkins, John Emms, John Santee (Showcase Promotions), K.K. Downing, Karen Atkins, Larsa Gustafsson, Laura Atkins, Manfred Hienstorfer (Iron Pages), Mark Stuart, Matthias Mader (Iron Pages), Michael Lliljhammer, Mike de Jager, Neil Daniels, Norman Hood, Paul May, Pete Boot, Pete MZ Emms, Rob Grohl, Robert Plant, Sharon Atkins, Shena Sear and Trevor Lunn.

Wherever relevant I have quoted from various magazines/newspapers that have referenced me and Judas Priest; I would like to thank them for their support over the years.

I'd also like to thank all those people who have contributed such kind words about me for the purpose of this book.

Apologies to those who I have forgotten but I've had a busy life. Here's to the next 60 years!

The author gratefully acknowledges permission to quote and use references from various publications. Every quote and reference taken from selected sources is fully acknowledged in the main text.

However, it has not been entirely possible to contact every copyright holder but every effort has been made to contact all copyright holders and to clear reprint permissions from the various publications. If notified, the publishers will be pleased to rectify any omission in future editions.

About The Authors

Al Atkins released the critically acclaimed album »Demon Deceiver« in 2007 via Diesel & Glory. After having formed many bands over the past 40 years he is happy tearing the Midlands apart with his latest heavy metal outfit The Holy Rage. Al is happily married and has five children. He continues to live in West Bromwich. Visit his website: www.alatkins.com.

Neil Daniels has written about classic rock and heavy metal for a wide range of magazines and fanzines. He currently writes for Fireworks, Powerplay and Get Ready To Rock.com, and occasionally contributes to Rock Sound and Record Collector. His reviews and articles have also appeared in the Guardian, Big Cheese, Drowned In Sound.com, Carling.com, Unbarred.co.uk and Planet Sound on CH4 Teletext. Neil has contributed articles and reviews on cinema to the academic publication MediaMagazine and the popular arts ezine musicOMH. More information is obtainable at neildaniels.com.

Books by Neil Daniels:
»Defenders Of The Faith: The Story Of Judas Priest« (Omnibus Press, 2007)
»Robert Plant: Led Zeppelin, Jimmy Page & The Solo Years« (Independent Music Press, 2008)
»The Bon Jovi Encyclopaedia« (Chrome Dreams, 2009)